Macmillan Computer Science Series
Consulting Editor
Professor F. H. Sumner, University of Manchester

S. T. Allworth and R. N. Zobel, *Introduction to Real-time Software Design, second edition*
Ian O. Angell and Gareth Griffith, *High-resolution Computer Graphics Using FORTRAN 77*
Ian O. Angell and Gareth Griffith, *High-resolution Computer Graphics Using Pascal*
M. Azmoodeh, *Abstract Data Types and Algorithms*
C. Bamford and P. Curran, *Data Structures, Files and Databases*
Philip Barker, *Author Languages for CAL*
A. N. Barrett and A. L. Mackay, *Spatial Structure and the Microcomputer*
R. E. Berry and B. A. E. Meekings, *A Book on C*
G. M. Birtwistle, *Discrete Event Modelling on Simula*
B. G. Blundell (Editor) *et al.*, *An Introductory Guide to Silvar Lisco and HILO Simulators*
T. B. Boffey, *Graph Theory in Operations Research*
Richard Bornat, *Understanding and Writing Compilers*
Linda E. M. Brackenbury, *Design of VLSI Systems – A Practical Introduction*
J. K. Buckle, *Software Configuration Management*
W. D. Burnham and A. R. Hall, *Prolog Programming and Applications*
J. C. Cluley, *Interfacing to Microprocessors*
J. C. Cluley, *Introduction to Low Level Programming for Microprocessors*
Robert Cole, *Computer Communications, second edition*
Derek Coleman, *A Structured Programming Approach to Data*
Andrew J. T. Colin, *Fundamentals of Computer Science*
Andrew J. T. Colin, *Programming and Problem-solving in Algol 68*
S. M. Deen, *Fundamentals of Data Base Systems*
S. M. Deen, *Principles and Practice of Database Systems*
Tim Denvir, *Introduction to Discrete Mathematics for Software Engineering*
P. M. Dew and K. R. James, *Introduction to Numerical Computation in Pascal*
M. R. M. Dunsmuir and G. J. Davies, *Programming the UNIX System*
D. England (Editor) *et al.*, *A Sun User's Guide*
K. C. E. Gee, *Introduction to Local Area Computer Networks*
J. B. Gosling, *Design of Arithmetic Units for Digital Computers*
Roger Hutty, *Z80 Assembly Language Programming for Students*
Roland N. Ibbett, *The Architecture of High Performance Computers*
Patrick Jaulent, *The 68000 – Hardware and Software*
J. M. King and J. P. Pardoe, *Program Design Using JSP – A Practical Introduction*
H. Kopetz, *Software Reliability*
E. V. Krishnamurthy, *Introductory Theory of Computer Science*
V. P. Lane, *Security of Computer Based Information Systems*
Graham Lee, *Form Hardware to Software – an introduction to computers*
A. M. Lister, *Fundamentals of Operating Systems, third edition*
G. P. McKeown and V. J. Rayward-Smith, *Mathematics for Computing*
Brian Meek, *Fortran, PL/1 and the Algols*
A. Mével and T. Guéguen, *Smalltalk-80*
Barry Morrell and Peter Whittle, *CP/M 80 Programmer's Guide*
Derrick Morris, *System Programming Based on the PDP11*
Y. Nishinuma and R. Espesser, *UNIX – First contact*
Pim Oets, *MS-DOS and PC-DOS – A Practical Guide*
Christian Queinnec, *LISP*
E. J. Redfern, *Introduction to Pascal for Computational Mathematics*
Gordon Reece, *Microcomputer Modelling by Finite Differences*
W. P. Salman, O. Tisserand and B. Toulout, *FORTH*
L. E. Scales, *Introduction to Non-linear Optimization*
Peter S. Sell, *Expert Systems – A Practical Introduction*
Colin J. Theaker and Graham R. Brookes, *A Practical Course on Operating Systems*
J-M. Trio, *8086-8088 Architecture and Programming*
M. J. Usher, *Information Theory for Information Technologists*
Colin Walls, *Programming Dedicated Microprocessors*
B. S. Walker, *Understanding Microprocessors*
Peter J. L. Wallis, *Portable Programming*
I. R. Wilson and A. M. Addyman, *A Practical Introduction to Pascal – with BS6192, second edition*

A Sun User's Guide

Stephen Beer
Stuart Borthwick
David Coffield
David England (Editor)
Peter Hurley
John Mariani
Howard Siwek
Jon Walpole

MACMILLAN
EDUCATION

First published 1987

Published by
MACMILLAN EDUCATION LTD
Houndmills, Basingstoke, Hampshire RG21 2XS
and London
Companies and representatives
throughout the world

Printed and bound in Great Britain at
The Camelot Press Ltd, Southampton

British Library Cataloguing in Publication Data
A Sun user's guide. — (MCSS).
1. Sun Workstation (Computer)
I. Beer, Stephen II. England, D.
004.165 QA76.8.S9
ISBN 0–333–44849–9

Contents

Preface

High-performance, high-resolution graphics workstations have been available for some ten years in specialist areas such as Artificial Intelligence and Computer Aided Design. However, the recent developments in powerful 16 and 32 bit microprocessors have led to the development of more general purpose machines. The Sun range of workstations is one example of this trend. These machines are bringing powerful computers out of the traditional machine room and into the offices of researchers and software developers.

Workstations provide new opportunities in addition to providing the individual user with more computing power. These opportunities require new skills. Window management can provide more "user-friendly" interfaces but requires knowledge of human-computer interaction. High-speed networking allows data distribution and rapid communication. It is hoped this book will help the user to realise the possibilities presented by Sun workstations.

About this book

A Sun User's Guide aims to be general and practical, being based on the authors´ own experiences. As well as concentrating on the strengths of the Sun workstation, such as window management, graphics and networking, we also introduce machine administration which the general user may not have met before. Sun UNIX is introduced and references to introductory UNIX books provided. It is expected that the reader will have had some exposure to C language programming and again introductory texts are recommended. Most of the programming-based chapters include some complete C programs which the reader can enter and compile. It is also assumed that the reader will have had some previous exposure to personal computers and will know how to use a keyboard and how to type in commands.

A Sun User's Guide is not meant to be read sequentially. It is possible to dip into a chapter of particular interest without reading the whole book. However some chapters are naturally linked, such as Chapter 1 on using windows and Chapter 3 on writing window-based programs. The reader should note that this book is based on release 3.2 of Sun software.

Chapter 1, *An introduction to using windows*, aims to teach the basics of using window and mouse-based tools. Not every possible tool is introduced. Instead the aim is to describe the common elements of all tools.

Chapter 2, *Sun UNIX*, introduces the UNIX operating system with many examples and particular references to the use of windows and networking.

Chapters 3 and 4 introduce programming in the SunView system so that window based programs can be produced. Chapter 3 shows how Frames and Panels can be constructed, while Chapter 4 considers the lower, and more flexible, Canvas level of Sunview. Chapter 5 then looks at the Pixrect imaging facilities, after a brief overview of the graphics packages available.

Chapter 6 describes the *SunCore* graphics package. Whereas SunView is aimed at producing window-based programs, SunCore is a general graphics system and provides facilities for image processing in 2 and 3 dimensions.

In Chapter 7 machine administration is introduced and includes topics such as tape backups and adding users to UNIX.

Networking is one of the Sun's strengths and Chapter 8 looks at the support available.

Finally Chapter 9 looks at the support available for software development on Sun Workstations.

We have endeavoured to remove any technical and typographical errors and are grateful to the various reviewers who have helped us in this task. Any errors which still remain are the responsibility of the authors. We would be grateful if readers could bring them to the attention of the editor or publisher for correction. This book was produced on various Sun workstations and a Sun laserwriter using ptroff, plus the occasional Macintosh diagram!

Acknowledgements

Much of the experience on which this book is based was gained on research projects supported by the Science and Engineering Research Council and the Alvey Directorate of Great Britain. The directory browser and the window-print software were developed as part of the Alvey ECLIPSE Software Engineering project for an earlier release of Sun Windows. We would like to thank Susan Coote, Andrew Howes, David Hutchison, Peter Sawyer, Doug Shepherd, Ian Sommerville, Catherine Taylor and Michael Twidale.

David England, (Editor)
Lancaster, 1987

1 An Introduction to Windows

1.1. Introduction

Developments in microelectronics over the last 10 to 15 years have led to several changes in the ways people work with computers. More powerful microprocessors and cheaper memory chips have led to personal workstations which have moved computing out of the traditional machine room and into the user's office. Developments in computer networks have also assisted the redistribution of computing power further into the hands of the users. And the introduction of high resolution displays, with associated pointing devices, has provided new opportunities for improving the interface between user and machine. In the jargon of Information Science, graphical workstations are able to offer more *cycles* and a greater *bandwith* of information communication, between user and machine, than was previously possible.

1.2. Interface metaphors

So the new machines, like Sun workstations, offer the possibility of communicating rich and complex information in a comprehensible way to the user. How is this achieved in practice? One of the most popular methods, adopted by many office personal computers, is to offer a *desk top* metaphor. In this approach, computer concepts like files, directories of files and command names, are represented on the screen as objects that users are familiar with in their everyday work. So the screen becomes an electronic desktop which has *icons* on it which represent *folders*. The user can point at folders and move them about, with the *mouse* pointing device, just as he or she would organise their own desktop. Folder icons can be opened to *windows* so the user can view their contents, which will again be represented as icons. When a folder is no longer required it can be closed back to its icon or moved into a trash can icon for disposal, or we may move one folder on top of another, just as we shuffle pieces of paper on a desk. The mouse can also be used to point at labels or areas of the screen which provide the user with a *pop-up menu* of choices. With menus, the user can perform some action on a previously selected folder window or icon, such as opening or closing a folder, or changing the way a folder displays its contents.

1.3. The suntools interface

The window interface on Sun workstations is similar in many ways to that described above. There are icons that can be opened up to windows. Windows and icons can be moved around and overlapped on the screen, and we can change the size of windows to make them fit. However, in the Sun windows system each window and icon represents a tool rather than a folder. Each tool has its own pop-up menu. The background window (similar to the underlying desktop described previously) also has a pop-up menu to start off more tools. The tool approach makes sense when you realise that the Sun uses the UNIX[1] operating system, and the main strength of UNIX is as a collection of tools which can be used to support the user's tasks. Mainly, these tasks have been concerned with the production of more tools, but UNIX is slowly making inroads into more general computer use.

The traditional way of working with UNIX is to use a character terminal with a screen, usually 80 characters by 24 lines in size. Using the Sun windows system, a terminal is just another tool window and several can be put on the screen, of various sizes, along with clocks, painting programs and other tools. And, because UNIX is a *multi-tasking* operating system, we can run several tasks on the screen simultaneously, switching our attention from one to the other as necessary.

In the rest of the chapter we are going to look at some of the window tools that are available. The general aim is to look at those tools which best show the common features of all tools. We shall look at the background window and its pop-up menu, the UNIX terminal tool, and other tools and facilities that allow users to tailor the working environment to their own requirements.

1.4. Hardware

Figure 1.1 shows a diagram of a Sun workstation. It consists of a screen, keyboard and optical mouse (the Sun pointing device). The mouse works by light reflected off the special mouse pad. Moving the mouse on its pad moves the cursor across the screen. The screen is 1152 x 900 pixels in size. On the Sun we use a three-button mouse. Throughout the book we will refer to the buttons as left, middle and right. Generally, the left and middle buttons are used to select items on the screen while the right button will provide a *pop-up menu* or list of available options. To select an item using the mouse you just *click* a mouse button and release it. To select a menu option you *hold* down the mouse button while you choose an item from the menu.

---

[1] The use of UNIX is explained in chapter 2.

The Sun is very much an interactive system and you should feel free to experiment with the window system as you read through this chapter.

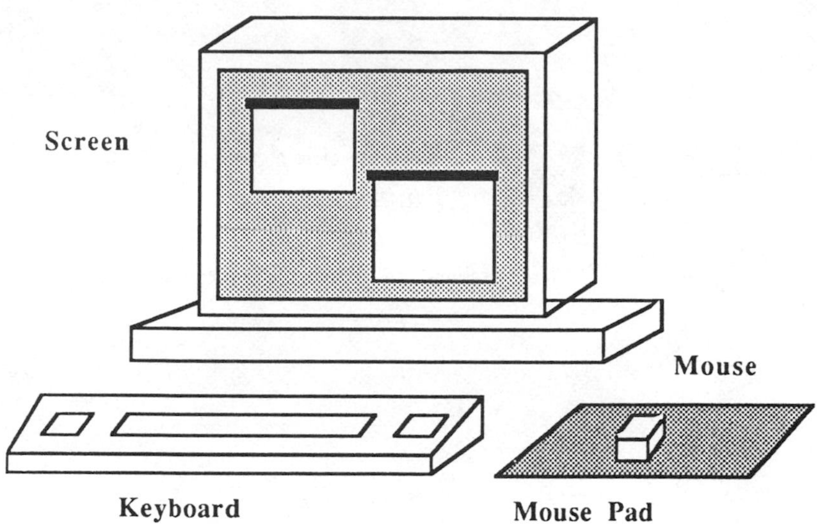

Figure 1.1 *Sun Workstation*

1.5. Logging on

To login to the Sun workstation a user name is needed which will probably be set up by the local machine administrator[2]. When you first use the machine it will either display a login message like

machine-name-login:

or will have a black screen with a changing pattern. The latter protects the screen from burn-out when it has not been used for long periods. To remove this protection and get to the login message press any letter key or mouse button. The screen will now look like figure 1.2.

---

[2] Or see chapter 7 for how to set up user names.

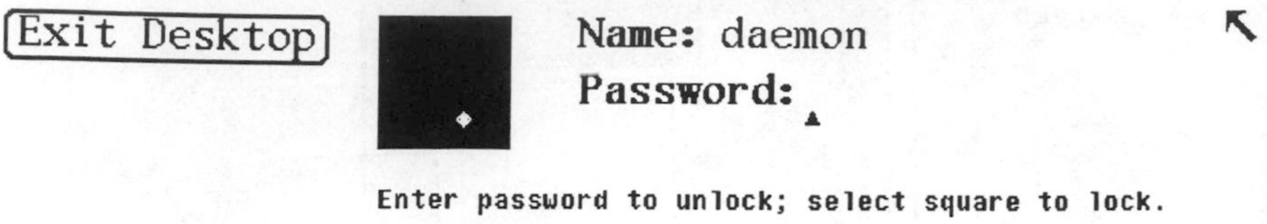

Figure 1.2 Lockscreen

Try moving the mouse on its pad until the arrow (or cursor) is positioned over the label Exit Desktop .

Click the left button and a message asking for confirmation of your action will appear - click the left or middle button again and the UNIX login message will appear. Now type in your login name.

After a few seconds, the UNIX prompt will appear, which will look something like (we will abbreviate this to %)

machine-name%:

as the Sun is waiting for you to type a UNIX command. We will leave UNIX until the next chapter. For now just type the command **suntools**. A grey pattern and an arrow cursor will appear on the screen followed by a default set up of windows similar to that of figure 1.3. What you see is an open window at the top left and four closed windows (or *icons*) to the right. The **suntools** command sets up the screen so window tools can now be used and controlled on the screen.

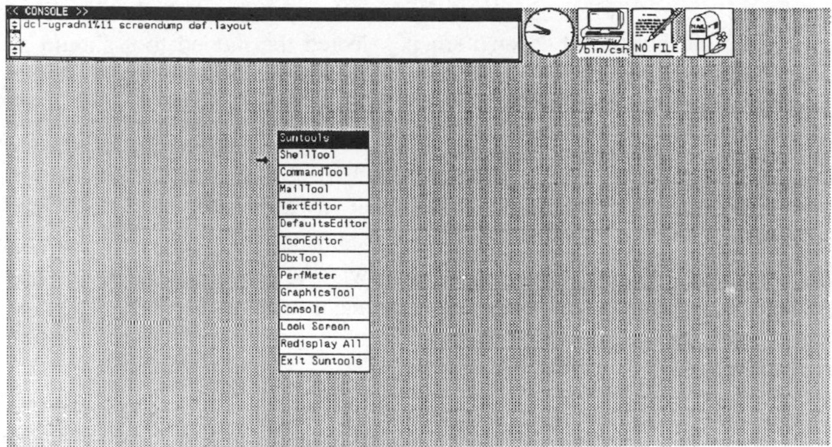

Figure 1.3 Default screen layout

1.6. Root menu

Try moving the mouse so that the cursor is somewhere over the grey background (or *root window*). Now hold down the right mouse button and the *root menu* will appear as in figure 1.4. The root menu has three basic functions; it allows other windows tools to be started (by selecting their name on the menu); the screen can be redrawn (by selecting *Redisplay*) and the **suntools** program can be stopped by selecting *Exit suntools.*

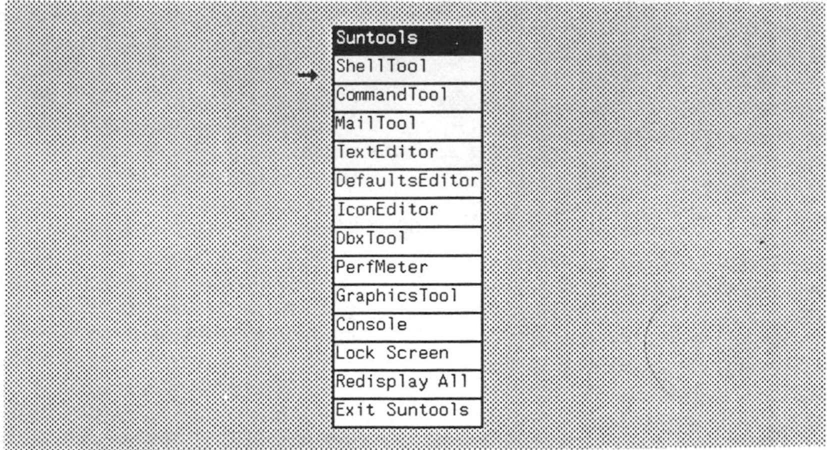

Figure 1.4 Root menu

As you move the cursor over an item in the root menu it becomes inverted (i.e. reverse video) indicating that the item has been selected. If you now release the right button while an item is selected the named tool should start up. Try selecting the Shelltool [3] item at the top of the menu. A shelltool window will appear after a few seconds. If you do not wish to start up any tools from the root menu, just move the cursor away from the menu box so that no items are selected and release the mouse button.

Selecting Exit Suntools at the bottom of the root menu takes you out of the suntools set up and back to the UNIX command prompt. Try that now and come back into suntools as before. If you wish to leave UNIX at this point, type the command **logout** at the UNIX command prompt.

1.7. Frame menu

Once you are back in suntools move the cursor either over an icon or over the black border of the open window. The cursor changes to a small circle. If you hold down the right mouse button now, the frame menu will appear (figure 1.5). This is used for controlling the appearance of windows on the screen.

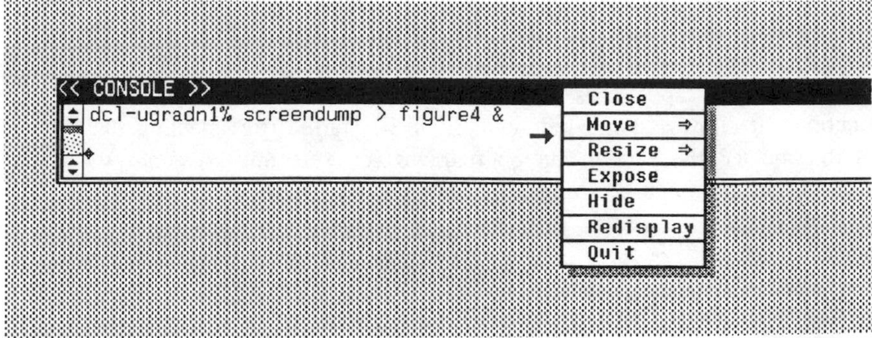

Figure 1.5 Frame menu

The frame menu items have the following actions.

Close/Open

This action closes a window down to its icon or opens an icon back to its respective window. Any programs running in a window will continue to run while the window is closed.

Move

A prompt box appears, asking you to hold the left or middle button to

[2] Shelltool is described in section 1.8.1 below.

move the window or the right button to cancel the action. Positioning the cursor on the centres of the borders allows you to move the window either vertically or horizontally, depending on the border, but positioning the cursor near a corner allows you to move the window in any direction.

Resize
: Again a prompt box appears, asking you to hold down the left or middle buttons to resize the window or the right button to cancel. Also, the direction in which you can resize the window depends on where you click the mouse button on the windows border.

Expose
: A window that may be partially hidden by other windows is made fully visible.

Hide
: The chosen window is placed behind any other windows that it may be covering.

Redisplay
: Occasionally, the display screen can contain garbage. This is caused by programs writing directly to the screen. This action restores a window to its proper state.

Quit
: The window is removed from the screen. A prompt will appear asking you to click the left or middle button to confirm your action or the right button to cancel it.

Accelerators can be used with the left and middle mouse buttons as a short cut to selecting some items from the tool menu. For example, clicking the left button on an icon causes the icon to open, while clicking the same button on a tool window boundary *exposes* that tool. Holding down the middle button on a icon or window boundary allows that window or icon to be moved about the screen.

1.8. Some Suntool utilities

Most of the available Suntool utilities that you might want to use are available from the root menu. They can also be started by typing commands in shelltool windows (this is described in more detail in section 1.8). This section describes the more useful tools and those which demonstrate the features which are the basis of all other tools. You should notice that there are apparently two types of *cursor* in some windows. One is the black arrow cursor moved around by the mouse and the other is a black rectangle or black triangle (or *caret*), which follows the text as you type in characters.

1.8.1. Shelltool

This tool gives you a window similar to a terminal running the UNIX command line interpreter (or *Shell*). It allows you to run the standard UNIX commands. Unlike a normal terminal, you can move and resize shelltool as with any other window. You can also have several shelltools running at once. Figure 1.6 shows one possible layout of shelltools. In one window we might be editing some text, while in another we might be running a program, so we can have two views of our work. In figure 1.6 the windows are shown as *tiled*, i.e. not overlapped.

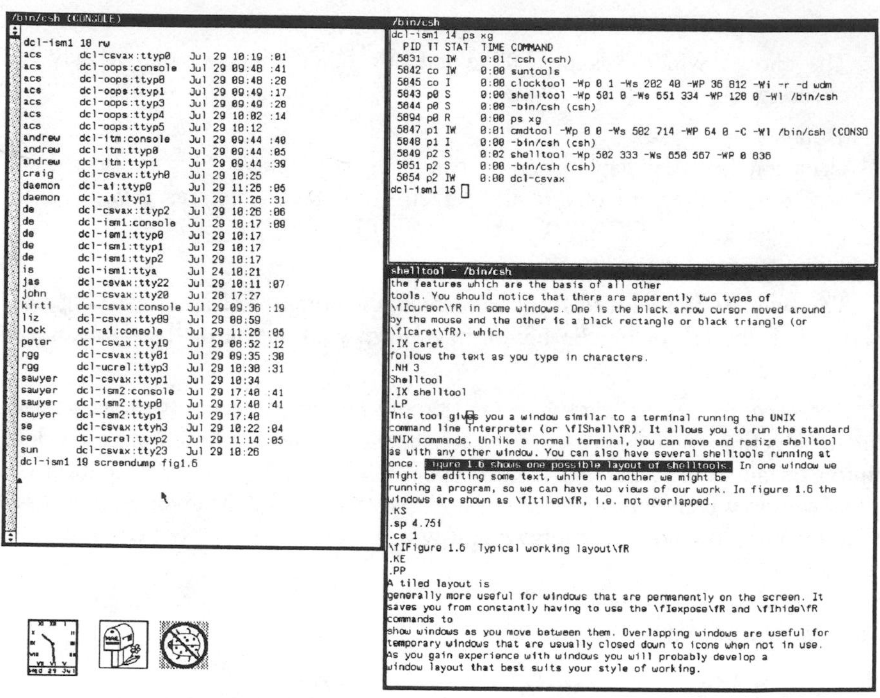

Figure 1.6 Typical working layout

A tiled layout is generally more useful for windows that are permanently on the screen. It saves you from constantly having to use the *expose* and *hide* commands to show windows as you move between them. Overlapping windows are useful for temporary windows that are usually closed down to icons when not in use. As you gain experience with windows you will probably develop a window layout that best suits your style of working.

To type commands into a shelltool window you must first move the cursor over that window. The border will change to black to indicate that this window is currently accepting keyboard commands. Also, the rectangular cursor will become black.

Shelltool menu

If you hold down the right button while you are inside a shelltool you will see the menu shown in figure 1.7. This is the ttysw (teletype sub window) menu. The items *Stuff* and *Put, then Get* are concerned with moving pieces of text within and between windows. The item *Page Mode On* stops sections of text longer than the current window from disappearing off the top of the window. Instead the text (output by a UNIX program) stops at each page until you press a key to see the next page.

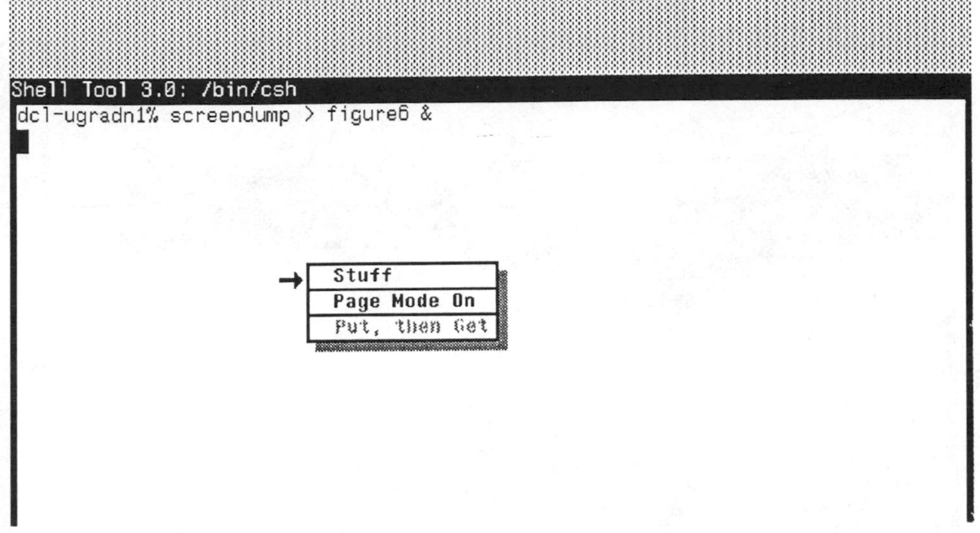

Figure 1.7 Shelltool menu

Selecting text

Pieces of text can be copied between different windows on the Sun screen. This can save time and prevent errors when the same piece of text is required by several tools. To use a piece of text it must first be marked as *selected.* To select a piece of text to be copied, mark the first character by clicking the left button over it. Then, while holding down the middle button, drag the cursor to the last character in the piece of text you wish to copy. As you drag the cursor over the text it will become inverted. Releasing the middle button then marks the inverted text as selected. To use this piece of text, move the cursor to the target shelltool and select the *Stuff* item in that window. Your piece of text will then appear in that window as though you had typed it there. This last point is important, because if you try to *stuff* text into a text editor like **vi** it will interpret the stuffed text as commands, so you should make sure that your editor is in insert mode if necessary. This problem does not occur with the **textedit** tool described below.

Stuff only works between shelltool windows. If you wish to move text between other types of windows, use the *Put, then Get* item. Putting and getting text is explained in the next section.

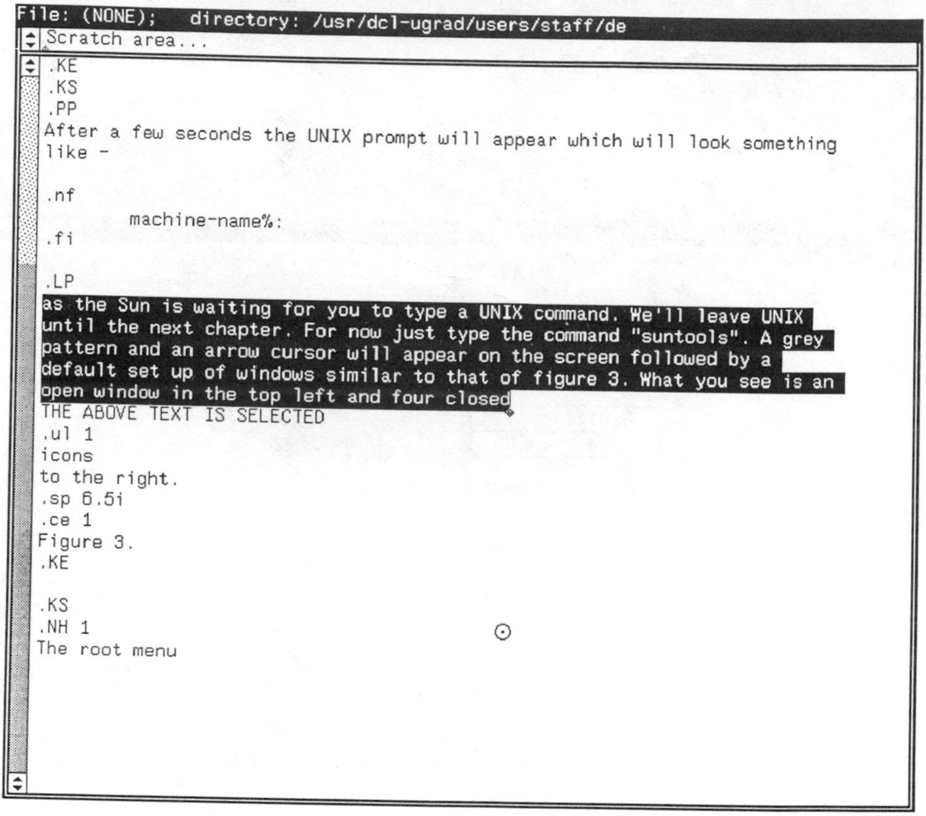

```
File: (NONE);   directory: /usr/dcl-ugrad/users/staff/de
Scratch area...
.KE
.KS
.PP
After a few seconds the UNIX prompt will appear which will look something
like -

.nf
        machine-name%:
.fi

.LP
as the Sun is waiting for you to type a UNIX command. We'll leave UNIX
until the next chapter. For now just type the command "suntools". A grey
pattern and an arrow cursor will appear on the screen followed by a
default set up of windows similar to that of figure 3. What you see is an
open window in the top left and four closed
THE ABOVE TEXT IS SELECTED
.ul 1
icons
to the right.
.sp 6.5i
.ce 1
Figure 3.
.KE

.KS
.NH 1
The root menu
```

Figure 1.8 Textedit

1.8.2. Text edit tool

The **textedit** tool allows you to type in and edit text. Most editing actions in **textedit** are based on the current position of the caret and the current text selection. The tool consists of two text *subwindows*. Figure 1.8 shows textedit as it appears when started from the root menu. The top border gives the name of the *file* being edited (NONE in this case) and the *directory* where that file resides. Directories and files are explained in Chapter 2. The tool contains two text subwindows, one main area for editing and a smaller area labelled the *scratch area* for typing and selecting temporary text which we do not want to appear in the main text. Each subwindow has a caret indicating where characters will appear as they are typed in. The caret is a black triangle in the selected window and a grey diamond in any unselected windows.

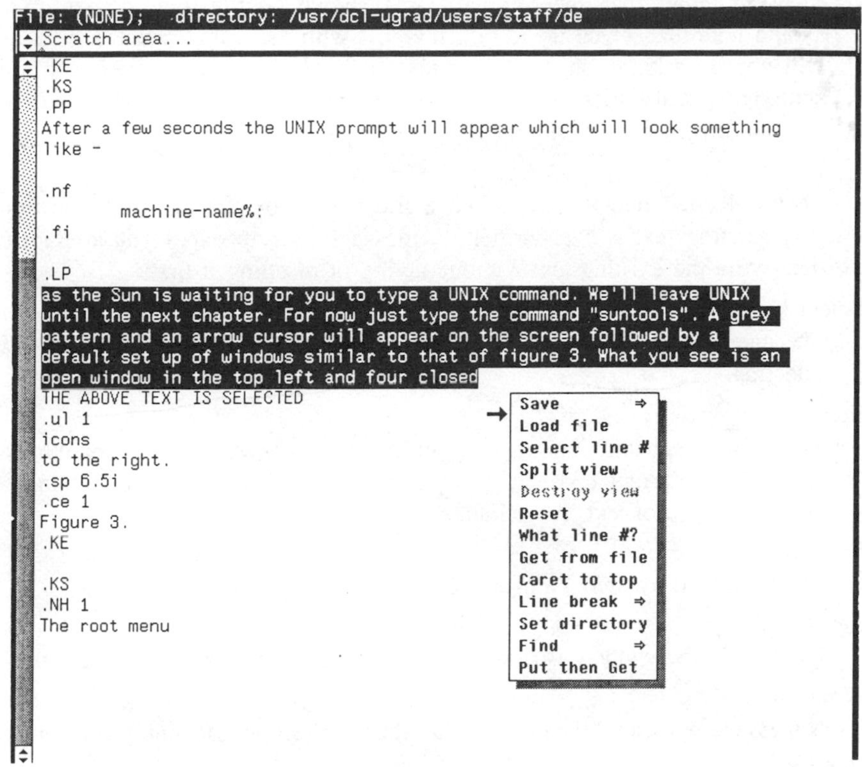

Figure 1.9 Textedit menu

Textedit menu

Each text subwindow has an identical right button menu (figure 1.9). Many of the items of this menu make use of the current text selection. So, for example, if the *load* item was chosen the current text selection would be used as the name of the file of text to be read. Similarly, if the *find* item was chosen the caret would move to the next set of characters which matched the text selection. Such text selections would be made in the upper *scratch area* so that the main window was not cluttered up with temporary filenames and so on. The menu items have the following actions:

Save =>

The current text is saved to the file named in the border label or to a file named by the last text selection if there is no original filename. The => symbol indicates that this item has a *walking menu* of further options to the right. This menu can be seen by moving the cursor (with the right button still down) over the => symbol. The options on this menu include saving, then quitting the tool and using the text selection to *store* as the filename rather than the original name shown on the tool border. You should note that if you try to quit **textedit** with the frame menu, a message will pop up asking you to save or reset the text first. However, if you quit suntools with the root menu no message appears and your changes will be lost, so remember to save first.

Load

Text is loaded into the tool from a file named by the last text selection. Any existing text is over-written. A message will appear if you attempt to over-write the existing text without saving or resetting it first.

Select line #

The caret moves to the line number in the text indicated by the last text selection.

Split view

The current subwindow can be split in two, with each half containing a copy of the current text. So it is possible to look at different sections of the same piece of text. Any changes made occur in both views.

Destroy view

Views created by *Split View* are restored to a single view.

Reset

The text in the window is reset to the contents at the start-up of the tool.

What line #

A message pops up indicating the number of the line containing the caret.

Get from file

A file of text is included into the current piece of text at the point indicated by the caret.

Caret at top

The line containing the caret is moved to the top of the window.

Line break =>

Controls how the line of text behaves when it reaches the right-hand border of the window. The options in the walking menu are either to put the next character on the next line or carry on with any characters disappearing off the right-hand edge. Unfortunately, there is no option to put (or *wrap*) complete words onto the next line.

Set directory

The directory where files are saved (and the directory label in the tool border) are changed to the current text selection.

Find =>

Searches forward for the next string of characters which match the current text selection. The optional walking menu allows searching backwards in the text and using the text string from the *shelf* rather than the current text selection.

Put then Get

The *shelf* is a temporary store where text selections can be held. If there has been a text selection in another window when **textedit** starts up, this item will have *Put then* in grey and **Get** in bold, indicating that text can be copied from the shelf to the current caret position. If the whole item is grey, then the shelf is empty. And if the item is all bold, the current text selection will be **Put** on the shelf then **Got** from the shelf and placed at the current caret position. Text stored on the shelf can also be copied to other tools.

Using function keys with textedit

The function keys to the left and right of the main keyboard can be used in conjunction with **textedit**. The key layout for the left-hand side is shown in figure 1.10. A set of stick-on labels is supplied for these keys. The labels can also be put on the right-hand keys, if you prefer, where the layout is the mirror image of the left.

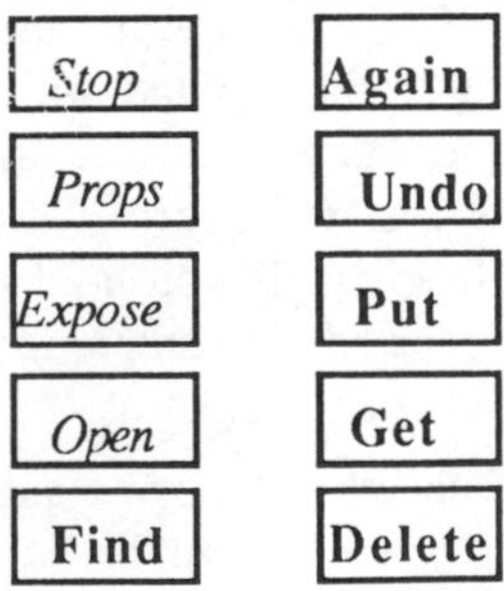

Figure 1.10 Function keys on left

Again

Repeats the last set of editing actions up to the previous text selection.

Undo

Undoes the last editing action. *Undo* remembers the last 50 editing actions.

Put

Puts the text selection on the shelf, and

Get

Gets the selection and puts it at the caret position.

Find

Uses the text selection to search for the next matching string in the text.

Delete

Removes the selected text from the screen.

Using the scrollbar

Scrollbars enable you to move through information which is too large to be displayed in the current window. Scrollbars (as seen in figure 1.9) consist of a long central grey band with a small darker grey *bubble*. The size of the bubble in relation to the band tells you what proportion of the complete information is currently shown in the window. So if the bubble fills the scrollbar all the information is visible. The position of the bubble within the band also gives an indication of what part of the information we are looking at. To try out the scrollbar, split the view in the main textedit window and type in enough text to fill the split window. As you reach the bottom, text at the top will disappear.

With the cursor in the central band, clicking the left button moves you forward and the right button backwards, about a page at a time. How far you actually move depends on the cursor's position in the scrollbar. The middle button moves you to the position in the text indicated by your position on the scrollbar. So if you click the middle button at the top of the scrollbar, the first lines of text will appear and if you click at the base, the last lines of text will appear and so on. Try moving to the top and bottom of your sample text. The two smaller squares with the black triangles (above and below the main scrollbar) allow you to move a step at a time through the text, forward with the left and backward with the right. If you hold the mouse buttons down for a moment, their actions are repeated. Try stepping through your sample text in either direction.

Scrollbars can be used with other types of subwindow. They can also be used horizontally, for example, when looking at graphics images which are too large in both dimensions for the current window.

1.8.3. Command tool

This is a combination of a shelltool and a text edit tool. It allows you to type in UNIX commands and edit and scroll through the text in the window. This is useful if you wish to scroll back through long program output or want to select the text of a previous command for re-execution. Some UNIX tools like **vi** and **more** do not work in a command tool, but their functions (editing and paging) are replaced by this tool. If you do move the caret away from the current UNIX prompt, remember to move it back again before you type the next command. If there is still no response, select the *Disable Edit* item at the bottom of the command tool edit menu, then hit the return key.

1.8.4. Iconedit

So far, we have seen two types of *subwindow* in tools; a *teletype* subwindow in **shelltool** and *textedit* subwindow in the **textedit** tool. **Iconedit** (figure 1.11) shows two new types of subwindows. The large window is a *canvas* window used by the user and the **iconedit** program to draw graphical images. Notice that the subwindows within a tool are tiled; their positions and sizes are fixed within the tool window boundary. The other main subwindow to the right is a *Panel*. Panels contain buttons, switches, messages and text input fields. They are the software equivalent of a control panel on a photocopier or video recorder.

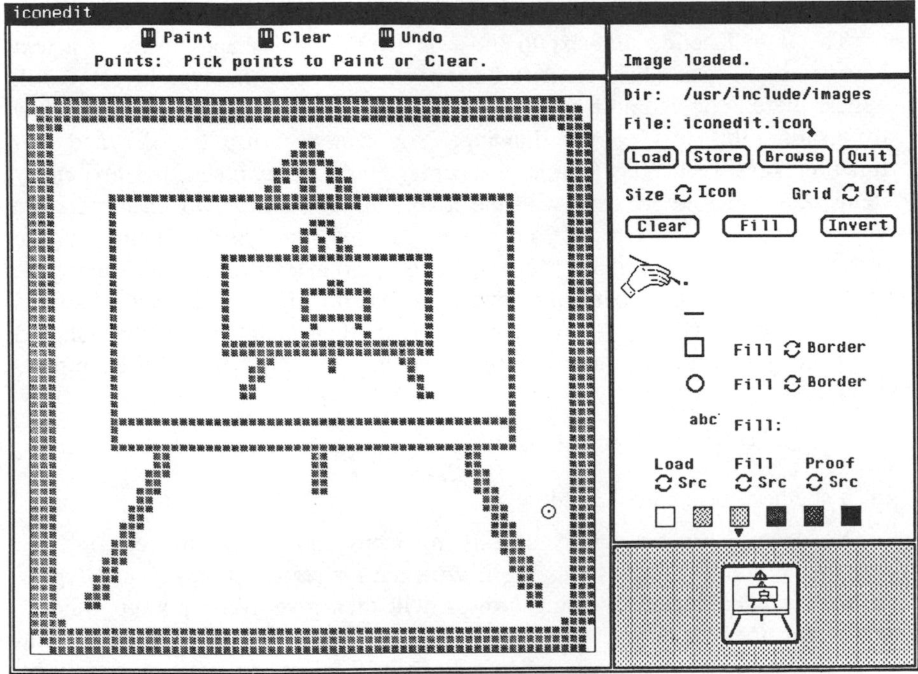

Figure 1.11 Iconedit

Canvas window

Starting up **iconedit** from the root menu gives you an initially empty canvas window in which you can use the mouse to draw shapes. At start-up the mouse is set up to draw dots and the message above the canvas window indicates the action of each mouse button, i.e. left to paint black dots, middle to paint white dots and right button to undo the last action.

Panel window and panel items

The panel window has a hand holding a paint brush next to the type of shape that can currently be drawn. Clicking the left button on a new shape allows you to draw lines, rectangles, circles or text in the canvas window. The painting hand symbol is part of a panel *choice item*, where all the choices available to you are shown on the screen. The items with two curved arrows are also choice items, but only the current choice is being shown. To see all the choices available with these items, hold down the right button on the item to see its pop-up menu. You can then select a choice from the menu or by *cycling* through the choices one by one with the left button. Try experimenting with the other choice items to see what effect they have on your picture.

The item labelled *fill* next to the *abc* item of the shapes menu is a text entry item. If you click the left button on this item the type-in caret will appear there. You can now enter text and use the mouse in the canvas window to position this text on the drawing. You can also use the *Put* and *Get* function keys to handle text in text entry items. The other two text entry items, *Dir* and *File* are used with the load and store *buttons* to load and store your completed picture to or from a file. Try selecting the *File* item with the mouse and type in the name you wish to give your icon or cursor. Then click on the *store* button to put your picture in that file. Buttons carry out actions indicated on their label. If you selected *clear*, then *load*, your picture should reappear. You can start iconedit with an existing icon by typing, for example

% iconedit myicon

in a shelltool or cmdtool window.

You can also get a gallery of existing icons and cursors by selecting the text in the *Dir* text item, removing it with the *Delete* function key and typing in */usr/include/images*. Selecting *browse* will then give you a pop-up window containing the standard set of icons and cursors. You can move through them with the scrollbar and select one to appear in the iconedit canvas window by selecting with the left button.

1.9. Saving a screen layout

So far, the screen layout that you start with has been set up by someone else. It would be more useful if you could start up with your own layout. If you would like to keep your present window layout, type the following line into a shelltool or cmdtool window:

% toolplaces > .suntools

This line writes some text into a file called *.suntools* which the suntools program will use to automatically layout the screen next time you execute suntools. The text is actually the UNIX commands that the user would have used to set up the windows in the size and position they currently occupy on the screen.

1.10. Window tool command line arguments

As well as starting tools from the root menu, you can also type the name of the tool in a shelltool or cmdtool window. Additionally, you can add options to the name in order to change the size or location of the window and so forth.

Table 1.1 shows a full list of the available options. The options **-Wf** and **-Wb** assume that you have a colour screen.

Table 1.1 Window tool command line arguments

Flag	(Long flag)	Arguments
-Ww	(-width)	columns
-Wh	(-height)	lines
-Ws	(-size)	x y
-Wp	(-position)	x y
-WP	(-icon_position)	x y
-Wl	(-label)	"string"
-Wi	(-iconic)	
-Wn	(-no_name_stripe)	
-Wt	(-font)	filename
-Wf	(-foreground_color)	red green blue
-Wb	(-background_color)	red green blue
-Wg	(-set_default_color)	
-WI	(-icon_image)	filename
-WL	(-icon_label)	"string"
-WT	(-icon_font)	filename
-WH	(-help)	

1.10.1. Some examples

Here is an example line created by the **toolplaces** command and placed in the *.suntools* file

shelltool -Wp 501 0 -Ws 651 334 -WP 128 0 -Wl /bin/csh

This would place a shelltool with its top left-hand corner (-Wp) at 501 pixels (or screen dots) across and zero pixels down. It is 651 pixels wide and 334 deep (-Ws). The icon is positioned at 128,0 (-WP). The top left-hand corner of the Sun screen is 0,0. In practice, you would hardly ever specify the size and position in this way. It is quite easy to use the mouse and frame menu to move and resize the window and then use **toolplaces** to work out and save the window layout. More useful options (from the user's point of view) are

% shelltool -Wl "This project" -WI myicon

which puts your own label on the tool border and uses the icon created by **iconedit** instead of the default icon.

% cmdtool -WL "Remote"

which puts a label on the closed icon to indicate its function. Also **-WH** prints out table 1.1.

1.11. Customising the root menu

The root menu at present is probably too long for convenient use. It can be tailored to your own needs by providing a new text description. This consists of a table similar to that shown in table 1.2. Each line starts with the text for the menu entry, followed by the name of the command to be executed when the item is selected. There are standard key words for the redisplay and exit entries. This example can be typed in and saved using the **textedit** tool.

Table 1.2

```
#
# First rootmenu description
#
"Shell"          shelltool
"MailTool"       mailtool
"IconEditor"     iconedit
"DbxTool"        dbxtool
"Console"        cmdtool -C
"Lock"           lockscreen
"Redisplay"      REFRESH
"Exit"           EXIT
```

It is also possible to have walking menus (as used in **textedit**) where the optional section is declared as in table 1.3 by putting the keywords MENU and END around the walking menu entry.

Table 1.3

```
#
# Nested rootmenu description
#
#
"Shell"            shelltool
"Tools"            MENU
"CommandTool"      cmdtool
"MailTool"         mailtool
"TextEditor"       textedit
"Defaults"         defaultsedit
"IconEditor"       iconedit
"DbxTool"          dbxtool
"PerfMeter"        perfmeter
"Gfx"              gfxtool
"Console"          cmdtool -C
"Tools"            END
"Lock"             lockscreen
"Redisplay"        REFRESH
"Exit"             EXIT
```

To use your new menu description and walking menus, see the following section on the **defaultsedit** tool.

1.12. The defaults edit tool

Figure 1.12 shows the **defaultedit** tool. This tool allows you to customise various features of your working environment. The top subwindow is a panel subwindow. The *category* choice item allows you to choose which set of features you wish to edit. The *save* and *quit* buttons allow you to save your current choices and quit the tool, respectively. The *Reset* button restores the choices to those that existed at the start-up of **defaultedit**. The *Edit item* permits you to edit certain features of the choices themselves.

The next window is a message window. Initially, as here, it gives a short help message. Help can be obtained for each item by clicking the left button on labels in the left-hand column.

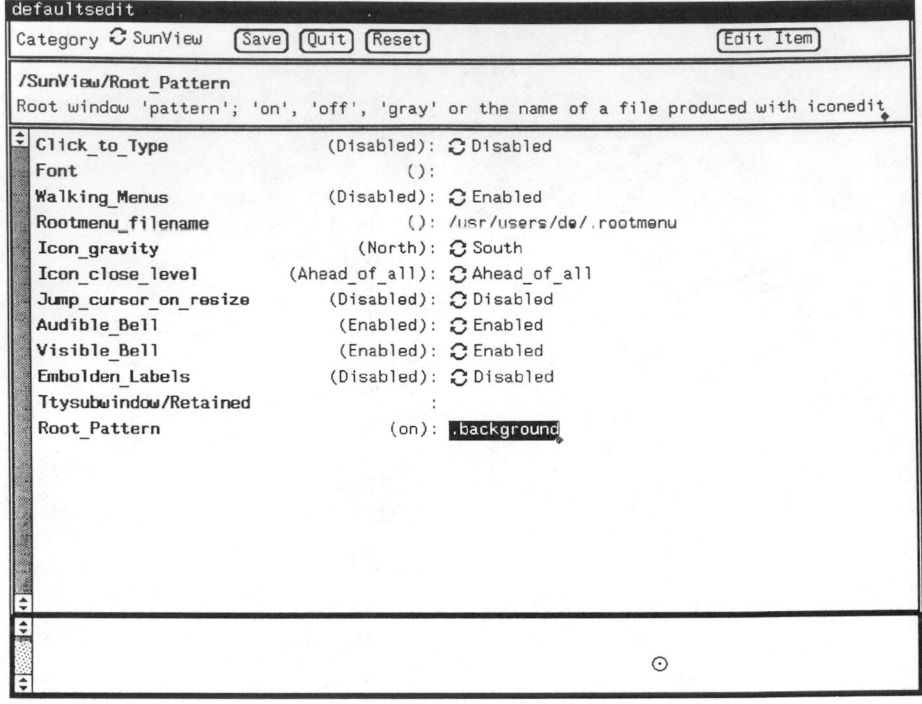

Figure 1.12

The main window is a panel window contain the choices available in each category. Initially it shows the *SunView* category. The left-hand column gives the names of the features, the next column is their default value and the final column is a choice or text input item which is modified by the user. The current user has modified features such as:

1. Switched on walking-style menus so that options can be obtained from this user's customised rootmenu shown in section 1.9.
2. Given the name of the file where the new menu description (also in section 1.9) is stored.
3. Changed *Icon_gravity* so that windows close to icons are placed at the bottom (or south) of the screen to fit in with this user's window layout.
4. Given the name of an icon file to be used as a repeated pattern for the root window, replacing the current uniformly grey background.

It is also possible, via the *category* choice item, to get choices for program source text indentation, basic mouse input, mail message tools, menus, scrollbars, textedit windows and tty windows. Generally, the need to modify the default features of your environment only begins to arise after some experience, so we will not expand on **defaultsedit** further. We will also say no more about the *Edit item* button other than, in conjunction with the lower text window, it allows you to copy features, delete them and edit the left-hand labels.

Further reading

The next step is to experiment with the above tools and occasionally dip into the relevant manuals when some aspect becomes unclear. The Sun manual to start with is:

Windows and Window Based Tools: Beginners' Guide.

For more detail, see the individual entries in section 1 of the UNIX manual, *Commands Reference Manual*. The entries are suntools, shelltool, cmdtool, textedit, defaultsedit, toolplaces, lockscreen and iconedit. Some further tools, not covered here, which you might like to explore are mailtool, clock, perfmon and traffic.

2 Sun UNIX

2.1. Introduction to UNIX

Many readers will be familiar with the UNIX operating system. Its growth and spread is perhaps one of the most unexpected success stories of computing. Originally implemented on an abandoned PDP-7 minicomputer in 1969 by Ken Thompson, (later joined by Dennis Ritchie), the system is now in widespread use in educational establishments and there are many UNIX look-alikes in the industrial marketplace. Sun UNIX is based on 4.2 BSD UNIX which was developed at the University of California, Berkeley, and has several extensions and improvements on the original version.

The purpose of this brief section is to imbue the UNIX novice with some of the central elements of UNIX and hopefully whet her/his appetite for further reading and exploration of the UNIX system. To try the examples given below you need to login to your machine, and perhaps start two or three shelltool windows within suntools as shown in Chapter 1.

2.1.1. Files and directories

Like most conventional operating systems, the user's data (programs, text, data etc.) is held on *files*. On UNIX, these files can be held in *directories*. Directories and files form a tree structure as described below.

The top of the UNIX directory hierarchy is called the *root* and is denoted by the '/' symbol.

We can specify any node in the tree by giving its name as a path from the root of the tree to the specific node. If we wish to refer to the node called *project*, we can say

```
/users/fred/programs/project
```

This is an *absolute pathname*, beginning from the root of the tree and taking us to the required node. The '/' character acts as a separator between node names.

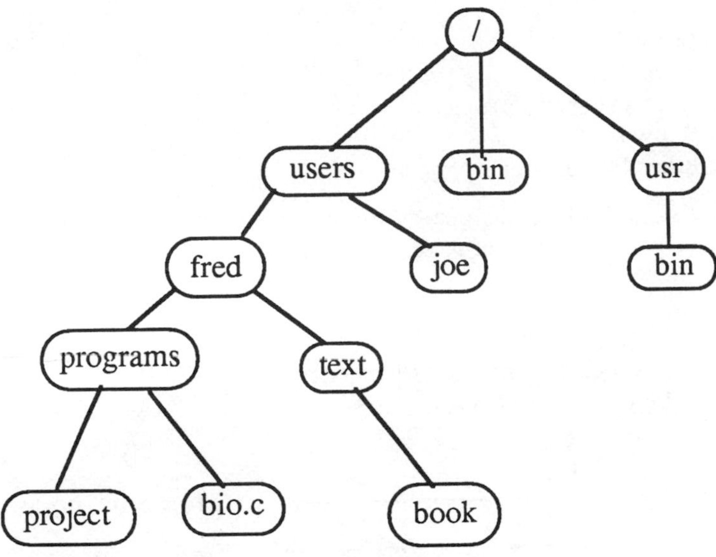

Figure 2.1 Directory Tree

When you login to UNIX, you will be positioned in an initial node of the tree; this node is referred to as your *home* (or login) directory. This may not be the node we wish to work in, so we can move to the *project* node (so we can work on our project) or to the *book* node (so we can work on our book). At any time during our tree traversals, we can find out where we are by typing **pwd** (print working directory).

If we login as *fred* and type **pwd** we should get the response

/users/fred

To change directories, we use the **cd** (change directory) command.

```
% pwd
/users/fred
% cd /users/fred/programs/project
% pwd
/users/fred/programs/project
```

In this example, we have quoted the absolute pathname from the root. We can give names in a *relative* form; that is, from our current position in the tree.

% **pwd**
/users/fred
% **cd programs/project**
% **pwd**
/users/fred/programs/project

We can also go back up the tree by using the '../' notation; this means, move to the node above my current node.

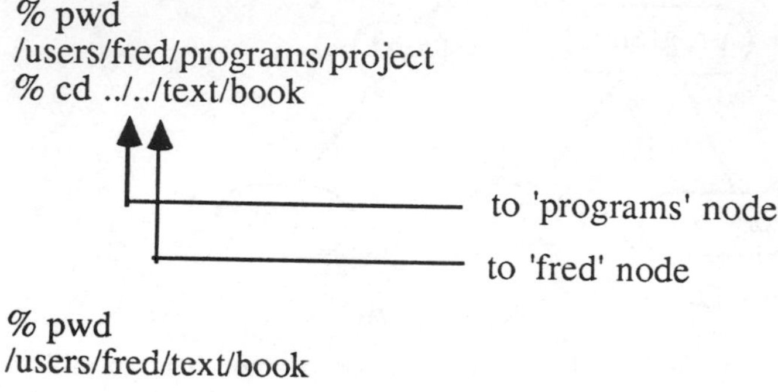
% pwd
/users/fred/programs/project
% cd ../../text/book
to 'programs' node
to 'fred' node
% pwd
/users/fred/text/book

Figure 2.2

At any time, we can return to our home directory by typing **cd** on its own.

% **pwd**
/users/fred/text/book
% **cd**
% **pwd**
/users/fred

Directories can contain other directories and files. Take the node called *programs*. It contains another directory called *project* and a file called *bio.c*. To find out what is in a directory, we use the **ls** command.

% **pwd**
/users/fred/programs
% **ls**
project
bio.c
%

We can use **ls** to find out the contents of other directories (other than our current working directory) by giving a pathname after the **ls.**

% **pwd**
/users/fred/programs
% **ls ../**
programs
text
% **pwd**
/users/fred/programs

Associated with files and directories are *access permissions.* The accesses can be

read (r)
write (w)
execute (x)

We can grant these permissions to

user (u) i.e. ourself
group (g) members
others (o) -- everybody else

We therefore have three groups of three permissions; these are viewed as nine permission flags.

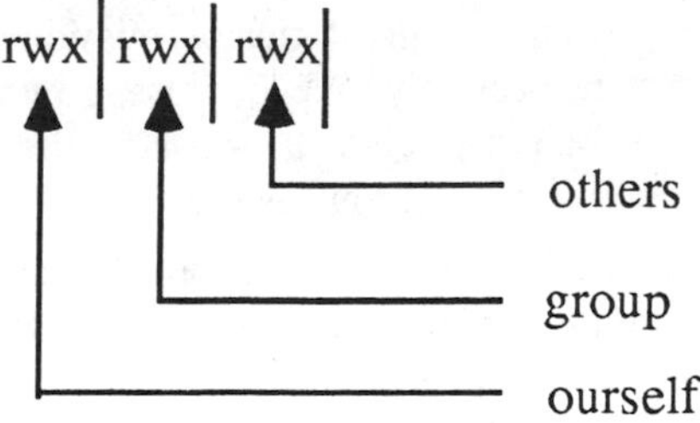

Figure 2.3

To find the current settings of these permissions for a file or directory, we can type **ls -l**.

```
% pwd
/users/fred/programs
% ls -l bio.c
-rw-r--r--  fred  30  Jun 5 11:09 bio.c
%
```

Here we see the three groups of three. Where a letter appears, that means that form of access is allowed; where a '-' (dash) appears, that means the form of access has been withheld. So, *bio.c* can be :

read and written by fred
read by his group
read by others

It cannot be:

executed by fred
written or executed by his group
written or executed by others

We can alter the permissions of files (and directories) that we own by using the **chmod** (change mode) command. For example:

```
% chmod u+rw,g+r,o+r bio.c
```

The plus (+) sign means to grant the permission. 'u', 'g' and 'o' mean user, group and others respectively. We can use a minus (-) sign to withhold the permission. If we simply give a + or - list of permissions, those permissions are assumed to hold for all users.

You may have noticed a tenth dash in our example; this is the directory flag. If the item we are examining is a directory, a 'd' appears in this position; if not (i.e. it is a file) a dash appears here.

```
% pwd
/users/fred/programs
% ls -l
-rw-r--r--  fred  30  Jun 5 11:09 bio.c
drwxr--r--  fred  24  Jul 2 01:20 project
```

To examine the contents of a file we can use the **cat** command. This displays a file on the screen.

```
% cat hi.there
hello
there
%
```

No matter how many lines there are in the file, **cat** will display them at an unhindered pace.

To peruse a file at a more leisurely pace, we can issue the **more** command. This prints out the contents of the file a *screenful* (normally 34 lines in a default-sized shelltool) at a time, and prompts us if we wish to see more. **more** has further capabilities than that; we refer the interested user to the appropriate manual entry. Manual entries can be viewed with the **man** command followed by the name of the UNIX command we need information on. **man** output is automatically sent to **more** (i.e. *redirected*) so we can see an entry page by page. You can refer to the printed Sun manuals supplied with your machine for a more leisurely read.

2.1.2. Input and output redirection

Much of the power and success of UNIX lies in its treatment of files, devices and processes, and the ability to redirect input and output among them. In the first case, UNIX views files, devices and processes as the same, in terms of i/o. Take the simple command **echo** that echoes its parameters to the screen.

```
% echo "hello"
hello
%
```

We can cause the output of any command to be passed to a file, device, or further command.

```
% echo "hello" > hello.file
% cat hello.file
hello
%
```

In the above example, we have created a file called *hello.file* and placed the five characters 'h', 'e', 'l', 'l', 'o' in the file. If the file existed before the command was issued, we would have overwritten its previous contents.

We can concatenate files together:

```
% cat f1 f2 f3 > ftotal
```

This creates a file called *ftotal* which consists of the contents of *f1*, *f2* and *f3*.

We can append to the end of files using >> ; i.e.

```
% echo "first line" > f1
% echo "second line" >> f1
% cat f1
first line
second line
%
```

Similarly, commands can take their input from files. Consider the **rev** command which reverses the data it reads.

```
% rev
hello
olleh
%    =    here we type CTRL and D together;
          signifies end of file
```

So we can carry out the following:

```
% echo "The deed is done Madam" > f1
% rev < f1
madaM enod si deed ehT
%
```

UNIX provides us with a mechanism for communicating between processes. In the above example, we wanted to see what "The deed is done Madam" looked like in reverse. To do this we created an intermediate file, *f1*. We could have used a *pipe* instead, as follows:

```
% echo "The deed is done Madam" | rev
madaM enod si deed ehT
%
```

Here, the standard output of *echo* is connected to the standard input of *rev*.

It is possible to build long, complex and powerful *chains* of commands (processes), files and pipes.

2.1.3. Some useful directory commands

We have already met the following:

```
ls   :   list contents of directory
pwd  :   print working directory
cd   :   change directory
```

Here are two more. We can create new directories with the **mkdir** (make directory) command.

```
% pwd
/users/fred/programs
% ls
bio.c
project
% mkdir syntax
% ls
bio.c
project
syntax
% cd syntax
% ls
%
```

We can also remove directories with the **rmdir** (remove directory) command. UNIX will, naturally enough, allow us to only remove empty directories. This is sensible (think about it!).

```
% pwd
/users/fred/programs
% ls
bio.c
project
syntax
% rmdir syntax
% ls
bio.c
project
%
```

2.1.4. Some useful file commands

Once we have a file, we may wish to copy it (in the same directory or indeed, elsewhere in the file hierarchy). This is done by the **cp** (copy) command.

```
% pwd
/users/fred/programs
% ls
bio.c
project
% cp bio.c original.bio.c
% ls
bio.c
original.bio.c
project
%
```

Here we have made a copy of *bio.c*; perhaps because we are about to change it and want to keep a *working* copy. What if the user called *joe* wants a copy of *bio.c* for his own purposes?

```
% pwd
/users/joe
% cp ../fred/programs/bio.c bio.c
%
```

Joe (if he is not a group member with Fred) can only carry out this copy if Fred's *bio.c* has read access set for others. Notice that he is free to give it the *same* name of *bio.c*; the two files/nodes are distinct when we consider the full pathnames:

/users/fred/programs/bio.c

and

/users/joe/bio.c

A useful shorthand to represent the *current* directory is to use the dot (.) character. In the example above,

```
cp ../fred/programs/bio.c .
```

would have had the same effect.

It is also possible to copy complete directories by using the **cp** command with the **-r** flag.

```
cp -r programs old.programs
```

Here, the destination of the copy command is a directory. The destination directory (here, old.programs) should exist before the command is issued. The command will cause a directory called *programs* to be created within the *old.programs* directory, and everything held within the original *programs* directory will be copied into the *old.programs/programs* directory.

We may also want to rename or move files (not making a copy). This is done with the **mv** (move) command. Say Fred has been *hacking around* with *bio.c* and it is now fouled up beyond belief, and he wants to return to his working copy (*original.bio.c*). He can issue the following command

```
% pwd
/users/fred/programs
% ls
bio.c
original.bio.c
project
% mv original.bio.c bio.c
% ls
bio.c
project
%
```

Again, we can use pathnames to move files across the tree.

We may wish to simply remove files; i.e. erasing or deleting them. This is done by the **rm** (remove) command. Consider this alternative scenario : Fred has managed to get his new *bio.c* into a working condition and no longer requires his *original.bio.c*.

```
% pwd
/users/fred/programs
% ls
bio.c
original.bio.c
project
% rm original.bio.c
% ls
bio.c
project
%
```

It is also possible to delete files interactively. If we type:

```
rm -i *
```

this will list the contents of the current directory, one file after another, followed by a colon. We can then type **y** if we wish to delete the file, **n** otherwise.

A user must have write permission to remove a file.

As we have seen, to examine the contents of a (text) file, we can use the **cat** command. The name of this command is derived from conCATenate, as we can use the **cat** command, with input/output redirection, to concatenate files.

> % **cat x**
> { the contents of the file named *x* appear unhindered on the screen }
> % **cat x y**
> { the contents of both *x* and *y* appear on the screen }
> % **cat x y > z**
> { the contents of *x* and *y* are concatenated into the file called *z* }

We can also use **cat** to create a new file by again using i/o redirection.

```
% cat > x
hello
there
CTRL-D
% cat x
hello
there
%
```

UNIX also provides us with several text editors. An editor like **ex** (or **ed**) is line oriented; we can only see the current line we are editing. An editor like **vi,** however, is screen oriented; we can see a screenful of text out of the file. Nevertheless, such editors are *vdu* based, and while **vi** is a far more satisfactory editor than the now obsolete line-oriented editors, none of the standard UNIX editors exploits the power of the Sun graphics capabilities. A full exploration of the editors is beyond the scope of this chapter; like most things in computing, the best way to learn the power and facilities of an editor is by using it.

2.1.5. Other users

UNIX is a multi-user system. This means more than one user can access the resources of the machine running UNIX. While Sun workstations are stand-alone, single user machines, we shall see later how they can be linked by networks and so may have more than one simultaneous user. To find out who else is using the machine, we can type **who** and this presents us with a list of users logged onto the machine.

```
% who
is        tty00   Feb  5 08:47
rgg       tty01   Feb  5 09:40
tony      tty02   Feb  5 15:32
```

```
dh        tty03   Feb  5 09:54
has       tty06   Feb  5 14:19
de        tty15   Feb  5 15:42
stephen   tty17   Feb  5 14:21
peter     tty19   Feb  5 09:04
john      tty20   Feb  5 09:16
jas       tty22   Feb  5 09:58
craig     ttyh0   Feb  5 10:04
jam       ttyh1   Feb  5 15:05
gordon    ttyh2   Feb  5 10:29
stuart    ttyp0   Feb  5 12:58(dcl-ipse1)
susan     ttyp1   Feb  5 10:23(dcl-oops)
csc316    ttyp2   Feb  5 15:09(dcl-ugrad)
%
```

Notice the bracketted information; this means that the user has logged onto our machine remotely from another machine; e.g. susan has logged in from the machine named *dcl-oops*. We shall investigate this further in a later section.

If we have had an attack of amnesia and have forgotten who we are, we can type **who am i.** More seriously, we may be logged on more than once and we need to know what terminal we are using now, so the **who am i** option can help us here.

We can communicate with the other users either interactively or not. There is a **write** command that allows us to write to other users. This is invoked by typing

```
write joe
```

Anything we type now will appear on Joe's terminal window (until we type CTRL-D to signify end of text). Joe can of course respond

```
write fred
```

and then he is in contact with us. Using **write** can lead to a bit of a mess if both users type simultaneously! Lines will appear intermingled on the screen. Most users adopt a protocol like 'o' (for over, meaning "I have now finished typing, you can please reply now") and ending with 'o+o' (for over and out).

There is also a **mail** system, which allows us to send electronic mail to users; because of the network connections, we can send inter-machine mail.

The **mail** program is invoked by typing

mail joe

We can send mail to several users by listing more than one user name. Here, we type our message again terminating with CTRL-D. This message does not appear directly on Joe's screen, but is placed in his mail box for his later perusal.

2.1.6. Programming

Because of the popularity of UNIX there are now compilers available for many of the better known programming languages; some of these are public domain and can be easily obtained. Among the languages supplied as standard are Fortran 77, ratfor, and Pascal. Another standard, of course, is the C programming language. This is the language that was developed at Bell Laboratories alongside the development of the UNIX system; it belongs to the class of language known as system development languages. Because it is so integral to UNIX, it is sometimes hard to separate the two. UNIX's extensive toolset includes many support tools for the C programming language, not least of which is the C compiler, **cc.**

Naturally, it is beyond the scope of this book to discuss C programming, but we have listed some C books at the end of this chapter.

Among the support tools are **lint** that carries out more intensive checks on your C programs than does the compiler (i.e. type checking of parameters, procedures having the correct number of parameters when called etc.) and **dbx,** a powerful debugging tool, which allows us to single-step through C programs, examine the contents of variables, etc. **Dbxtool,** the window version of **dbx,** and the tools **make** and *SCCS* are discussed in Chapter 9.

For those readers keen to write compilers, there are two aids -- **yacc** (yet another compiler-compiler) and **lex** (a lexical analyser). **yacc** will take a syntax and produce a syntax analyser (written in C); similarly, **lex** will take a list of strings and their tokens and produce a lexical analyser. Both these analysers can then be included in a C program and called as necessary.

2.1.7. The C shell

The program that acts as the command interpreter for UNIX is known as a *shell.* There are several well-known shells -- the Bourne shell (sh) and the C shell (csh), to name but two. Indeed, there is nothing to prevent the user from writing and using her/his own shell program.

The C shell is usually the preferred shell when working in Sun UNIX. It is this program that supplies the % prompt, used in this chapter, and that reads in our commands, interprets them, and finally executes them.

Pattern matching

We can give incomplete filenames containing patterns and the C shell will find those files that match the pattern. We will only consider two metacharacters used for this purpose; * and ?. There are more powerful matching mechanisms, but they are beyond the introductory scope of this chapter.

The symbol '*' is used to mean any number (including zero) of characters. For example, "*a" would match "ta", "beta" and "a" on its own. Similarly, "a*" would match "alpha" as well as "a". The expression "*a*b*" can match "samba" and "ab".

If we use "*" on its own, it will match all the files in our current directory. A dangerous command to type would be

```
rm *
```

as this will erase all the files.

```
% ls
bio.c
original.bio.c
header.h
% rm *
% ls
%
```

When we issue the command **rm ***, the shell expands the '*' into a list of parameters, as if we had typed

```
rm bio.c original.bio.c header.h
```

The '?' metacharacter will match exactly one character in the filename.

```
% ls
one
two
f1
f2
% rm f?
% ls
one
two
%
```

Here, the pattern *f?* will only match those filenames with two characters, the first one of which is *f*. We could also have tried

```
rm ??
```

which would erase all files with names two characters long.

Shell variables

Shells can support powerful concepts such as programming at the shell level (which is beyond the scope of this chapter) and, to help with this (and other facilities), the shells have internal variables that we will refer to as *shell variables.*

For example, we have the shell prompt that is initially set to %. This is contained in a shell variable called *prompt*. By using the shell command **set** (i.e. this is not the name of a program but a shell directive) we can change the value of any shell variable, and therefore we can customise our prompt.

```
% set prompt='what now rodge babe?'
what now rodge babe?who
  "      "
what now rodge babe?set prompt = '% '
% who
```

Start up commands

When we login, the C shell begins by reading commands stored in a file called *.cshrc*, held in our home directory. Any later shells we start will also read from this file. However, if we do not yet have a *.cshrc* file, the C shell does not complain and carries on. A login shell will then go on to read from a file called *.login*; these commands are only executed once, when we login. Therefore, we can place commands that we wish to be executed when we login in our *.login* file. For example, we could execute the **suntools** command in *.login* to automatically start the window system everytime we login. As a bracket to *.login*, we can also have a *.logout* file that contains commands to be executed when we logout -- this could include the lines;

```
if ( `tty` =~ /dev/console ) then
      login lock
endif
```

which starts the **lockscreen** program to protect the screen until the next user comes to use the machine. The **if** statement is needed as we only want to lock the screen if we logout from the main console, not if we logout from a remote connection.

In the *.cshrc* file, then, we might include a **set prompt** directive. A useful prompt to set up is \!%. This issues a prompt like **5%**. The number represents the number of the current command. These command numbers are kept internally by the C shell, regardless of our prompt, as they form the basis of the C shell's *history* mechanism. Note that we use *.cshrc* to set the prompt if we wish the same prompt to occur in any shelltool we start. Shelltool reads *.cshrc* but not *.login* which is only read by the login shell.

History mechanism

The C shell maintains a list of the last N commands executed. N can be given a value by setting the shell variable called *history*. By typing the shell command

% **history**

we will get a numbered list of commands. We can re-execute any of these commands by typing the number of the command, preceded by the history symbol, !

% **!5**

would re-execute the fifth command in the history list. To re-execute the command that we have just typed

% **!!**

We can also pattern match using the metacharacters listed earlier.

% **!vi**

will execute the last **vi** command issued and

% **!?h**

will execute the last command instruction that had an argument containing the letter 'h'.

Aliasing

We can set up a translation between what we type and the command that the C shell executes.

If, when we type the **ls** command, we always want it to show the size of files, i.e. to always use the **-s** flag, we can say

% alias ls ls -s

Now, whenever we type **ls** the C shell interprets it as **ls -s.**

We can put a list of alias commands in our *.cshrc* file, to be obeyed whenever we start a shell.

We can alias commands that use pipes etc. A useful alias when using **nroff** might be

alias nrpr "nroff -Trpr \!* | lpr"

Here, we wish to specify a shorthand way of using **nroff** to produce output for our rapid printer (here denoted by -Trpr) and that we want the output to go directly to the 'list this on the rapid line printer' command, **lpr.** The \!* parameter is replaced by any parameters we give when issuing **nrpr.** so

nrpr -ms chap.two

is interpreted as

nroff -Trpr -ms chap.two | lpr

If we find that we always use the same set of **nroff** macros (say **-ms**) we could include this in the alias set up

alias nrpr "nroff -Trpr -ms \!* | lpr"

Search Paths

When we type the name of a command, the C shell has to find the file that contains that command. We can specify the places that the C shell looks by setting up a search path in the shell variable, *path*.

In earlier versions of UNIX, the search rule was first your current directory, then */bin*, then */usr/bin*. The latter two directories contain the UNIX utility programs, such as those we have met in this chapter, i.e. **cat, ls, nroff** etc. To set this up for the C shell, we can type set path = (. ~/bin /usr/local /usr/ucb /bin /usr/bin)

The shell searches the path variable from left to right, so if we had a program in our own directory *~/bin* called nroff, our version of nroff would be executed rather than that in */usr/bin/*. Similarly, we may have commands which are local to our own machines and these would be found in */usr/local* (or possibly */usr/local/bin*). */usr/ucb* contains commands specific to the version of UNIX on which Sun UNIX is based, i.e. Berkeley 4.2. Of course, we can set up any path that we choose.

Conclusion

We have only touched on the power of the C shell. For example, it is possible to program in the C shell, as it supports control structures such as **if-then-endif, while-end,** and **switch-case-endsw** etc.

We can create files containing shell commands involving the above structures.

The C shell also supports extensive job management; any command we start can be temporarily suspended, or placed in foreground or background mode.

2.2. Using windows with UNIX

Sun UNIX is Berkeley 4.2 BSD. Everything we have discussed so far will work happily on a simple terminal hooked up to a Sun workstation or (say) a VAX 750 running 4.2. How then can we exploit the additional graphics facilities of the Sun workstation?

Well, to begin with, as we know, the Sun workstation supports the concept of windows on the screen. We can regard each window as a single terminal. Within each window, then, we can run anything we might do on a single terminal. Each window has the C shell executing within it.

Because we can have as many windows on the screen as we like, each one executing a C shell, we can allocate a conceptual activity to each window. If we are trapped in the {edit, compile, test and debug} cycle, we can devote each activity to a single window. For example, we might have an edit permanently running in one window. In another, we can be compiling the program. If the compiler produces any error messages, these will be listed in our compiler-window. We can easily move to our edit-window to rectify these errors, which remain on the screen in our compiler-window. Once we have completed our edit, we can move to the compiler-window. If it compiles with no errors, we can move to a third (execution) window to run the program. If it fails, we can move to the edit-window to effect alterations, and then to the compiler-window and so on (see Chapter 1).

Each activity then has a window devoted to it. The results of each activity are not lost (as they would be on a terminal) when we context switch to a different activity. While there are (as far as the author is aware) no quantitative measures of this kind of environment, personal experience unhesitatingly recommends this qualitatively!

Invoking the suntool menu, we can launch further shelltools; this starts a new C shell window. Once it is on screen, we can move and change its size by invoking the window menu. We can lay out the screen as we require.

2.3. Networking

2.3.1. Remote logins and shells

Because of the extensive hardware and software support for networking, it is possible to link Suns in an ethernet configuration. Every machine is given a symbolic name, and we can refer to those machines by those names. It is possible to login to these remote machines. This is done with the **rlogin** command.

Each *host* system on the net has a file called */etc/hosts* which stores all the names of the *remote* systems it knows about. There is also a file called */etc/hosts.equiv* which contains a list of remote hosts (rhosts) with which it shares user names. When you login as the same user on an equivalent host, you do not need to give a password.

% **rlogin ugrad** = *ugrad* is the symbolic name of another Sun

This example assumes that the host, *ugrad*, has an entry for the machine you are currently working on in its equivalence file. The */etc/hosts.equiv* file is system wide, and will be maintained by the system manager. On a per-user level, we can have an *.rhosts* file in our home directory; this contains a private equivalence list. Each line contains an rhost name and a username, separated by a space. This allows us to specify additional cases where a remote login can occur without a password.

If you remotely login to a machine for which you do not have an equivalence, then a login and password will prompted for, as with a local login.

% **rlogin ugrad -l fred2**
Password:

If you do not wish to login to the remote machine, but only wish to execute a single command on that machine, you can use the **rsh** (remote shell) command.

% **rsh ugrad who**

will execute the **who** command on the *ugrad* machine. If you have a different username on the remote machine, you can specify it using the **-l** option.

% **rsh ugrad -l young.fred who**

You must have an equivalence on the remote host to use **rsh;** the remote shell will not prompt for a password, nor can you supply one in the command line. If you omit the command (i.e. omit the **who** in the above example), you will be remotely logged in by **rlogin.**

The names of the remote hosts are also commands, held in a directory called */usr/hosts*. If you include this directory in your search path, you can simply type

% **ugrad who**

to execute a single command on the remote machine. To remotely login, you can again omit the command and type

% **ugrad**

2.3.2. Remote file copy

You may wish to copy (several) file(s) from a remote machine to your local machine, to carry out some local processing. A UNIX utility called **rcp** is provided for this purpose. The format of the command, for single file copies, is

rcp file1 file2

Each file is of the form

"rhost:path"

or

"path"

where *path* is a pathname as we have seen. Naturally, one filename is a remote one, and this is signified by prefixing the pathname identifying the remote file with the name of the remote host, separated by a colon.

If *path* is not a full pathname (i.e. not beginning with '/'), it is taken to be relative to your login directory -- if it is a remote name, it is relative to your login directory on the remote machine. We must have an entry in our *.rhosts* file on *rhost:* to give us permission to copy the file.

If you are using metacharacters within the remote file name, you should enclose the name in quotes so that the metacharacters are resolved on the remote machine and not locally. We will see an example of this in a few lines.

We can copy files in both directions.

```
rcp ugrad:list list
```

copies the file called *list* under our login directory on the remote host called *ugrad* into our local file, also called *list*. We could have used metacharacters as follows:

```
rcp ugrad:"l*" list
```

```
rcp list ugrad:list
```

copies the local file *list* to the remote file *list* under our login directory on the remote host *ugrad*.

We can also copy files from other users by giving the remote user name after the remote host name as follows :

```
rcp ugrad.fred:list mylist
```

This copies a file called *list* held under fred's login directory on the *ugrad* machine into our local file called *mylist*.

Just as with the local copy command **cp,** we can remotely copy directories using the **-r** flag. Here, the destination must be a directory:

```
rcp -r ugrad.dir1 local.dir
```

At this point, we can consider the use of windows again when accessing remote machines.

We may be in the position of wanting to copy files from a remote host to our local host, but unsure of where it is on the remote host. We can create a window and through it remotely login to the remote host in question. Now, we can use that window to locate the file/directory in question, and carry out the **rcp** in a local window, using any information required and gained in the remote window. In brief, we can use the remote and local windows to synchronise and co-ordinate the copy.

2.3.3. Forwarding mail

We can also arrange for our mail to be forwarded from the machine it arrived on to the machine we want it to be on; typically, the machine we tend to log onto most frequently.

This is done by placing a file called *.forward* in our home directory on the mail arrival machine. This file contains lines in the form

fred@ugrad

2.3.4. File transfer

ftp (file transfer program) is a user interface to the ARPANET standard file transfer protocol. To invoke **ftp,** type

ftp> **ftp rhost**

Once the rhost is named, the local **ftp** program will attempt to talk to a **ftp** server on the rhost. The **ftp** program will await instructions from the local user by presenting a **ftp**> prompt.

ftp is a powerful program with an extensive set of commands. With such programs, there are always two commands worth knowing:

* **bye** (or **quit**) : end the ftp session
* **help** [command] : display information on the specified command i.e.

ftp> **help bye**

if **command** is omitted, a list of available commands is output.

At any time during an **ftp** session, it is possible to issue a local command preceded by an '!'.

Among **ftp's** command set are several for examining, traversing and manipulating the rhost's directory structure:

cd
ls -- an abbreviated listing of the directory's contents
dir -- a full listing
pwd
rmdir
mkdir

We can also manipulate the remote files:

delete remote_file
rename f1 f2 -- rename the file *f1* to *f2*.

We can also issue some commands regarding the local file system, i.e. lcd (or change local directory).

Single file transfers

get remote_file [local_file]

We can get a single remote file and copy it into a local file. If we omit the name of the local file, the remote file will be copied into a local file of the same name.

put local_file [remote_file]

This stores a local file on the remote machine. If we omit a remote filename, it is given the same name as the local file.

Multiple file transfers

We can prefix the **get** and **put** commands with the letter 'm' to form the **mget** and **mput** multiple file commands.

mget remote_files

This will retrieve the specified remote files and place them in the local directory. Conversely,

mput local_files

will copy the local files into the remote directory.

It is possible to use metacharacters within **ftp,** if we first issue a **glob** command, i.e.

ftp> **glob**

Therefore, we could issue commands such as

ftp> **mget l***

The **glob** command is a *toggle* command; we can switch the global capabilities on and off by repeated issuing of the **glob** command.

When issuing a command dealing with multiple files, ftp interactively prompts us with each name, expecting a **y** or **n** reply, depending upon whether we really want to transfer each individual file. We can disable this prompting by originally issuing the **ftp** command with a **-i** flag.

If, at any time, we are unsure of **ftp's** actions, we can switch on *verbose* mode. Under this mode, **ftp** will show all responses from the remote **ftp** server. **ftp** is automatically in verbose mode when it starts running. To toggle between verbose and non-verbose mode, we use the **verbose** command.

The various commands **ftp** provides for local and remote file system traversal allow us to position ourselves in the required directories on both the rhost and lhost before commencing file transfer. However, the use of windows with ftp should be obvious.

ftp has the advantage over **rcp** in that no *.rhosts* entry is required, rather, the password is entered each time **ftp** is used. This is useful if you are worried about the security of your files on a particular machine.

2.3.5. Network file system

To conclude this section on networking, we shall look briefly at Sun's Network File System (NFS). Whereas **ftp, rsh, rlogin** and **rcp** are common to all machines with Berkeley UNIX, NFS is specific to the Sun. NFS provides the facility of sharing files on the disks of different machines in a network. The sharing is transparent to the user who uses standard pathnames, in the usual way, to access files. For example, the directory */usr/local/* may exist on one machine but be shared, by NFS, across several machines. So the users, on the machines with NFS access to **/usr/local/**, need only one entry in their path variable to execute the commands in this directory. They do not need to use **rsh** or **rlogin**. Similarly with data files, **rcp** and **ftp** are not needed to access files shared by NFS. Theses commands are still needed, however, for files and directories not shared by NFS, and also when there are non-Sun machines on our ethernet network (though NFS is becoming available on other hardware).

The ideas behind NFS are explained in Chapter 8, while the procedures for sharing files via NFS are dealt with in Chapter 7.

Recommended reading

Getting Started with UNIX: Beginner's Guide, Sun Microsystems Inc.,

Doing More with UNIX: Beginner's Guide, Sun Microsystems Inc., Mountain View CA, 1986.

Games, Demos and Other Pursuits: Beginner's Guide, Sun Microsystems Inc., Mountain View CA, 1986.

R.E. Berry, B.A.E. Meekings,
A Book on C, Macmillan, London, 1984.

M.R.M. Dunsmuir, G.J. Davies,
Programming the UNIX System, Macmillan, London, 1985.

Y. Nishinuma, R. Espesser,
UNIX - First Contact, Macmillan, London, 1987.

R.J. Whiddett et al.,
UNIX: a practical introduction for users, Ellis Horwood, Chichester, 1985.

3 Introduction to SunView

3.1. Introduction

SunView is a toolkit of C objects and functions which allow the construction of window tools. The tools introduced in Chapter 1 were written using SunView and C. This chapter will consider how tools are written, starting with the tool layout, then handling the interaction between user and tool and finally looking at the internal non-window functions of the tool. The example given will look mainly at the *Panel* subwindow package. Chapter 4 will look at the *Canvas* package and Chapter 5 will consider the *Pixrect* imaging facilities, as well as introducing other graphics packages.

Before writing window-based tools, it is important to understand tools from the user's point of view. In this way the tool designer can have some idea of the user's needs and problems and can avoid some bad design decisions. Also, by looking at other tools, designers can ensure that their particular tool is consistent in terms of layout and interaction. Consistency between tools helps user learning and understanding.

3.2. Directory browser

The example tool in this chapter is a directory browser. This combines, in a visual way, several of the functions given by UNIX commands described in Chapter 2. For example

cd	Change directory
rm	remove a file
cp	copy a file
vi	edit a text file
ls	list a directory

3.3. Tool layout

In this section we consider how objects are placed on the screen, and the functions and parameters that are provided for this purpose.

Constructing the tool layout first brings two advantages

(1) The tool is being designed from the user's point of view, so the designer can appreciate how the user's requirements are being satisfied.

(2) The user can get an early look at the tool and can influence its design more readily than if it just existed as a text description.

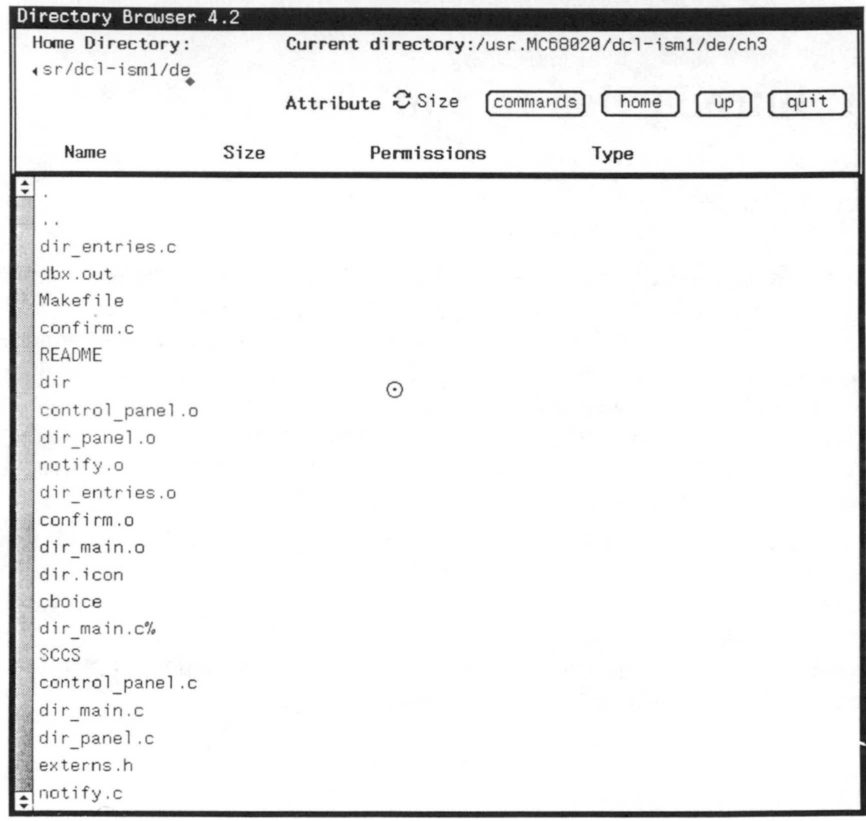

Figure 3.1 Directory browser

Figure 3.1 gives one layout of the directory browser. In practice, the designer would sketch or construct a number of alternative layouts for the user to evaluate. The layout shows some of the functions that were set out in section 3.2 above. It consists of a tool *Frame*, containing two *Panel* subwindows. The top panel contains panel items such as

Buttons

Like **Quit** and **Home** which initiate actions.

Choice items

Such as the **Commands** menu and the **Attribute** cycle item which allow choices to be made.

Text items

Home Directory lets the user type in short pieces of text.

The lower window contains entries for the directory currently in view. It changes as the user interacts with items in the top panel. This panel also has a scrollbar attached, as there may be more directory entries than can be actually shown in the lower window.

3.4. SunView objects

SunView provides a hierarchy of screen objects for the designer, as shown in figure 3.2.

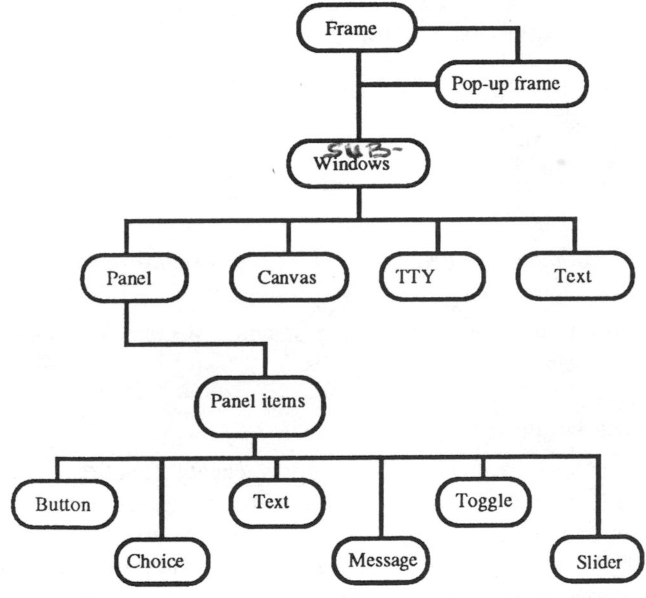

Figure 3.2 SunView object hierarchy

Higher level *parent* objects have to be created before the lower level *child* objects. The names of higher level objects are then used in the creation of lower level objects to indicate which parent item contains them on the screen. To create the tool frame and the panels for the directory browser, the designer would write the code shown in example 3.1.

```
#include <suntool/sunview.h>
#include <suntool/panel.h>

Frame base_frame;
Panel control_panel, directory_panel;

main ()
{
    base_frame = window_create (NULL, FRAME,
            FRAME_ARGS, argc, argv,
            FRAME_LABEL, "Directory Browser 3.2",
            0);

    control_panel = window_create (base_frame, PANEL,
            WIN_ROWS, 5,
            0);

    directory_panel = window_create (base_frame, PANEL,
            WIN_ROWS, 20,
            WIN_VERTICAL_SCROLLBAR, scrollbar_create (0),
            0);

    window_fit (base_frame);

    window_main_loop (base_frame);

    exit (0);
}
```

Example 3.1 Frame and panel construction code

Here the **#include** lines bring in the standard declarations needed to use SunView and Panels.

3.4.1. Creating windows

Window objects are created by the **window_create** function. This function returns a handle to the object created (as declared at the top of the source file). **Window_create** takes as parameters a list of attributes to control the appearance of the object created. The first parameter is the name of the parent item. **Base_frame** being the first item created has no parent, so takes the parameter **NULL**. The two panel subwindows belong to **base_frame** and take this as their first parameter. The second parameter is the type of the window being created, i.e. PANEL ,TEXTSW, TTY or FRAME.

You should note that most functions in SunView take pairs of attributes and values, and the number of pairs can be vary depending on how many attributes we wish to set. If you have used the **printf** function in C programming previously then you have already used this concept of *variable* *length* arguments lists. If you are more used to other languages the concept may, at first, seem strange.

Frame attributes

The parent name and item type are then followed by a list of *Attribute-pairs* which control the appearance and behaviour of the item. **Base_frame** has had the attributes **FRAME_LABEL** and **FRAME_ARGS** set. **FRAME_LABEL** takes the string "Directory Browser" as the border label. **FRAME_ARGS** interprets the window arguments from the command line (as described in Chapter 1, table 1.1). There are several other attributes (with the prefix **FRAME_**) which could be set, such as the name of the icon to use and the size of the tool frame. The size will be set by an alternative method below.

Please take note that functions with **_create** and **_set** suffixes have their parameter list terminated by 0 (i.e. the character zero).

Window attributes

Subwindows, such as panels, can also take several window attributes with the prefix **WIN_**. In the example the **WIN_ROWS** attribute has been used to set the height of each panel. The width of the panels has been left to the default size of 80 columns, but this could be set by the attribute **WIN_COLUMNS. WIN_VERTICAL_SCROLLBAR** uses the function **scrollbar_create(0)** to attach a vertical scrollbar to the window.

The order of the creation of subwindow items is important, as subwindows are laid out in the frame window from top to bottom and left to right in the order of their creation. Thus, if the two panel creation routines were switched round, **directory_panel** would be at the top and **control_panel** at the bottom.

Of the last two window functions, **window_fit(base_frame)** sets the size of **base_frame** to contain its child items (**directory_panel** and **control_panel**), and **window_main_loop(base_frame)** displays all the created (and visible) objects on the screen. It also puts the tool in a loop waiting for user input. All objects that should appear on the screen at tool start up should be created before **window_main_loop()** is called.

Panel items

Panel items provide the programmer with the components needed to build the software equivalent of control panels on photocopiers and video recorders. So there are equivalent devices for selection switches, buttons, data input, slider volume controls and so on. The programmer can decide how these items appear on the screen and how they provide feedback to the user. Panel items, such as buttons and choice items, are created by the **panel_create_item()** function which takes the parent panel as its first parameter, followed by the panel item type and then a list of panel item attributes, i.e.

```
Panel_item item_name;

item_name = panel_create_item (parent_panel, PANEL_ITEM_TYPE,
                    list of panel attributes and values,
                    0);
```

In the directory browser, **control_panel** has:

Two text items, PANEL_TEXT
Home Directory: and one presently hidden text item.

Three button items, PANEL_BUTTON
home, up and **quit**.

Two Choice items, PANEL_CHOICE and PANEL_CYCLE
The **commands** menu and the **Attribute** cycle item.

Two message items, PANEL_MESSAGE
One showing the current directory the other providing column labels for the lower panel.

3.5. Compiling the tool

If all the functions, required to build the directory browser, were in one text file named *main.c* they would be compiled by

% cc main.c -lsuntool -lsunwindow -lpixrect

where the **-l** option tells the compiler to *load* functions from the SunView toolkit libraries.

In practice, the functions would be split into an number of files, e.g. the control panel item creation routines would be in *init_control_panel.c* and the notification procedures for that panel would be in *notify.c*. This *modular* approach is discussed further in Chapter 9.

Text items

The following code creates the **Home Directory:** text item:

```
home_dir = panel_create_item (control_panel,PANEL_TEXT
                    PANEL_ITEM_X,           ATTR_COL(1),
                    PANEL_ITEM_Y,           ATTR_ROW(0),
                    PANEL_LAYOUT,           PANEL_VERTICAL,
                    PANEL_LABEL_BOLD,       TRUE,
                    PANEL_LABEL_STRING,     "Home Directory:",
                    PANEL_VALUE,            "/usr/users/de",
                    0);
```

Example 3.2

This creates a text item, **home_dir**, in **control_panel** at column 1, row 0, where 0,0 is the top left of the panel. **PANEL_LABEL_STRING** gives the item the label "Home Directory:" and **PANEL_LABEL_BOLD**, TRUE sets the label to bold font. The value part of a text item can be edited by the user and here it is initialised to a string value. It could also be left blank. In the final version of the tool, the UNIX system function **getenv("HOME")** would replace the string to initialise the value of home_dir. **PANEL_LAYOUT, PANEL_VERTICAL**
puts the label part of the item above the value part. Alternatively, **PANEL_HORIZONTAL** could be used to put the label to the left of the value.

In the space beneath **home_dir** a text item could be created called **prompt box**. Its visibility is initially set to false by **PANEL_SHOW_ITEM, FALSE.** It is reset to true when the tool needs to prompt the user for some additional text input.

Choice Items - Menus

As would be expected, choice items give the user a range of alternatives to select from. However, there are a number of ways of presenting choices. Example 3.3 below shows the create function for the **commands** menu in the directory browser. The position is set as shown for text items. In addition, choice items have a list of choice strings as set by **PANEL_CHOICE_STRINGS.**

```
commands = panel_create_item(control_panel,PANEL_CHOICE,
                PANEL_ITEM_X,               ATTR_COL(44),
                PANEL_ITEM_Y,               ATTR_ROW(2),
                PANEL_CHOICE_STRINGS,       "Display",
                                            "Remove",
                                            "Rename",
                                            "Edit",
                                            "Copy",
                                            0,
                PANEL_DISPLAY_LEVEL,        PANEL_NONE,
                PANEL_LABEL_IMAGE,          panel_button_image(
                                            control_panel,
                                            "commands",
                                            8,
                                            NULL),
                PANEL_NOTIFY_PROC,          command_proc,
                0);
```

Example 3.3

Note that the list of strings after **PANEL_CHOICE_STRINGS** is terminated by zero. This should not be confused with the zero character terminating the full parameter list; *both* are needed.

The attribute **PANEL_DISPLAY_LEVEL, PANEL_NONE** means that none of the choices set is directly visible to the user. Only the label is visible and the user must hold down the right button on the item's label to get a pop-up menu of the choice list. The alternative **PANEL_CHOICE** presentations are:

PANEL_NONE
: The choices are only available through a pop-up menu.

PANEL_CURRENT
: The value of the current selection is shown. Where it appears is controlled by **PANEL_LAYOUT**.

PANEL_ALL
: All the choices are visible on the screen. Usually a tick mark indicates the current choice. Again **PANEL_LAYOUT** controls the layout of the items.

Deciding which arrangement to use, depends of the number of choices and the space available in the panel.

The attribute **PANEL_NOTIFY_PROC** is described later in section 3.6.

Figure 3.3 Alternative choice item layouts

Choice items - cycle

There is a pre-packaged choice item of type **PANEL_CYCLE.** In this item **PANEL_LAYOUT** and **PANEL_DISPLAY_LEVEL** are preset. In addition a *cycle* image is placed between the label and value parts. The **Attribute** item is an example of a cycle item.

```
attribute = panel_create_item(control_panel,PANEL_CYCLE,
                    PANEL_ITEM_X,           ATTR_COL(25),
                    PANEL_ITEM_Y,           ATTR_ROW(2),
                    PANEL_CHOICE_STRINGS,   "Size",
                                            "Group",
                                            "Owner",
                                            0,
                    PANEL_LABEL_BOLD,       TRUE,
                    PANEL_LABEL_STRING,     "Attribute",
                    PANEL_NOTIFY_PROC,      attrs_proc,
                    0);
```

Example 3.4 Attribute cycle item

Button items

Buttons are created as in the following example for the **home** button of the directory browser.

```
home = panel_create_item(control_panel, PANEL_BUTTON,
                    PANEL_ITEM_X,           ATTR_COL(55),
                    PANEL_ITEM_Y,           ATTR_COL(2),
                    PANEL_LABEL_IMAGE,      panel_button_image(
                                            control_panel,
                                            "home",
                                            6,
                                            NULL),
                    PANEL_NOTIFY_PROC,      home_proc,
                    0);
```

Example 3.5 Home button

The new attribute here (which was also used for the **commands** menu) is **PANEL_LABEL_IMAGE**. This takes a pixrect[1] image as the label of the item rather than a text string, as previously. There is a standard macro **panel_button_image** which returns a pixrect with the item label in a rounded box. The macro takes as parameters, the parent panel name, the text string for the label, the width of the label and finally the font to use for the text. The font parameter **NULL** means use the standard font for this panel.

Other Items

The other item type in the control panel is **PANEL_MESSAGE**. This simply puts a text or pixrect message in the panel. Other panel item types which are less often used are; **PANEL_TOGGLE** which is a multiple choice version of **PANEL_CHOICE**; **PANEL_SLIDER**, which looks like a sliding volume control and allows a numerical value to be set in a given range.

---

[1] Pixrects are described in Chapter 5

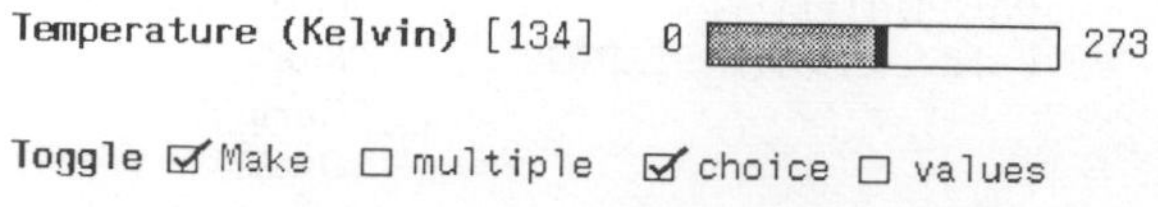

Temperature (Kelvin) [134] 0 273

Toggle ☑ Make ☐ multiple ☑ choice ☐ values

Figure 3.4 Slider and Toggle items

Dynamic panel

The control panel items are fairly static, only the value parts of items change and the visibility of the prompt box is switched on and off. In the directory panel, however, items change each time a user causes an action which moves to a new directory or updates the current directory. Example 3.6 shows the function **draw_dir_panel()** which is called when the tool is initialised and each time the panel needs updating. It assumes that a call has been previously made to another function, **buildlist()**, which uses UNIX system calls to put the names of the files in the current directory into a string array declared as **char *entry_list[256]**[2] and keep a count of the number of entries in an integer variable **count**. The function also updates the current directory message item.

```
char   *entry_list[256];
int     count;
Panel_item dir_entry_item[256];

draw_dir_panel ()
{
   int    i;

   panel_set (current_dir,
          PANEL_LABEL_STRING, getwd (path), 0);

   for (i = 0; i < count; i++)
   {
       dir_entry[i] = panel_create_item (directory_panel, PANEL_BUTTON,
             PANEL_ITEM_X, ATTR_COL (0),
             PANEL_ITEM_Y, ATTR_ROW (i),
             PANEL_LABEL_STRING, entry_list[i],
```

[2] For simplicity, and to avoid getting into explanations of dynamic space allocation, it is assumed that directories are not bigger than 256 entries.

```
                PANEL_SHOW_ITEM, TRUE,
                PANEL_NOTIFY_PROC, dir_select,
                PANEL_CLIENT_DATA, (int) i,
                0);

        panel_set (dir_entry[i],
                PANEL_PAINT, PANEL_CLEAR,
                0);
    }
    panel_update_scrolling_size (dir_panel);
}
```

Example 3.6

The function creates an array of button items to be displayed in **directory_panel**, placing each one in the next available row. **PANEL_SHOW_ITEM** is also set to **TRUE** as it may have been set to false by a previous operation. The attribute **PANEL_CLIENT_DATA** permits non-window data to be associated with the panel item. In this case the index number of the item in the array is stored.

Draw_dir_panel is called once before **window_main_loop()**, but for subsequent calls it is necessary to explicitly re-paint the panel items for them to appear on the screen. This is done via the **panel_set()** function and the **PANEL_PAINT, PANEL_CLEAR** attribute. **Panel_set()** takes the panel item name followed by a list of attributes to be set.

Finally, because the number of items will change each time the panel is updated, the scrollbar has to be notified of the change. This is done by **panel_update_scrolling_size(dir_panel)**.

3.6. Handling interaction

So far, no actions have been associated with the items on the screen. The tool just exists as an image. Selecting panel items will cause some visual feedback but no other actions. In the examples for **PANEL_CHOICE** and **PANEL_BUTTON** items shown above, the attribute **PANEL_NOTIFY_PROC** was used. This attribute takes the name of a function to call when an that item is selected. So when the user selects the **home** button the function **home_proc** is called. When the **Attribute** cycle item is selected **attrs_proc** is called.

One of the functions of **window_main_loop()** is to register functions set with **PANEL_NOTIFY_PROC** with a process called the *notifier*. The notifier gets low level inputs, such as keyboard depressions or mouse clicks, and distributes them to the right window. With Panel subwindows and Canvas subwindows (described in Chapter 5) the programmer rarely has to deal with the notifier directly; instead the programmer works at the higher level of notification procedures for Panels, and event procedures for Canvases.

Notify procedures are used in conjunction with the functions

```
window_set()
window_get()
panel_get()
panel_set()
```

to enquire about and change the contents of the tool windows. In addition they are used to call internal, non-window functions, such as **buildlist()** which handle non-window data.

3.6.1. Handling button events

When a button is selected the button item's notify procedure is sent the name of the item and a code indicating the *event* which caused its selection. The examples below will consider the functions **home_proc, dir_selected** and **quit_proc** which are called by the **home** button, the directory entries and the **quit** button respectively.

Home_proc

This procedure returns users to their home directory as entered in the **Home Directory:** text item. The value of the text is obtained by **panel_get()** and the UNIX function **chdir()** changes the current directory of the tool to that directory. As the current directory has changed, the block of statements in the **for** loop removes the old values from the screen and throws away the space used to store them. The information for the new directory is then rebuilt and re-displayed by **buildlist()** and **draw_dir_panel()**.

```
home_proc (item, event)
Panel_item item;
Event * event;
{
    register int    i;

    chdir ((char *) panel_get (home_dir, PANEL_VALUE, 0));
    for (i = 0; i < count; i++)
    {
        panel_set (dir_entry[i], PANEL_SHOW_ITEM, FALSE, 0);
        panel_free (dir_entry[i]);
        free (entry_list[i]);
    }
    build_list (".");
    draw_dir_panel ();
}
```

Example 3.7

Quit_proc

Quit_proc calls **window_done(base_frame)**, which causes the program to leave **window_main_loop()** and hence exit and disappear from the screen. Tools should always provide a quit item so that any tidying up can be done before exiting. For example, a tool may make some changes that may require saving. In this case **quit_proc** would pop-up a frame which asked the user to either save the changes or confirm the quit operation. Pop-up frames are described below.

```
quit_proc (item, event)
Panel_item item;
Event * event;
{
    window_done (base_frame);
}
```

Example 3.8

Dir_selected

Dir_selected differs in that it can be called by any of the button items in **directory_panel**. It uses the parameter **item** to identify the particular entry that was selected. Then, via **panel_get()**, the attribute **PANEL_CLIENT_DATA** can be retrieved to get the array index of that item. Finally, two calls to **panel_set()** are used to highlight the newly selected item in bold font and restore the last selected item to normal font.

```
dir_select (item, event)
Panel_item item;
Event * event;
{
    register int    i;

    panel_set (dir_entry[selected_object], PANEL_LABEL_BOLD, FALSE, 0);
    i = (int) panel_get (item, PANEL_CLIENT_DATA, 0);
    panel_set (item, PANEL_LABEL_BOLD, TRUE, 0);
    selected_object = i;
}
```

Example 3.9

3.6.2. Handling choice events

In addition to passing the item handle and the event to their notify procedure, choice items pass the value of the chosen option. Earlier the choices for **Attribute** were defined as:

PANEL_CHOICE_STRINGS, "Size", "Group", "Owner", 0,

Size, Group and Owner pass the values 0, 1 and 2 respectively to the notify procedure when they are selected. So the ordering of the strings in **PANEL_CHOICE_STRINGS** controls their order of appearance on the screen and the value the chosen string passes to the procedure.

Attrs_proc

Given the value passed from the **Attribute** item, **attrs_proc** sets the message item to the appropriate string. In the final version, UNIX system calls would be used to update the information for the size, group and owner columns of **directory_panel** which are currently empty. The code is shown below.

```
attrs_proc(item, value, event)
Panel_item item;
int value;
Event *event;
{
        switch (value) {
        case 0:
                panel_set(dir_title,PANEL_LABEL_STRING,
       "   Name            Size          Permissions          Type",
            0);
       break;
        case 1:
                panel_set(dir_title,PANEL_LABEL_STRING,
       "   Name            Group         Permissions          Type",
            0);
        break;
       case 2:
                panel_set(dir_title,PANEL_LABEL_STRING,
       "   Name            Owner         Permissions          Type",
            0);
       break;
        default:
        break;
        }
}
```

Example 3.10

Command_proc

Command_proc similarly uses the **value** parameter in a **switch** statement to execute the required statements. This example concentrates on the handling of the **delete** option and the handling of the **event** parameter.

```
command_proc (item, value, event)
Panel_item item;
int    value;
Event * event;
{
   int    i;

   if (event_id (event) == MS_LEFT)
        return;
```

```
    panel_set (prompt_box, PANEL_SHOW_ITEM, FALSE, 0);

    switch (value)
    {
        case 0:
            if (chdir (entry_list[selected_object]) == 0)
            {
                for (i = 0; i < count; i++)
                {
                    panel_set (dir_entry[i], PANEL_SHOW_ITEM, FALSE, 0);
                    panel_free (dir_entry[i]);
                    free (entry_list[i]);
                }
                build_list (".");
                draw_dir_panel ();
            }           /* else try to "view" the object in a TTY
                           frame */
            break;

        case 1:
            window_loop(confirm_del_frame);
            break;

        case 2:
            panel_set (prompt_box,
                    PANEL_LABEL_STRING, "Enter new name:",
                    PANEL_SHOW_ITEM, TRUE,
                    0);
        /* get new name, rename file, remove box */
            break;

        case 3:
        /* edit by popping up a ttysw with vi */
            break;

        case 4:
            panel_set (prompt_box,
                    PANEL_LABEL_STRING, "Enter name to copy:",
                    PANEL_SHOW_ITEM, TRUE,
                    0);
        /* get new name, copy file, remove box */
            break;

        default:
            break;
    }

    selected_object = 0;
    panel_set (dir_entry[selected_object],
            PANEL_LABEL_BOLD, FALSE,
            0);
}
```

Example 3.11

The user can move through the options of a choice item one by one with the left button, or make a choice via a pop-up menu with the right button. For **commands**, we wish to prevent the user cycling through the options with the left mouse button, as none of the options is visible. This is done by checking the code of the event passed to **commands_proc**. The codes for the the mouse button presses are **MS_LEFT, MS_MIDDLE** and **MS_RIGHT**. Exiting from the function when the left button is pressed means that the left button is ignored.

When the **delete** option is chosen, we may wish to ask the user to confirm the delete action. This is done by popping up a new frame on the screen as shown below.

```
Do you want to delete this item?
            YES   NO
```

Figure 3.5 Pop-up Confirmation frame

The frame is created by **window_create**(), i.e.

```
Frame confirm_delete_frame
confirm_delete_frame = window_create(base_frame, FRAME, 0);
```

A panel and the panel items shown in figure 3.5 would be created in the same way as those in **base_frame**. The confirmation frame would not appear until called from **commands_proc**.

There are two ways in which it could appear:

(1) Blocking mode
The frame would appear via the call

```
window_loop(confirm_delete_frame);
```

The confirm frame would remain on the screen until the **yes** or **no** buttons made a call to the function **window_return**(). While the pop-up frame remains on the screen all other inputs are ignored. The user has to confirm or cancel the delete operation via the pop-up frame. **Window_return**() can take an integer parameter which is returned by **window_loop**(). This value can be tested to see if the delete operation should be executed or skipped in

command_proc.

(2) Non-blocking mode
The confirmation frame and its child objects are created as before but this time they are made to appear by

```
window_set(confirm_delete_frame, WIN_SHOW, TRUE, 0);
```

and removed from the screen when required by

```
window_set(confirm_delete_frame, WIN_SHOW, FALSE, 0);
```

The user can still interact with the directory browse and other tools.

3.7. Cursors and icons

The icons and cursor images created by **iconedit** can be associated with a particular tool. For example, to have a tool Frame closed down to the icon described in the file *my_icon* one would include the following declaration statements;

```
static short icon_image[] = {
#include "my_icon"
};
DEFINE_ICON_FROM_IMAGE(icon, icon_image);
```

Example 3.12

Here the array *icon_image* is initialised with values read in from the icon file *my_icon*, where *my_icon* would have been previously drawn and saved using **iconedit**. The *icon* structure defined from *icon_image* is them associated with the tool frame using the attribute **WIN_ICON** in **window_create**, e.g.

```
window_create(NULL, FRAME, WIN_ICON, &icon,0);
```

Similarly, a cursor file created by **iconedit** can be linked to a window. For example

```
short cursor_image[] = {
#include "my_cursor"
};
mpr_static(cursor_pixrect, 16, 16, 1, cursor_pixrect_image);
```

Example 3.13[3]

[3] **mpr_static( )** is explained in Chapter 5.

creates a pxirect **cursor_pixrect_image** which can be associated with a window by the **WIN_CURSOR** attribute, i.e.

```
window_set(control_panel,
        WIN_CURSOR,
        cursor_create(CURSOR_IMAGE, &cursor_pixrect_image),
        0);
```

The pixrect images obtained from **iconedit** files can also be used with the **PANEL_LABEL_IMAGE** attribute to create a new image for a panel item and a list of pixrects can be used with the **PANEL_CHOICES_IMAGES** attribute to create an image for each option in a choice item. The images are also used in the item's pop-up menu.

3.8. Summary

In this chapter we have looked at how to create the tool layout from the objects available in the SunView toolkit. Create routines take, as parameter, the parent item and the object type, followed by a list of attributes. The tool is then displayed and put into a loop, waiting for user input. Inputs are handled by notify routines that are used to called get/set functions, UNIX systems calls and other, user-supplied non-window functions.

3.9. Future of SunView

At the time of writting a new window system is due to appear on Sun Workstations. This is *SunNeWS*. NeWS stands for Network extensible Window System. Briefly NeWS would allow a tool like the directory browser to run the window part of the tool on one machine, while browsing through the files of another machine. SunNeWS will continue to support SunView, so programs written using the features described in this chapter and Chapter 4 will still work. However, the Pixrect level, described in Chapter 5, may not move across. Tool writers and designers should bear this in mind when planning new tools and committing themselves to a particular system.

Further reading

Chapter 4 will now go on to look at Canvas windows, scrollbars and menus.

SunView Programmers Guide
Sun Microsystems Inc, Mountain View CA, 1986.

SunNeWS Preliminary Technical Overview,
Sun Microsystems Inc, Mountain View CA, 1987.

A R Hartson,
Advances in Human Computer Interaction - Vol.1, Ablex, New Jersey, 1985.

B W Kernighan, D M Ritchie,
The C Programming Language, Prentice-Hall, Englewood Cliff NJ, 1978.

A Monk,
Fundamentals of Human Computer Interaction, Academic Press, London, 1984.

D A Norman, S W Draper,
User Centered System Design, Lawrence Erlbaum, Hillsdale NJ, 1986.

Ben Shneiderman
Designing the User Interface: Strategies for Effective Human-Computer Interaction, Addison-Wesley, Reading MA, 1987.

M E Sime, M J Coombs,
Designing for Human-Computer Communication, Academic Press, London, 1983.

4 Lower Level SunView Facilities

4.1. Introduction

SunView is a hierarchical system; it allows a tool writer to choose which level of the hierarchy is appropriate for a given application. At the top of the hierarchy is the Panel subwindow package which was described in Chapter 3. This provides a set of powerful objects (panel items) which follow certain conventions and are constrained to the panel type of interface. Panel windows are essentially control windows from which commands are issued and in which control information is displayed. Many applications, however, in addition to control panels, will also require an area in which to display data - this may be graphical objects, text or a mixture of the two. For this type of window, the tool writer would move down the SunView hierarchy to a level which provides more basic facilities.

This chapter discusses the low level facilities provided by the SunView system. These facilities allow an application program to define its own interface, handle user inputs and use a variety of packages such as scrollbars, menus, etc.

4.1.1. Canvas subwindow

All the examples in the chapter use the canvas subwindow. This is the most basic type of window provided by SunView. It is essentially a window into which you can draw lines, text or more complex shapes.

The canvas subwindow provides a greater degree of flexibility than panels. It allows the application to define its own interface and is not constrained to a set of standard items. The price paid for this flexibility is that applications use lower level functions to access the window and have to provide their own routines to handle user inputs.

In order to use the canvas subwindow package, the header file <suntool/canvas.h> must be included. A canvas is declared as type *Canvas* and is created using the **window_create()** procedure, i.e.

```
#include <suntool/sunview.h>
#include <suntool/canvas.h>
```

```
main(argc, argv)
int argc;
char **argv;
{
    Frame base_frame;
    Canvas canvas;

    base_frame = window_create (NULL, FRAME, 0);
    canvas = window_create (base_frame, CANVAS, 0);

    ...
}
```

This chapter shows how an interface can be built using the canvas subwindow and its associated functions. The examples in this chapter construct the directory browser tool which was implemented in Chapter 3 using panel subwindows.

4.1.2. Pixwins

To render images in the canvas, the canvas pixwin must be used. A pixwin is a rectangular area which provides a coordinate system of pixels and a set of functions for accessing the pixels. In addition to pixwins, this chapter will also introduce the concept of pixrects. A pixrect is device independent area which may have text or graphical data drawn into it. A pixrect is used as the drawing surface for a pixwin, but a pixwin also has data which specifies the position of the surface on the screen, the position in the window hierarchy, etc. A pixwin can essentially be thought of as a pixrect which is displayed on the screen. This chapter introduces some basic functions which apply to pixwins. All of these functions have corresponding functions which apply to pixrects. A detailed description of these is given in Chapter 5.

All subwindows, regardless of their type, have an associated pixwin, but it only has to be accessed directly when we use the canvas subwindow. Other types of subwindow use higher level routines such as **panel_create_item().**

A canvas pixwin is created by calling the **canvas_pixwin()** macro. This returns a handle to the pixwin which can be used by the pixwin functions. The macro takes the canvas name as parameter and returns a pointer to a pixwin, i.e.

```
Canvas  canvas;
Pixwin  *pw;

pw = canvas_create (canvas);
```

4.2. Output to pixwins

4.2.1. Basic pixwin functions

A large number of functions are available for accessing a pixwin. Some functions allow text, vectors or polygons to be drawn in the pixwin. Others allow source pixrects to be copied into the pixwin or areas of the pixwin to be copied into other pixrects.

Most functions have a set of coordinates as parameters which indicate the pixel at which the function is to begin or end. Other parameters are specific to the function used.

In this section we introduce some of the basic pixwin functions.

(a) Drawing vectors

```
pw_vector (pw, x0, y0, x1, y1, op, value)
Pixwin    *pw;
int       x0, y0, x1, y1, op, value;
```

This draws a vector from pixel location (x0, y0) to (x1, y1). **pw** is the handle to the pixwin returned by canvas_pixwin(). **op** is the raster operation to be performed. It allows logical operations to be carried out between source and destination pixels. Standard operations such as **PIX_SRC** and **PIX_DST** are provided by the SunView package and these may be combined together to provide all logical operations (see section 5.5.1 for details). For example,

```
pw_vector (pw, 5, 5, 10, 10, PIX_NOT(PIX_DST), 1)
```

draws a vector from (5, 5) to (10, 10) on the pixwin **pw**. **PIX_NOT(PIX_DST)** indicates the logical operation to be used, in this case, if the pixwin is black, a white vector is drawn, if the pixwin is white, a black vector is drawn. The most common operation is **PIX_SRC** which draws the source object with no regard to the current state of the pixwin. **value** specifies the value of the pixels in the vector and should normally be set to 1.

(b) Writing text

```
pw_text (pw, x, y, op, font, s)
Pixwin          *pw;
int             x, y, op;
struct pixfont *font;
char            *s;
```

This draws the character string *s* into the pixwin **pw** at location (x, y). This is the pixel at which the left edge and baseline of the first character will appear. **font** is the font in which the string appears. If this is set to **NULL** the standard system font is used. **op** is the raster operation to use as before, e.g.

```
pw_text(pw, 5, 10, PIX_NOT(PIX_SRC), NULL, "Quit");
```

draws the string "Quit" at location (5, 10) in the standard system font. The operation **PIX_NOT(PIX_SRC)** indicates that the string will appear inverted.

(c) Clearing the pixwin

```
pw_writebackground (pw, x, y, width, height, op)
Pixwin *pw;
int    x, y, width, height, op;
```

This clears a rectangle of **width** x **height** pixels whose top left vertex is at location (x, y). If **op** is **PIX_SRC** the rectangle is cleared. If **op** is **PIX_NOT(PIX_SRC)** the rectangle is blacked.

We can now write a simple program which draws into a canvas subwindow. Example 4.1 below sets up a canvas and draws a box with the word "Quit" in it.

```
#include <suntool/sunview.h>
#include <suntool/canvas.h>

main(argc, argv)
        int         argc;
        char        **argv;
{
        Frame       base_frame;
        Canvas      canvas;
        Pixwin      *pw;

        /* create frame and canvas */
        base_frame = window_create(NULL, FRAME, 0);
        canvas = window_create(base_frame, CANVAS, 0);

        /* create pixwin */
        pw = canvas_pixwin(canvas);

        draw_box(pw, 100, 100, "Quit");

        window_main_loop(base_frame);
        exit(0);
}
```

```
draw_box(pw, x, y, string)
        Pixwin      *pw;
        int         x, y;
        char        *string;
/*
 * writes the string on pixwin pw surrounded by a box whose top left
 * vertex is at (x, y)
 */
{
        int         boxlength;          /* length in pixels of the box */
        int         x2, y2;  /* bottom right vertex coordinates */

        /* length = no. of chars. x pixel width of font */
        boxlength = strlen(string) * 8;

        x2 = x + boxlength + 3;         /* leave a 3 pixel margin */
        y2 = y + 15;                    /* height of font + margin */

        pw_text(pw, x + 2, y + 12, PIX_SRC, NULL, string);
        pw_vector(pw, x, y, x, y2, PIX_SRC, 1);
        pw_vector(pw, x, y, x2, y, PIX_SRC, 1);
        pw_vector(pw, x, y2, x2, y2, PIX_SRC, 1);
        pw_vector(pw, x2, y2, x2, y, PIX_SRC, 1);
}
```

Example 4.1

4.2.2. The pw_rop function

This section introduces a more complex pixwin function - **pw_rop**. The **pw_rop** function allows an image to be copied from a pixrect into a pixwin.

```
pw_rop (pw, dx, dy, width, height, op, sp, sx, sy)
Pixwin          *pw;
struct pixrect *sp;
int             dx, dy, width, height, op, sx, sy;
```

This copies the source pixrect **sp** into the pixwin **pw.** A rectangle of the pixwin is made available to draw in. The rectangle starts at location (dx, dy) and is of dimensions **width x height.** The source pixrect is clipped if it is larger than this area. If the source pixrect is smaller, the resulting image may contain garbage. (sx, sy) indicates the location within the source pixrect at which the copy will start from.

This function is most useful for displaying predefined images. A predefined image can be loaded into a pixrect, then displayed in a window using **pw_rop.** One way of doing this is to define an image using **iconedit** then load the data file created by **iconedit** into a pixrect. This is done as shown below

```
char data[] = {
#include "iconedit.out"
}
mpr_static (pr, x, y, 1, data);
```

mpr_static creates a static memory pixrect **pr.** We do not have to declare **pr** elsewhere - **mpr_static** defines the variable and initialises it. **pr** however is not a pointer, it is a pixrect variable. When used in functions such as **pw_rop,** the address of **pr** must be given (i.e. &pr). The values **x** and **y** are the width and height of the pixrect.

As an example, suppose we wish to display a character string surrounded by the box shown below.

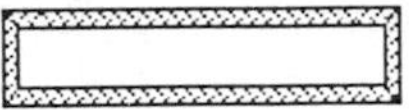

The box has three components -

a left end of size 12 x 28 pixels

a right end of size 12 x 28 pixels

an edge piece of size 8 x 6 pixels

The following code fragment loads the three components from files (created using **iconedit**) and displays a character string in a pixwin surrounded by a box of the correct size.

```
#include <suntool/sunview.h>
#include <suntool/canvas.h>

/* load in the left end */
static short    data[] = {
#include "left-file"
};

/* load in the right end */
static short    data2[] = {
#include "right-file"
```

```
};

/* load in the edge piece */
static short    data3[] = {
#include "edge-file"
};

/* create the pixrects */
static          mpr_static(left_end, 64, 64, 1, data);
static          mpr_static(right_end, 64, 64, 1, data2);
static          mpr_static(edge_piece, 64, 64, 1, data3);


draw_button(pw, x, y, string)
        Pixwin          *pw;
        int             x, y;
        char            *string;
/*
 * draws a shaded box (top left vertex at (x, y)) and writes the string in
 * the box
 */
{
        int             i;
        int             boxlength;              /* size in pixels of box */
        int             boxsize;/* size in chars. of box */

        boxsize = strlen(string);
        boxlength = boxsize * 8;

        /* write the text */
        pw_text(pw, x + 12, y + 19, PIX_SRC, NULL, string);

        /* display left and right edge of box */
        pw_rop(pw, x, y, 12, 28, PIX_SRC, &left_end, 0, 0);
        pw_rop(pw, x + 11 + boxlength, y, 12, 28, PIX_SRC, &right_end, 0, 0);

        /* loop for top and bottom edges */
        for (i = 0; i < boxsize; ++i)
        {
                pw_rop(pw, x + 12 + (i * 8), y, 8, 6, PIX_SRC, &edge_piece, 0, 0);
                pw_rop(pw, x + 12 + (i * 8), y + 22, 8, 6, PIX_SRC, &edge_piece, 0, 0);
        }
}
```

Example 4.2

Using the procedures given in examples 4.1 and 4.2, we can write the following code which produces the window shown in figure 4.1. This window is similar to the top subwindow of the directory browser which was introduced in Chapter 3 (see figure 3.1).

```
#include <suntool/sunview.h>
#include <suntool/canvas.h>
```

```
main(argc, argv)
        int         argc;
        char        **argv;
{
        Frame       base_frame;
        Canvas      canvas;
        Pixwin      *pw;

        base_frame = window_create(NULL, FRAME,
                                        WIN_HEIGHT, 140,
                                        0);
        canvas = window_create(base_frame, CANVAS, 0);

        pw = canvas_pixwin(canvas);

        draw_button(pw, 430, 20, "Home");
        draw_button(pw, 500, 20, "Up");
        draw_button(pw, 560, 20, "Quit");

        draw_box(pw, 220, 55, "Command");
        draw_box(pw, 50, 35, "                ");
        pw_text(pw, 50, 30, PIX_NOT(PIX_SRC), NULL, " Home Directory ");

        draw_box(pw, 300, 45, "  Attribute  ");
        draw_box(pw, 300, 60, "Size in Bytes");
        window_main_loop(base_frame);
        exit(0);
}
```

Example 4.3

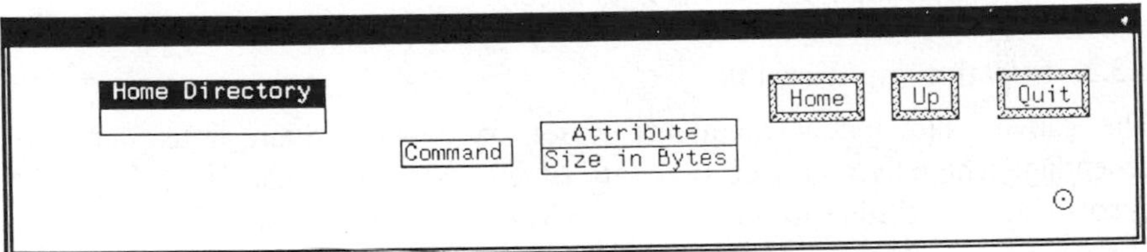

Figure 4.1

4.3. Handling inputs to pixwins

4.3.1. Event handling procedure

As mentioned earlier, if canvas subwindows are to accept user inputs, they must provide their own event handling routines. There are a number of possible user-initiated events which a canvas can handle

- pressing or releasing a mouse button

- moving the mouse

- pressing an ASCII key

- pressing a function key

A canvas can choose to accept or ignore events or can accept a subset of events. Whenever an event occurs which the canvas has chosen to accept, the SunView system will call the window's event handling procedure which the application program must supply. The procedure is given as the value for the **WIN_EVENT_PROC** attribute of the canvas subwindow. This can be specified as shown below when the canvas is created

```
Frame base_frame;
Canvas canvas;

base_frame = window_create (NULL, FRAME, 0);
canvas = window_create (base_frame, CANVAS,
            WIN_EVENT_PROC, my_event_proc,
            0);
```

my_event_proc is the name of a procedure which will be called whenever an event occurs which the canvas is to accept.

4.3.2. Selecting input events

The canvas subwindow maintains a set of events which it is currently accepting. There are in fact two sets of events - one relating to keyboard events and one relating to mouse events. The event sets are stored in **WIN_KBD_INPUT_MASK** and **WIN_PICK_INPUT_MASK.**

Events may be added to the sets by using the attributes

```
WIN_CONSUME_KBD_EVENT
WIN_CONSUME_PICK_EVENT
```

These attributes take *event codes* as value. There is an event code related to each possible user input. Some examples are **MS_RIGHT, MS_MIDDLE, MS_LEFT** and **WIN_ASCII_EVENT** which correspond to the user pressing the right mouse button, middle button, left button or an ASCII key respectively.

A canvas may be created as shown below

```
canvas = window_create (base_frame, CANVAS,
            WIN_EVENT_PROC, my_event_proc,
            WIN_CONSUME_KBD_EVENT, WIN_ASCII_EVENT,
            0);
```

If the cursor is within the canvas window and the user presses an ASCII key, the procedure **my_event_proc** will be called.

New events may be added to the window event sets, after the window is created, by using the **window_set()** procedure, e.g.

```
window_set (canvas,
        WIN_CONSUME_PICK_EVENT, MS_RIGHT,
        0);
```

adds the right mouse button to the set of mouse input events. Rather than specifying a single event, a null terminated list of events may be added by using the attributes:
WIN_CONSUME_KBD_EVENTS and **WIN_CONSUME_PICK_EVENTS**
For example,

```
window_set (canvas,
        WIN_CONSUME_PICK_EVENTS, MS_RIGHT,
                                 MS_MIDDLE,
                                 MS_LEFT,
                                 0,
        0);
```

adds the three mouse button events to the set of mouse input events.

Events may also be removed from the sets using the four attributes **WIN_IGNORE_PICK_EVENT, WIN_IGNORE_PICK_EVENTS, WIN_IGNORE_KBD_EVENT, WIN_IGNORE_KBD_EVENTS** which are used in the same manner as shown above.

Note that these attributes add or remove events from the sets - they do not change the entire set. A canvas subwindow by default enables the following events - **LOC_WINENTER, LOC_WINEXIT, LOC_MOVE, MS_LEFT, MS_MIDDLE, MS_RIGHT**. It expects to receive these events and will not function properly if they are disabled. (See [1] for an explanation of event codes.)

Events take place when a button or key is pressed **or** released. Button or key releases are called UP events and may be ignored by removing the **WIN_UP_EVENTS** event code from the input sets.

4.3.3. Information returned from events

When an event occurs which a window is interested in, the event handling routine is called. This is given as parameters to the identifier of the window in which the event took place and a pointer to an *Event* type which contains information about the event. The event handling procedure should be declared as shown below

```
my_event_proc (canvas, event)
Canvas canvas;
Event *event;
```

The event parameter contains information about the type of event, the location of the event and the time that the event took place. This information can be retrieved using a set of macros which take the event pointer as parameter

```
event_id(event)
```

which returns the identifying code of the event. This may be an ASCII value or one of the event codes described in the previous section.

```
event_x(event)  and event_y(event)
```

return the x and y coordinates of the cursor when the event took place.

Example 4.4 below displays a box in a canvas (using the procedure given in example 4.2) and prints a message whenever a mouse button is pressed or released over the box.

```
#include <suntool/sunview.h>
#include <suntool/canvas.h>

static void     my_event_proc();

main(argc, argv)
        int         argc;
        char        **argv;
{
        Frame          base_frame;
        Canvas         canvas;

        base_frame = window_create(NULL, FRAME, 0);
        canvas = window_create(base_frame, CANVAS,
                                WIN_EVENT_PROC, my_event_proc,
                                0);
        /* use default canvas input sets */

        draw_box(canvas_pixwin(canvas), 100, 100, "Quit");
```

```
        window_main_loop(base_frame);
        exit(0);
}

static void
my_event_proc(canvas, event)
        Canvas          canvas;
        Event           *event;
{
        Pixwin          *pw;
        int             xpos, ypos;             /* position of event */

        pw = canvas_pixwin(canvas);
        xpos = event_x(event);
        ypos = event_y(event);

        if ((xpos >= 100) && (xpos <= 137)
            && (ypos >= 100) && (ypos <= 115))
                switch (event_id(event))
                {
                case MS_LEFT:
                        pw_text(pw, 100, 150, PIX_SRC, NULL, "Left Button  ");
                        break;
                case MS_MIDDLE:
                        pw_text(pw, 100, 150, PIX_SRC, NULL, "Middle Button");
                        break;
                case MS_RIGHT:
                        pw_text(pw, 100, 150, PIX_SRC, NULL, "Right Button ");
                        break;
                default:
                        pw_text(pw, 100, 150, PIX_SRC, NULL, "             ");
                        break;
                }
        else
                pw_text(pw, 100, 150, PIX_SRC, NULL, "             ");
}
```

Example 4.4

4.4. Window damage

The SunView system is an overlapping window system: when frames are created, they may appear on top of other frames on the screen. The interface allows frames to be resized, closed to icons, hidden beneath other frames or moved around the screen. This type of interface may cause a window to become damaged - an area of the window becomes exposed on the screen which was not previously visible. The SunView system recognises two types of window damage

(a) if an existing portion of a window is exposed, either by moving another window or by opening a window's icon.

(b) if the size of a window changes.

4.4.1. Repainting

By default, the SunView system will automatically repaint a canvas window when an existing portion of it becomes exposed. SunView handles this by maintaining a pixrect copy of the canvas window. If anything is written to the canvas, it is also written to the copy. When SunView detects damage to a canvas, the image is automatically copied from the backing pixrect into the canvas pixwin. The canvas window is said to be 'retained' and the window attribute **CANVAS_RETAINED** is set to **TRUE.**

An application program may choose to do its own repainting. This may be done setting the **CANVAS_RETAINED** attribute to **FALSE** and supplying a repaint procedure as the value of the **CANVAS_REPAINT_PROC** attribute. There are two occasions on which this may be necessary: when the time penalty in writing to both the canvas and the backing copy is too great, and when the extra memory required for the copy is too great. For most applications, however, a retained window should be used.

The repaint procedure should be declared as shown below

```
my_repaint_proc (canvas, pixwin, repaint_area)
Canvas   canvas;
Pixwin   *pixwin;
Rectlist *repaint_area;
```

The third argument is a pointer to a list of rectangles which define the damaged area. The application may choose to repaint this area, the whole canvas or the rectangle given by **repaint_area->rl_bound**, which is the bounding rectangle for the repaint area.

4.4.2. Resizing

An application program may wish to take into account changes to the window size. This can be quite difficult, especially for complex windows which have a large number of images displayed. Many window tools (e.g. **iconedit**) simply ignore resizing. It is possible, however, to specify a procedure to be called when the window is stretched. This is done by giving the procedure name as value to the **CANVAS_RESIZE_PROC** attribute. The procedure should be declared as shown below

```
my_resize_proc (canvas, width, height)
Canvas canvas;
int    width, height;
```

where **width** and **height** are the new dimension of the window. Note that the window should not be repainted inside this procedure, as the repaint procedure will be called automatically by SunView after the resize procedure.

4.5. Scrollbars

Canvas subwindows, in common with text and panel subwindows, support scrollbars. The canvas can be defined as a large area which is manipulated through a smaller window. The small window can be regarded as a viewing window which may be moved around the canvas using the scrollbars. The canvas subwindow package has been designed to work with scrollbars and an application has to do very little extra work to use them.

The SunView package provides two types of scrollbar - vertical and horizontal to allow up/down and left/right scrolling. A canvas may have one, two or no scrollbars, and the scrollbars may be positioned at the left or right, or the top or bottom of the window.

4.5.1. Creating scrollbars

When a canvas is created with scrollbars, there are in effect two windows - the canvas and the viewing window. The attributes **WIN_WIDTH** and **WIN_HEIGHT** specify the dimensions of the viewing window, while the attributes **CANVAS_WIDTH** and **CANVAS_HEIGHT** specify the dimensions of the canvas.

Scrollbars are created using the **scrollbar_create()** function. This returns a structure of type *Scrollbar*. To associate a scrollbar with a canvas, this structure should be given as value to the **WIN_VERTICAL_SCROLLBAR** or **WIN_HORIZONTAL_SCROLLBAR** attributes of the canvas. As an example, a canvas may be created as shown below

```
canvas = window_create (base_frame, CANVAS,
                CANVAS_AUTO_SHRINK, FALSE
                 CANVAS_WIDTH, 1000,
                 CANVAS_HEIGHT, 1000,
                 WIN_VERTICAL_SCROLLBAR, scrollbar_create(0),
                 WIN_HORIZONTAL_SCROLLBAR, scrollbar_create(0),
                 0);
```

The canvas is of size 1000 x 1000. The viewing window is the size of the frame (this is not explicitly set but defaults to that size) and may be scrolled in both directions.

Note that canvas windows are set to expand or shrink automatically to the size of the parent frame. To ensure that the canvas is at least 1000 x 1000 pixels, the attribute **CANVAS_AUTO_SHRINK** is set to **FALSE**.

4.5.2. Reading and writing

When pixwin functions are used to draw into a canvas which has scrollbars, the arguments should be given in the canvas coordinate system. The whole of the canvas is available for drawing, irrespective of the current position of the viewing window.

If user input events occur, these will also be in the canvas coordinate system. The viewing window simply provides visual access to an area of the canvas, and in general an application will rarely require to use its coordinate system.

There are a few occasions, however, on which it is necessary to use the viewing window coordinates - if an application uses menus (see section 4.6), the menu location must be specified in the viewing window. SunView provides a function which translates from canvas space to viewing window space - **canvas_window_event()**. This takes an event structure as parameter; the location of the event is translated from canvas to viewing window location. For example, if the user presses a mouse button in a canvas and the application program then wants to display a menu at the current cursor position, the following code would be placed in the application's event handling procedure.

```
my_event_proc (canvas, event)
Canvas canvas;
Event  *event;
{
        event = canvas_window_event (event);
        display_menu (event_x(event), event_y(event));

        ...
}
```

An application can also translate from viewing window to canvas coordinates using the **canvas_event()** function in a similar manner. This would only be used by applications which read their own events.

4.5.3. Scrollbar attributes

As mentioned above, an application can specify the position at which a scrollbar will appear. Scrollbars, in common with all other SunView items, have a list of attributes which dictate their appearance and behaviour. The example in section 4.5.1 created scrollbars with default attributes. The example below creates a non-default scrollbar by using attributes which specify its thickness, position, etc. (For a full list of scrollbar attributes see [2].)

```
my_bar = scrollbar_create(
        SCROLL_PLACEMENT, SCROLL_NORTH,
        SCROLL_THICKNESS, 20,
        SCROLL_BUBBLE_COLOR, SCROLL_BLACK, 0);
```

4.6. Menus

Another facility provided by SunView is the capability to display a pop-up menu. A typical menu is shown in Chapter 1. The user releases the mouse button over the item which he or she wishes to select.

A menu is created using the **menu_create()** function and can be displayed on the screen using **menu_show()**.

4.6.1. Creating simple menus

The **menu_create()** function returns a Menu structure. It takes menu attributes as arguments in a similar manner to **scrollbar_create()**. The **MENU_STRINGS** attribute allows a list of string to be defined which are displayed as items in the menu.

We can define a simple menu as shown below

```
Menu my_menu;

my_menu = menu_create(MENU_STRINGS, "display", "remove", 0,
                0);
```

We can then use **menu_show()** to display the menu when desired. This takes parameters as shown below

```
menu_show ( menu, window, event, attributes )
Menu            menu;
Window          window;
Event           *event;
<attribute-list> attributes;
```

This will display **menu** on the subwindow **window** at the location specified in the **event** structure. **menu_show()** returns the value of the selected item; i.e. if the first string is selected, it returns 1, if the second string is selected, it returns 2 and so on. If no item in the menu is selected, **menu_show()** returns 0. The location of the menu or the default menu notify procedure may be changed by giving different values in the **attributes** parameter.

We can now write a simple program which uses menus. The program shown below displays a menu at the cursor position when a mouse button is pressed. It displays a message which tells which selection has occurred.

```
#include <suntool/sunview.h>
#include <suntool/canvas.h>
static void     my_event_proc();

main(argc, argv)
          int            argc;
          char         **argv;
{
          Frame          base_frame;
          Canvas         canvas;

          base_frame = window_create(NULL, FRAME, 0);
          canvas = window_create(base_frame, CANVAS,
                                   WIN_EVENT_PROC, my_event_proc, 0);

          window_main_loop(base_frame);
          exit(0);
}

static void
my_event_proc(canvas, event)
          Canvas         canvas;
          Event         *event;
{
          Pixwin         *pw;
          int           selection;
          Menu           my_menu;
          char          message[20];

          if ((event_id(event) == MS_LEFT) ||
             (event_id(event) == MS_MIDDLE) ||
             (event_id(event) == MS_RIGHT))
          {
                    /*
                     * if a button is pressed, open pixwin, create the menu and
                     * display it
                     */
                    pw = canvas_pixwin(canvas);
                    my_menu = menu_create(MENU_STRINGS, "display",
                                          "remove",
                                          "chmod", 0,
                                          0);

                    /*
                     * we convert the event to window coordinates although this
                     * is not necessary since no scrollbars are used
                     */
                    selection = (int) menu_show(my_menu, canvas,
                                          canvas_event(canvas, event),
                                          NULL);
```

```
                switch (selection)
                {
                case 0:
                                strcpy(message, "No item selected");
                                break;
                case 1:
                                strcpy(message, "display selected");
                                break;
                case 2:
                                strcpy(message, "remove selected ");
                                break;
                case 3:
                                strcpy(message, "chmod selected  ");
                }
                pw_text(pw, 100, 20, PIX_SRC, NULL, message);
        }
}
```

Example 4.5

4.6.2. Walking menus

SunView provides *walking menus*, in which a menu may actually be a hierarchy of individual menus. Some of the selections in the menu will have a small arrow pointing to the right. This indicates to the user that if he/she slides the mouse to the right of that selection, a "pullright" submenu will appear.

A simple pullright menu is shown below.

```
Menu first, second;

second = menu_create ( MENU_STRINGS, "a1", "a2", "a3", 0,
                       0);

first = menu_create ( MENU_PULLRIGHT_ITEM, "a", second,
                      MENU_STRINGS, "b", "c", 0,
                      0);
```

When using walking menus, the value returned from **menu_show** may not distinguish between some of the possible selections. For example, in the menu shown above, if the selection 'a2' is chosen or the selection 'b' is chosen, **menu_show** will return the value 2 in both cases. To distinguish between these selections, it is necessary to use the **MENU_NOTIFY_PROC** attribute. This can be used as shown below,

```
second = menu_create ( MENU_STRINGS, "a1", "a2", "a3", 0,
                       MENU_NOTIFY_PROC, handle_second,
                       0 );
```

If a selection is made from the menu **second,** the procedure **handle_second** will then be invoked.

4.6.3. Menu attributes

There are a large number of attributes which apply to menus. We have already seen **MENU_STRINGS** and **MENU_PULLRIGHT_ITEM.** Other attributes allow pixrect images rather than character strings to be used as the menu items; menus may be defined as two-dimensional by using the **MENU_NCOLS** and **MENU_NROWS** attributes, or a shadow may be placed behind the menu by using the **MENU_SHADOW** attribute. (For a full list of attributes see [3].)

4.7. Example program

Example 4.6 uses all the features we have looked at. It is a fuller implementation of the directory browser which has been used in this chapter, although some of the procedures have still been omitted. Figure 4.2 shows the directory browser frame.

```
#include <suntool/sunview.h>
#include <suntool/canvas.h>

static void     my_event_proc(), fill_top_window(), display_contents();
static void     up_proc(), display_attribute(), do_command();
static void     home_proc(), quit_proc();
Canvas          display_window;
static int      ATT_FLAG = 1;
/* ATT_FLAG indicates which attribute is currently being displayed */
static char     homedir[256];
/* homedir contains the initial directory of the browser */

main(argc, argv)
        int             argc;
        char            **argv;
{
        Frame           base_frame;
        Canvas          control_window;

        getwd(homedir);

        base_frame = window_create(NULL, FRAME,
                                        FRAME_LABEL, "Directory Browser",
                                        0);

        control_window = window_create(base_frame, CANVAS,
                                        WIN_EVENT_PROC, my_event_proc,
                                        WIN_HEIGHT, 140,
                                        0);
```

```
        display_window = window_create(base_frame, CANVAS,
                                CANVAS_AUTO_SHRINK, FALSE,
                                CANVAS_HEIGHT, 1000,
                            WIN_VERTICAL_SCROLLBAR, scrollbar_create(0),
                                0);

        window_set(control_window, WIN_IGNORE_PICK_EVENT, WIN_UP_EVENTS, 0);
        /* not interested in button releases - only presses */
        fill_top_window(control_window);
        display_contents(display_window);

        window_main_loop(base_frame);
        exit(0);
}

static void
fill_top_window(canvas_name)
        Canvas          canvas_name;
/* this procedure displays the buttons and menus in the control panel */
{
        Pixwin          *pw;
        char            *homeptr;

        pw = canvas_pixwin(canvas_name);

        draw_button(pw, 430, 20, "Home");
        draw_button(pw, 500, 20, "Up");
        draw_button(pw, 560, 20, "Quit");

        draw_box(pw, 220, 55, "Command");
        draw_box(pw, 300, 45, "  Attribute  ");

        switch (ATT_FLAG)
        {
        case 1:
                draw_box(pw, 300, 60, "Size in Bytes");
                break;
        case 2:
                draw_box(pw, 300, 60, "Permissions  ");
                break;
        case 3:
        default:
                draw_box(pw, 300, 60, "Owner        ");
                break;
        }

        /* only display the last 15 characters of the home directory */
        for (homeptr = homedir; strlen(homeptr) > 15; ++homeptr);
        draw_box(pw, 50, 35, homeptr);
        pw_text(pw, 50, 30, PIX_NOT(PIX_SRC), NULL, " Home Directory ");
}
```

```
#include <sys/dir.h>
static void
display_contents(canvas_name)
        Canvas          canvas_name;
/*
 * This procedure displays the contents of the directory in the display
 * window with a header above each field
 */
{
        DIR             *directory;
        struct direct   *entry;
        int             xpos, ypos;
        Pixwin          *pw;

        pw = canvas_pixwin(canvas_name);
        xpos = 150;
        ypos = 45;
        switch (ATT_FLAG)
        {
        case 1:
                pw_text(pw, 20, 25, PIX_SRC, NULL, "Size        ");
                break;
        case 2:
                pw_text(pw, 20, 25, PIX_SRC, NULL, "Permissions");
                break;
        case 3:
        default:
                pw_text(pw, 20, 25, PIX_SRC, NULL, "Owner       ");
                break;
        }
        pw_vector(pw, 20, 30, 110, 30, PIX_SRC, 1);
        pw_text(pw, 150, 25, PIX_SRC, NULL, "Contents");
        pw_vector(pw, 150, 30, 210, 30, PIX_SRC, 1);
        directory = opendir(".");
        while ((entry = readdir(directory)) != NULL)
        {
                pw_text(pw, xpos, ypos, PIX_SRC, NULL, entry->d_name);
                display_attribute(entry->d_name, ypos);
                ypos = ypos + 20;
        }
}


static void
my_event_proc(canvas, event)
        Canvas          canvas;
        Event           *event;
/*
 * Handles user inputs in the control panel - it only reacts to the user
 * pressing the right mouse button
 */
{
        int             xpos, ypos, selection;
```

```
        Menu            my_menu;

        xpos = event_x(event);
        ypos = event_y(event);

        if (event_id(event) == MS_RIGHT)
                if ((xpos > 300) && (xpos < 411) && (ypos > 45) && (ypos < 75))
                {
                        my_menu = menu_create(MENU_STRINGS, "Size in Bytes",
                                                "Permissions  ",
                                                "Owner        ",
                                                0,
                                                0);
                        selection = (int) menu_show(my_menu, canvas,
                                        canvas_event(canvas, event),
                                                NULL);
                        if (selection > 0)
                        {
                                ATT_FLAG = selection;
                                fill_top_window(canvas);
                                display_contents(display_window);
                        }
                } else if ((xpos > 220) && (xpos < 310) && (ypos > 55) && (ypos < 70))
                {
                        my_menu = menu_create(MENU_STRINGS, "Rename",
                                                "Chmod",
                                                "Display",
                                                0,
                                                0);
                        selection = (int) menu_show(my_menu, canvas,
                                        canvas_event(canvas, event),
                                                NULL);
                        if (selection > 0)
                                do_command(selection);
                } else if ((xpos > 500) && (xpos < 520) && (ypos > 20) && (ypos < 48))
                        up_proc();
                else if ((xpos > 430) && (xpos < 490) && (ypos > 20) && (ypos < 48))
                        home_proc();
                else if ((xpos > 560) && (xpos < 620) && (ypos > 20) && (ypos < 48))
                        quit_proc();
}

static void
up_proc()
/* Changes the working directory to the parent of the current one */
{
        chdir("..");
        display_contents(display_window);
}

static void
home_proc()
/* Changes the working directory to the home directory of the browser */
```

```
{
        Pixwin *pw;

        pw = canvas_pixwin(display_window);
        chdir(homedir);
        pw_writebackground(pw, 0, 31, 1000, 1000, PIX_SRC);
        display_contents(display_window);
}

static void
quit_proc()
{
        exit(0);
}

static void
display_attribute(filename, position)
        char        *filename;
        int         position;
{

        /*
         * This procedure should check the global variable ATT_FLAG and issue
         * the appropriate UNIX call on "filename". It should then display
         * the resulting attribute value at (10, position) using "pw_text"
         */

}


static void
do_command(which)
        int         which;
{
        /*
         * The command procedures are not implemented - a procedure must be
         * provided to allow user inputs in the display window. The user can
         * then select the object names displayed in the window and issue
         * commands on the objects
         */
}
```

Example 4.6

4.8. Colour

All the examples given so far have been in monochrome. It is also possible to output colour to pixwins on a colour workstation e.g. a Sun 3/110. This is achieved by first associating a *colour map segment* with a pixwin, and then setting the raster op value of an output function to use a colour defined in the colour map.

In example 4.7 a pre-defined colour map, reproducing the colours of the rainbow, is used. The map is defined in *<sunwindow/cms_rainbow.h>* and

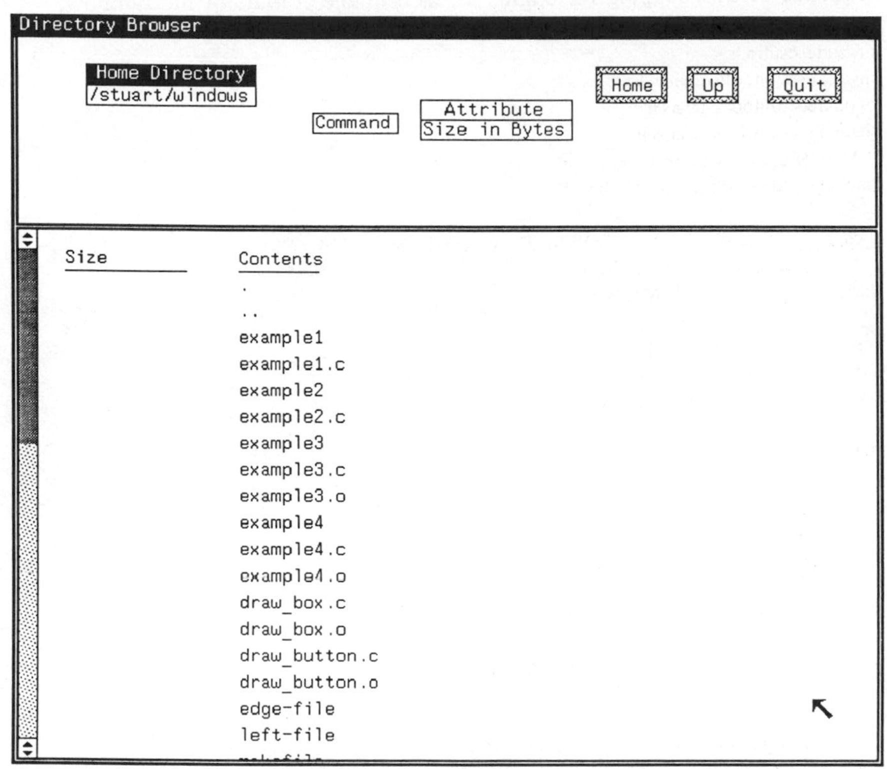

Figure 4.2

consists of eight colors, (**CMS_RAINBOWSIZE** equals eight.) A colour is composed from a mixture of red, green and blue components. The arrays storing the colour values, red, green and blue, are initialised by **cms_rainbowsetup**(). The colour map segement is then associated with the pixwin by **pw_putcolormap**(). It is possible to create more colours and modify existing ones by editing a private copy of *cms_rainbow.h*. The complete colour map can have 256 colours.

The colour value is then set in the raster op value by or'ing it with the **PIX_COLOR()** macro. For example,

op = PIX_SRC | PIXCOLOR(0);

uses the first colour in the colour map, i.e. white. Example 4.7 draws a sequence of over-lapping rectangles in each of the colours of the rainbow.

```
#include <stdio.h>
#include <suntool/sunview.h>
#include <suntool/canvas.h>
#include <sunwindow/cms.h>
/* Map of the colours of the rainbow */
#include <sunwindow/cms_rainbow.h>

u_char      red[CMS_RAINBOWSIZE], green[CMS_RAINBOWSIZE],
            blue[CMS_RAINBOWSIZE];
char        cmsname[CMS_NAMESIZE];

Frame       base_frame;
Canvas      color_canvas;
Pixwin      *color_pix;

main()
{

        int         op, i;
        int         x, y = 0;

        base_frame = window_create(NULL, FRAME,
                                WIN_WIDTH, 800,
                                WIN_HEIGHT, 800,
                                0);

        color_canvas = window_create(base_frame, CANVAS,
                                CANVAS_HEIGHT, 800,
                                CANVAS_WIDTH, 800,
                                CANVAS_RETAINED, TRUE,
                                0);

        color_pix = canvas_pixwin(color_canvas);

/* Associate the colour map name with the pixwin */
        strncpy(cmsname, CMS_RAINBOW, CMS_NAMESIZE);
        pw_setcmsname(color_pix, cmsname);

/* initialise the colour arrays */
        cms_rainbowsetup(red, green, blue);

/* associate the colour map values with the pixwin */
        pw_putcolormap(color_pix, 0, CMS_RAINBOWSIZE, red, green, blue);

        for (i = 0; i < CMS_RAINBOWSIZE; i++)
        {
```

```
        op = PIX_SRC | PIX_COLOR(i);
        pw_rop(color_pix, x += 40, y += 40, 100, 100, op, NULL, 0, 0);
    }

    window_main_loop(base_frame);

}
```

Example 4.7 Colour

Further reading

[1] *SunView Programmer's Guide*, Chapter 6 - Handling Input pp. 61-73 Sun Microsystems, 1986.

[2] *SunView Programmer's Guide*, Chapter 14 - Scrollbars pp. 231-244 Sun Microsystems, 1986.

[3] *SunView Programmer's Guide*, Chapter 11 - Menus pp. 169-208 Sun Microsystems, 1986.

[4] *SunView Programmer's Guide*, Chapter 5 - Canvases pp. 47-57 Sun Microsystems, 1986.

[5] W H Newman, R F Sproull, *Principles of Interactive Computer Graphics*, McGraw-Hill, New York, 1979.

5 Pixrect Layer and Graphics Packages

5.1. Introduction

Computer graphics have been applied successfully in many different application areas over the last 30 years or so. The application areas have been as diverse as desktop publishing, computer aided design of bridges, electronic circuits, cartography, business and advertising. The tremendous increase witnessed in the past few decades of the application of computer graphics has been partly due to the advent of cheaper, higher resolution displays and the falling cost of digital memory.

The Sun workstation is of the modern family of computer graphics displays. These generally comprise a high resolution, bitmapped graphics display, a pointing device (such as a mouse) and a keyboard. Sun workstations are suitable for applications in engineering, CAD/CAM, desktop publishing, business graphics and general dynamic graphics applications.

5.2. Basic concepts

A raster-scan, or bitmapped, display consists of a screen similar to that of a TV, a display controller and a refresh buffer (frame buffer). The frame buffer is a 2D array of picture elements. The task of the display controller subsystem is to take the contents of the frame buffer and display it on the screen approximately 60 times per second. A picture element is normally referred to as a pixel and each pixel in the frame buffer corresponds to a unique point on the display screen.

In the case of monochrome displays, each pixel value in the frame buffer has a value of either 1 or 0. This is translated by the display controller into setting the corresponding point on the display screen to be either black or white. Colour displays have pixel values which indicate the mixture of red, green and blue hue intensities to be used in displaying the point on the screen.

The major decrease in the cost of digital memory, as well as the performance and dynamic picture capabilities, have been the major reasons for the proliferation of raster-scan display systems such as the Sun.

For further reading on the history of computer graphics, hardware and software, see the definitive texts on the subject [NEWMAN 79] and [FOLEY 82].

5.3. Graphics packages

The answer to the question "Why have graphics packages?" is similar to the answer to "Why have high level languages and code libraries?". High level languages provide a high degree of portability across different machine architectures. They also provide a means of describing the problem domain using higher level concepts than low level assembly languages. They allow the programmer to think more in the terms of the actual problem at hand than in the low level details of the particular machine or language being used for implementation. Similarly, the main advantages of using graphics packages when writing graphics applications are that the programmer can think more in terms of the user interface and the problem at hand rather than low level implementation details. Graphics packages can also guarantee a fair degree of portability across different types of display.

The graphics packages to be discussed in this chapter are SunCORE, SunCGI and the Pixrect package.

5.3.1. SunCORE

The CORE standard describes a graphics package proposed by the special interest group on graphics of the ACM (Association for Computing Machinery). This has been reviewed by US and European standards bodies. The standard defines the set of capabilities required by a specific language binding (implementation) of the CORE system. The main aims of CORE are to provide both program and programmer portability across different machines.

SunCORE is a specific implementation of the CORE standard, providing interfaces to the C, FORTRAN and Pascal programming languages. The CORE standard is defined at different levels related to the input and output capabilities of a particular CORE implementation. SunCORE supports the following levels:

output level 3C
- including 2D and 3D translation, scaling and rotation

input level 2
- including the pick device

dimension level 2
- supports 3D operations

The SunCORE implementation provides facilities in addition to the CORE standard in order to exploit the full capabilities of the Sun workstation. These include textured polygon fill algorithms, raster primitives, shaded surface polygon rendering and hidden surface elimination. For an introduction to SunCORE see Chapter 6 and also the reference manual [SUNCORE 86].

5.3.2. SunCGI

SunCGI is an implementation of the ANSI Computer Graphics Interface. It provides high level graphics capabilities without the overhead of many of the functions of SunCORE. In a sense it can be thought of as a lower level SunCORE providing much, but not all of the functionality.

A certain number of the optional functions of CGI are not supported in order to ensure optimum run-time speed of application programs using CGI.

SunCGI differs from SunCORE in the areas of output primitives, input and segmentation. These are:

- no 3D output primitives are supported
- no rotation or translation of geometrical output primitives
- no segmentation (i.e. no ability to collect output primitives together for manipulation as one unit)

SunCGI does provide extra geometrical and raster primitives not available in SunCORE. These are routines for the generation of circles and ellipses (filled and hollow) and the cell array primitive. The cell array is a raster array whose dimensions vary as the view surface size varies, thus providing built-in scaling of raster images. For further reading on using SunCGI, see the manual [SUNCGI 86].

The Graphical Kernel System (GKS) is an emerging ISO graphics standard which is similar in many respects to SunCORE and SunCGI. GKS is not provided as part of the standard Sun software distribution, however. The model of input devices in CGI is based directly on the GKS model and CGI supports the output primitives defined for GKS. GKS, in addition, also provides segmentation like SunCORE and application portability is greatly enhanced by the concept of a generalised workstation.

5.3.3. Pixrect layer

The pixrect layer is the the layer sitting above low level device drivers and routines in this layer to some extent parallel those in the pixwin layer. The pixrect layer allows all Sun displays, whether screen, printer, memory, etc., to be accessed in a device independent fashion, at least in theory. The routines for accessing a pixrect are the same no matter which medium the pixrect is stored on, therefore, the programmer need not be concerned with the low level implementation details of the media.

The pixwin layer, as described in Chapter 4, is built using pixrects. These pixrects are displayed on the screen and input to each pixwin is handled by the overall input handler. Each pixwin can be either retained or non-retained. A retained pixwin is one which has a copy of its image stored on a memory pixrect. Therefore, a retained pixwin is constructed from 2 pixrects, a pixrect existing on the screen and a pixrect retained in memory.

Programming at the pixrect layer is for lowest level image creation; it is generally used in conjunction with the higher level facilities of SunView for interactive window-based programming.

5.4. Pixrect concepts

To introduce you to the pixrect layer, this section will present a number of small programs demonstrating some of the powerful imaging facilities available. Many different functions exist at the pixrect layer for manipulating pixrects and in the next few sections we will look at ways of combining pixrects to produce different images, clearing and inverting pixrects, how to draw lines and more complex shapes, how to display text, simulate moving images, create offscreen images and load and store pixrects via UNIX files. To actually see the effects, the Sun workstation screen will be used as a pixrect.

First of all, though, it is necessary to introduce the basic concepts of the pixrect layer.

Pixel
: A pixel is an individual picture element.

Bitmap
: A bitmap can be thought of as a rectangular region of pixels.

Pixrect
: A pixrect is a bitmap with a set of defined operations which may be performed on it. The defined operations are the same, regardless of the media on which the bitmap is stored.

RasterOp
: A raster operation is one which combines two rasters (bitmaps) using some Boolean operation. The two bitmaps are commonly referred to as the source and destination bitmaps.

5.4.1. RasterOp operation

A pixrect can be used to store graphical and textual images and certain visual effects can be achieved by combining two pixrects using a RasterOp. The RasterOp is in essence one of a number of Boolean operations and some of the common RasterOp functions available include:

PIX_SRC
source overwrites the destination

PIX_DST
effectively does nothing - destination remains the same

PIX_SRC | PIX_DST
OR the source and destination - any black pixel in either source or destination is set to black in the destination

PIX_SRC & PIX_DST
AND the source and destination - a pixel is set to black in the destination if the corresponding pixel is black in both the source and destination before the operation is applied

PIX_NOT(PIX_SRC) & PIX_DST
erases the sources image from the destination

PIX_NOT(PIX_DST)
inverts the destination's pixels

PIX_SRC ^ PIX_DST
inverting paint - inverts the source image contained in the destination

Very complex RasterOp functions can be constructed from **PIX_SRC, PIX_DST, PIX_NOT** and the Boolean operators **|, &** and **^**. The above table lists those most commonly used functions and the following sections now present programs demonstrating the different use of such functions.

5.4.2. Combining pixrects

The **pr_rop()** function is used for combining two pixrects

```
pr_rop(dpr, dx, dy, dw, dh, op, spr, sx, sy)
struct pixrect *dpr, *spr;
int dx, dy, dw, dh, op, sx, sy;
```

This performs a Raster operation **op** from a source pixrect **spr** to a destination pixrect **dpr**. The area of the destination pixrect to be affected is defined by the rectangle whose origin is (**dx, dy**) and whose width and height are **dw** and **dh** respectively. Pixels are taken from the source pixrect beginning at position (**sx, sy**). As previously mentioned, altering the **op** argument has many different effects which will be illustrated in the following short examples and the program in example 5.1.

Note **pr_rop()** is in fact a macro created with the C preprocessor facilities. Its definition will be included in any program which includes the pixrect header file **<pixrect/pixrect_hs.h>**.

5.4.3. Clearing a pixrect to white

One of the simplest applications of the **pr_rop()** routine is to clear a pixrect to all white pixels[1].

```
clear_pixrect(pr)
struct pixrect *pr;
{
        pr_rop(pr, 0, 0, pr->pr_size.x, pr->pr_size.y,
               PIX_CLR, NULL, 0, 0);
}
```

The above presents a function which takes a pointer to a pixrect structure and clears all its pixels to zero. The whole of the pixrect is affected, since (0,0) specifies the origin and **pr->pr_size.x** and **pr->pr_size.y** specify the total width and height of the pixrect respectively. Notice that in this example we have supplied NULL as the source pixrect. This implies that the Raster operation will use a constant source - in this case it uses a constant source of zeros.

5.4.4. Inverting a pixrect

Another simple but powerful use of the **pr_rop()** function is for inverting each pixel within a pixrect

```
invert_pixrect(pr)
struct pixrect *pr;
{
        pr_rop(pr, 0, 0, pr->pr_size.x, pr->pr_size.y,
               PIX_NOT(PIX_DST), NULL, 0, 0);
}
```

The function **invert_pixrect()** takes a pointer to a pixrect as a parameter and inverts every pixel within the pixrect. Again the whole of the pixrect is affected by virtue of the 0, 0, **pr->pr_size.x**, **pr->pr_size.y** parameters. The operation used is the negate operator and **PIX_NOT(PIX_DST)** means "negate every pixel of the destination pixrect" - therefore all 1's are changed to 0's and vice versa. As in **clear_pixrect()** the source pixrect plays no part in this operation.

---

[1] This assumes that the maximum and minimum intensities are 0 and 1. This is usually the default for monochrome pixrects but can be altered by the function **pr_reversevideo( )**.

5.4.5. Flashing screen program

To demonstrate the functions **invert_pixrect()** and **clear_pixrect()** we will present a small program in example 5.1 which claims the screen as a pixrect, clears it and repeatedly flashes it.

```
#include <stdio.h>
#include <pixrect/pixrect_hs.h>

main ()
{
    struct pixrect *screen;
    int     loop;

    screen = pr_open ("/dev/fb");
    clear_pixrect (screen);

    for (loop = 0; loop < 11; loop++)
    {
        invert_pixrect (screen);
        sleep (1);
        loop++;
    }
    pr_close (screen);
}

clear_pixrect (pr)
struct pixrect *pr;
{
    pr_rop (pr, 0, 0, pr -> pr_size.x, pr -> pr_size.y, PIX_CLR,
            NULL, 0, 0);
}

invert_pixrect (pr)
struct pixrect *pr;
{
    pr_rop (pr, 0, 0, pr -> pr_size.x, pr -> pr_size.y, PIX_NOT (PIX_DST),
            NULL, 0, 0);
}
```

Example 5.1 invert.c - repeatedly inverts the screen

This program, held in a file called *invert.c*, is compiled with the command

```
cc -o invert invert.c -lpixrect
```

This produces a program named **invert** which can be executed to invert the screen.

Note

header file
: **/usr/include/pixrect/pixrect_hs.h** is the header file to be included in programs using pixrect facilities

pr_open()
: This opens a pixrect device. In this case **/dev/fb** is the screen (or frame buffer). Subsequent to this function call, we can regard the screen as an ordinary pixrect.

5.4.6. Shading the screen

On monochrome workstations it is possible to display pseudo-grey scaled[2] areas using pixel patterns. This next example presents a program which first clears the screen to white and then changes it to a grey tone. This demonstrates the use of both memory pixrects (to be discussed in a further section) and how to replicate a source pixrect across a destination pixrect.

```
#include <stdio.h>
#include <pixrect/pixrect_hs.h>

#define SCREENWIDTH        (screen->pr_size.x)
#define SCREENHEIGHT       (screen->pr_size.y)

static unsigned short   grey_data[16] =
{
    0x8420, 0x2108, 0x0842, 0x4210,
    0x1084, 0x8420, 0x2108, 0x0842,
    0x4210, 0x1084, 0x8420, 0x2108,
    0x0842, 0x4210, 0x1084, 0x0000
};
mpr_static (grey_pr, 15, 15, 1, grey_data);


main ()
{
    struct pixrect *screen;

    screen = pr_open ("/dev/fb");
    clear_pixrect (screen);

    pr_replrop (screen, 0, 0, SCREENWIDTH, SCREENHEIGHT, PIX_SRC,
            &grey_pr, 0, 0);
    sleep (5);
    pr_close (screen);
}
```

---

[2] Real grey scale systems allow a value to be specified for each pixel indicating its black intensity. Pseudo-grey scales are implemented using pixel patterns where each pixel can only be white or black.

```
clear_pixrect (pr)
struct pixrect *pr;
{
    pr_rop (pr, 0, 0, pr -> pr_size.x, pr -> pr_size.y, PIX_CLR,
            NULL, 0, 0);
}
```

Example 5.2 grey.c - paints the screen grey

The main aim of the program in example 5.2 is to use one small memory pixrect to cover the whole screen (for the purposes of this section a memory pixrect can be thought of as being a pixrect held somewhere other than the screen; it is really only a collection of bits). The screen is actually painted by replicating the small pixrect **grey_pr** using the **pr_replrop()** routine which takes the same parameters as the **pr_rop()** routine. **pr_replrop()** takes the pixrect **grey_pr** and affects the region defined by 0, 0, SCREENWIDTH, SCREENHEIGHT in the destination pixrect screen. Pixels are taken from the origin 0,0 from pixrect **grey_pr** and replicated on *screen* until all of the affected region has been covered. The process can be visualised as a **pr_rop()** operation, where the source pixrect is constructed from an infinite number of **grey_pr** pixrects laid side by side in both dimensions.

5.4.7. Demonstrating the raster operations

This next section will present an example demonstrating the effects that may be produced by combining two pixrects with different raster ops. The program in example 5.3 was executed and produced the output shown in figure 5.1.

```
#include <stdio.h>
#include <pixrect/pixrect_hs.h>

#define SCREENWIDTH     (screen->pr_size.x)
#define SCREENHEIGHT    (screen->pr_size.y)
#define NUM_OPS         (sizeof(rastcrop)/sizeof(int))
#define CHECKWIDTH      ((SCREENWIDTH - 100) / (NUM_OPS) - 50)
#define CHECKHEIGHT     600

static unsigned short   checked_data[16] =
{
    0xFF00, 0xFF00, 0xFF00, 0xFF00, 0xFF00, 0xFF00, 0xFF00, 0xFF00,
    0x00FF, 0x00FF, 0x00FF, 0x00FF, 0x00FF, 0x00FF, 0x00FF, 0x00FF
};
mpr_static (checked_pr, 15, 15, 1, checked_data);

int     rastcrop[] =
{
    PIX_SRC,                    /* src overwrites dst */
    PIX_SRC | PIX_DST,          /* OR src with dst */
    PIX_SRC & PIX_DST,          /* AND the src and dst */
    PIX_SRC ^ PIX_DST,          /* exclusive OR src with dst */
    PIX_NOT (PIX_SRC) & PIX_DST /* invert src contained in dst */
};
```

```
main ()
{
    struct pixrect *screen;
    int     x,
            y,
            count;

    screen = pr_open ("/dev/fb");
    clear_pixrect (screen);

 /* Draw a black band across the screen */
    pr_rop (screen, 0, 200, SCREENWIDTH, 400, PIX_NOT (PIX_DST),
            screen, 0, 200);

 /* Display the checked pixrect using different RasterOps */
    for (count = 0, x = 50, y = 100; count < NUM_OPS;
            count++, x += 50 + CHECKWIDTH)
    {
        pr_replrop (screen, x, y, CHECKWIDTH, CHECKHEIGHT,
                rasterop[count], &checked_pr, 0, 0);
    }
    pr_close (screen);
}

clear_pixrect (pr)
struct pixrect *pr;
{
    pr_rop (pr, 0, 0, pr -> pr_size.x, pr -> pr_size.y, PIX_CLR,
            NULL, 0, 0);
}
```

Example 5.3 rop.c - combining pixrects with pr_rop()

Type this program in to a file *rop.c*, compile using **cc rop.c -o rop -lpixrect** and then type **rop** to execute. This will produce the patterns shown in figure 5.1.

In the example presented, the most common raster operations have been used. In each **pr_rop()** call the source pixrect is the checked pattern and the destination pixrect is the white screen with a black band running across it. Try adding the raster operations described in section 5.4.1 to the array **raster_op** and check if the output produced is as you expect.

5.4.8. Displaying text

The Sun workstation has the capability of displaying text on pixrects using a number of different fonts and raster operations. Before a text string can be displayed the font to be used must be opened. This is achieved using the following function

Figure 5.1 Patterns using common rasterOps.

```
struct pixfont *pf_open(fontname)
char *fontname;
```

where **fontname** should be the pathname of the file containing the font's definition. Font definition files are usually to be found in the directory */usr/lib/fonts/fixedwidthfonts*. If the font file cannot be opened then NULL is returned. Alternatively, the default font used by the system can be opened with the following:

```
struct pixfont *pf_default()
```

If the environment variable *DEFAULT_FONT* is preset to some font definition file, then this font will be opened. In either case, when a font is no longer required in a program, it is advisable to close it so as to free the space in memory taken up by the font. This can be done by calling the procedure

```
pf_close(pf)
struct pixfont *pf;
```

Having opened a font, the function for displaying text is:

```
pf_text(pos, op, font, string)
struct pr_prpos pos;
int op;
struct pixfont *font;
char *text;
```

where **pos** defines the position within a pixrect for the text to start (this position defines the left edge and baseline of the string), **op** is the raster operation in combining the text with the pixrect, **font** is the font to be used and **string** is the null terminated string to be displayed.

A useful routine for calculating the width of a text string, once it is displayed on a pixrect, is the following:

```
struct pr_size pf_textwidth(len, font, text)
int len;
struct pixfont *font;
char *text;
```

This calculates the width and height, in pixels, of **len** characters of the string text.

This next example shows how to display a message on a pixrect using different raster operations. The program is listed in example 5.4 and the resultant output is shown in figure 5.2.

```
#include <stdio.h>
#include <pixrect/pixrect_hs.h>

#define NUM_FONTS (sizeof(font_table)/sizeof(char *))
char   *font_table[] =
{
    "/usr/lib/fonts/fixedwidthfonts/apl.r.10",
    "/usr/lib/fonts/fixedwidthfonts/cmr.b.14",
    "/usr/lib/fonts/fixedwidthfonts/cmr.b.8",
    "/usr/lib/fonts/fixedwidthfonts/cmr.r.14",
    "/usr/lib/fonts/fixedwidthfonts/cmr.r.8",
    "/usr/lib/fonts/fixedwidthfonts/gacha.b.7",
    "/usr/lib/fonts/fixedwidthfonts/gacha.b.8",
    "/usr/lib/fonts/fixedwidthfonts/gacha.r.7",
    "/usr/lib/fonts/fixedwidthfonts/gacha.r.8",
    "/usr/lib/fonts/fixedwidthfonts/gallant.r.10",
    "/usr/lib/fonts/fixedwidthfonts/gallant.r.19",
    "/usr/lib/fonts/fixedwidthfonts/sail.r.6",
    "/usr/lib/fonts/fixedwidthfonts/screen.b.12",
    "/usr/lib/fonts/fixedwidthfonts/screen.b.14",
    "/usr/lib/fonts/fixedwidthfonts/screen.r.11",
    "/usr/lib/fonts/fixedwidthfonts/screen.r.12",
    "/usr/lib/fonts/fixedwidthfonts/screen.r.14",
    "/usr/lib/fonts/fixedwidthfonts/screen.r.7"
};
```

```
main ()
{
    struct pixrect *screen;
    struct pixfont *font;
    struct pr_prpos where;
    struct pr_size textsize;
    int     i;

    screen = pr_open ("/dev/fb");
    clear_pixrect (screen);
    where.pr = screen;
    where.pos.x = 100;
    where.pos.y = 100;

    for (i = 0; i < NUM_FONTS; i++)
    {
        font = pf_open (font_table[i]);
        textsize = pf_textwidth (strlen (font_table[i]), font,
                font_table[i]);
        where.pos.y += textsize.y + 10;
        pf_text (where, PIX_SRC, font, font_table[i]);
        pf_close (font);
    }
    pr_close (screen);
}

clear_pixrect (pr)
struct pixrect *pr;
{
    pr_rop (pr, 0, 0, pr -> pr_size.x, pr -> pr_size.y, PIX_CLR,
            NULL, 0, 0);
}

invert_pixrect (pr)
struct pixrect *pr;
{
    pr_rop (pr, 0, 0, pr -> pr_size.x, pr -> pr_size.y, PIX_NOT (PIX_DST),
            NULL, 0, 0);
}
```

Example 5.4 font.c - displaying text using different fonts

The purpose of the program is to display a number of text strings on the screen using a different font for each one. Each string printed actually represents the name of the file which contains the definition of the font being used to display the string.[3]

The main part of the program is a for statement which loops round once for each string to be displayed on the screen. The strings to be displayed are

[3] In most Sun systems the font definition files are held in the directory /usr/lib/fonts/fixedwidthfonts.

```
/USR/LIB/FONTS/FIXEDWIDTHFONTS/APL.R.10
/usr/lib/fonts/fixedwidthfonts/cmr.b.14
/usr/lib/fonts/fixedwidthfonts/cmr.b.8
/usr/lib/fonts/fixedwidthfonts/cmr.r.14
/usr/lib/fonts/fixedwidthfonts/cmr.r.8
/usr/lib/fonts/fixedwidthfonts/gacha.b.7
/usr/lib/fonts/fixedwidthfonts/gacha.b.8
/usr/lib/fonts/fixedwidthfonts/gacha.r.7
/usr/lib/fonts/fixedwidthfonts/gacha.r.8
/usr/lib/fonts/fixedwidthfonts/gallant.r.10
/usr/lib/fonts/fixedwidthfonts/gallant.r.19
/usr/lib/fonts/fixedwidthfonts/sail.r.6
/usr/lib/fonts/fixedwidthfonts/screen.b.12
/usr/lib/fonts/fixedwidthfonts/screen.b.14
/usr/lib/fonts/fixedwidthfonts/screen.r.11
/usr/lib/fonts/fixedwidthfonts/screen.r.12
/usr/lib/fonts/fixedwidthfonts/screen.r.14
/usr/lib/fonts/fixedwidthfonts/screen.r.7
```

Figure 5.2 Common fonts on Sun systems

taken from an array of character strings named *font_table*. Within the loop the font is opened up and assigned to *font* - the font pointer. The width and height of the string in pixels, once it is displayed on the pixrect, is calculated using the routine **pf_textwidth()**. The actual y-starting position of the text string is calculated using the height returned from **pf_textwidth()** and the string is then printed. In this example, the raster operation used was **PIX_SRC**, but any operation may be used. In this particular example, however, changing the operation will have little effect since all of the background is white.

A character in a font can be visualised as being held on a very small pixrect. Therefore, only the actual pixels within the outline of the character will be set to black; all others (those in the background) will be set to white. This should be taken into account when displaying text, because these white (background) pixels can disturb their corresponding destination pixels. For example, suppose we want to display black text on a grey background. If the raster operation **PIX_SRC** is used, then a white outline will appear around the text since the white pixels as well as the black pixels of each character image are copied to the destination pixrect. If, however, the boolean OR operation **PIX_SRC | PIX_DST** is used then the procedure will display "transparent" text. Thus, those parts of the destination pixrect untouched by the characters' actual outline, will be left undisturbed. The procedure **pf_ttext()** does exactly this operation, but is more specifically aimed at colour pixrects.

5.4.9. Drawing line shapes

The function for this is:

```
pr_vector(pr, x0, y0, x1, y1, op, value)
struct pixrect *pr;
int x0, y0, x1, y1, op, value;
```

This draws a one unit wide vector from the point (x0, y0) to the point (x1, y1) on the pixrect pointed to by **pr**. The parameter **op** is the raster operation and **value** specifies the resulting values in the vector, if **op** is zero.

The program shown in example 5.5 demonstrates a kaleidoscope effect as shown in figure 5.3. This simple program draws a number of vectors from a fixed point to randomly generated points. Each vector is drawn using the **PIX_SRC** operation, and altering this value can dramatically alter the resulting output - try it and see. In the example, the macro **RANDOM(maxval)** will generate a random number in the range 0 to maxval. Note that the function **invert_pixrect()** is included for completeness sake but is not actually used.

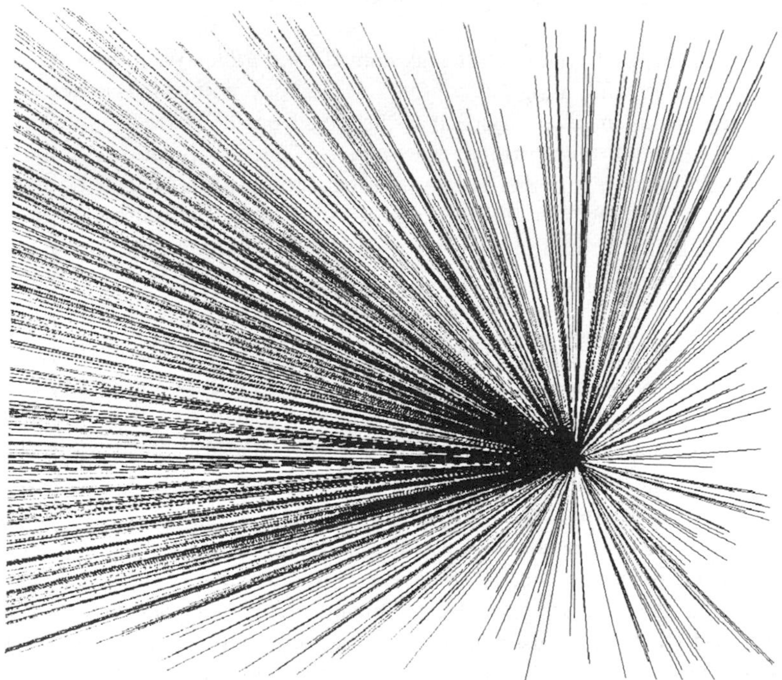

Figure 5.3 A kaleidoscope pattern

```
#include <stdio.h>
#include <pixrect/pixrect_hs.h>
#define RANDOM(maxval)   (random()%maxval)

main ()
{
    struct pixrect *screen;
    int     loop;
    int     randx,
            randy;

    screen = pr_open ("/dev/fb");
    clear_pixrect (screen);

    for (loop = 0; loop < 1000; loop++)
    {
        randx = RANDOM (1500);
        randy = RANDOM (900);
        pr_vector (screen, 300, 300, randx, randy, PIX_SRC, 1);
    }
    pr_close (screen);
}

clear_pixrect (pr)
struct pixrect *pr;
{
    pr_rop (pr, 0, 0, pr -> pr_size.x, pr -> pr_size.y, PIX_CLR,
            NULL, 0, 0);
}

invert_pixrect (pr)
struct pixrect *pr;
{
    pr_rop (pr, 0, 0, pr -> pr_size.x, pr -> pr_size.y, PIX_NOT (PIX_DST),
            NULL, 0, 0);
}
```

Example 5.5 kaleidoscope.c - drawing randomly generated lines

It will be noticed from the output that most of the lines do not have a smooth representation on the screen pixrect. This situation is known as aliasing and arises when displaying a line other than a straight horizontal or vertical line. This is a well known computer graphics problem and techniques such as *anti-aliasing* - where the intensity of each pixel is altered in proportion to the actual area of the line being represented by that pixel, or by simply increasing the resolution of the display screen, can display more pleasing lines to the human eye. These techniques are expensive, however, in terms of time and cost and are used mainly in very specialised graphics systems.

5.4.10. Memory Pixrects

Memory pixrects can be used to great advantage in retaining images for later manipulation. This can be most useful when the time taken to reconstruct an image becomes overlong. Creating a memory pixrect and constructing the image on it means that the image can then be used and manipulated without being reconstructed every time it is required. A concrete example is the case of a simple graphics editor which allows the user to pick shapes from a menu, place them in some editing area and subsequently manipulate them. Such a manipulation could be a move command, where a shape in the editing area is first selected and then moved to a new position. To simulate movement of the object across the editing area it is required to display the object (or at least its outline) at small intervals along the move path. There are at least two methods in achieving this effect:

(1) redraw the shape at each interval along the move path

(2) first create a memory pixrect containing the image and then copy this pixrect at each interval.

Method (1) requires no extra memory but is generally much slower and subsequently causes much "flickering" of the image as it moves than does method (2).

5.4.11. Static and dynamic memory pixrects

There are basically three methods of creating a memory pixrect. These are:

(a) statically, from an array of constant values at compilation time of a program;

(b) dynamically create the pixrect and apply pixrect ops to build the image during program execution;

(c) dynamically generate the image from data already held in memory during program execution.

The first of these methods uses the **mpr_static()** macro defined below

```
#define mpr_static(name, w, h, depth, image)
int   w, h, depth;
short       *image;
```

which generates the following data structures

```
struct mpr_data name_data;
struct pixrect name;
```

The memory pixrect name will thus contain an image as defined by the data given in the array of short integers pointed to by image.

Essentially then, any array of short integers can be transformed into a displayable image using **mpr_static()**. In the earlier example of shading a pixrect in example 5.2, a grey pattern was created using the following code:

```
static unsigned short grey_data[16] = {
        0x8420, 0x2108, 0x0842, 0x4210,
        0x1084, 0x8420, 0x2108, 0x0842,
        0x4210, 0x1084, 0x8420, 0x2108,
        0x0842, 0x4210, 0x1084, 0x0000
};
mpr_static(grey_pr, 15, 15, 1, grey_data)
```

The pixrect generated from this is **grey_pr** and the address of this can subsequently be used with any routine requiring a pixrect pointer as a parameter.

The second way of creating a memory pixrect is to use the **mem_create()** function.

```
struct pixrect *mem_create(w, h, depth)
int     w, h, depth;
```

This returns a pointer to a pixrect **w** pixels wide and **h** pixels high. This essentially returns a white canvas upon which further pixrect operations, such as **pr_rop()**, **pf_text()**, **pr_vector()**, etc. can be applied to create an image.

The third way of creating a memory pixrect is essentially a mix of the previous methods. If the data for an image already exists in memory (as an array of short integers), then the routine **mem_point()** can be used to transfer that image onto a pixrect structure.

```
struct pixrect *mem_point(width, height, depth, data)
int     width, height, depth;
short   *data;
```

Dynamic pixrects are most suitable when at least one of the following statements is true:

(a) the dimensions of an image can only be computed during execution of a program;

(b) the image itself is not known until during execution;

(c) the image is only required for a short time.

When creation of an image will take some time, a memory pixrect could be used to build the image "behind" the user interface and then be displayed once complete. Whilst this does not actually reduce the time to display the complete image, techniques such as this can significantly enhance a user interface. Also, memory pixrects may be suitable when an image is not required for display but more for combination with other pixrect images. Memory pixrects can be interfaced to pixwins via the routines **pw_read()**, **pw_rop()**, and **pw_write()**. (See [SUNVIEW] for more details.)

5.4.12. Saving and loading pixrects via files

As previously mentioned, the image on a pixrect consists of a sequence of bits set to 1 or 0 (for monochrome displays) or some colour value. Pixrects are therefore suitable for storing into a file. Such a file can be subsequently loaded into a pixrect for further use. This facility is useful in the application of a graphical editor, for example, where shapes or pictures created by the user may be stored away on files and retrieved at a later date if necessary.

The two principal routines for file I/O of pixrects are **pr_dump()** and **pr_load()**.

```
int pr_dump(pr, outfile, colormap, type, copyflag)
struct pixrect  *pr;
FILE            *outfile;
colormap_t      colormap;
int             type, copyflag;
```

This takes a pixrect **pr** and stores it away in a file pointed to by **outfile**. For monochrome displays **colormap** should be NULL, while **type** specifies which format is to be used in storing the pixrect. **copyflag** indicates whether or not the pixrect should be copied before it is dumped. This should be TRUE when dumping a pixrect that is liable to be changed by other processes whilst dumping is taking place. An example is of dumping a portion of the screen where other processes can, and do, asynchronously access and update the screen.

```
struct pixrect  *pr_load(infile, colormap)
FILE            *infile;
colormap_t      colormap;
```

This returns a pointer to a pixrect containing the image loaded from the file referenced by **infile**. Again, for monochrome displays **colormap** should be NULL.

Additionally, pixrects can be stored and loaded with user defined formats. Further functions exist to aid this task; however, for the majority of users the existing formats will be sufficient - for more details see [PIXRECT 86] Chapter 5.

The following example will show how to use the routines **pr_dump()** and **pr_load()** together. The file *save_image.c* in example 5.6 is the source code of a program which creates a memory pixrect, inverts it (thus making it all black), and outputs it to standard output. The file *load_image.c* (example 5.7) is the source for a program which reads an image from the standard input into a pixrect. This is then displayed at position (200, 200).

```
#include <stdio.h>
#include <pixrect/pixrect_hs.h>
#define FALSE   0
#define TRUE    1

main ()
{
    struct pixrect *image;
    FILE * output = stdout;

    image = mem_create (400, 400, 1);
    invert_pixrect (image);
    pr_dump (image, output, NULL, RT_STANDARD, FALSE);
}
invert_pixrect (pr)
struct pixrect *pr;
{
    pr_rop (pr, 0, 0, pr -> pr_size.x, pr -> pr_size.y, PIX_NOT (PIX_DST),
            NULL, 0, 0);
}
```

Example 5.6 save_image.c - saving a pixrect image to a file

```
#include <stdio.h>
#include <pixrect/pixrect_hs.h>
#define FALSE   0
#define TRUE    ! FALSE

main ()
{
    struct pixrect *screen,
                   *image,
                   *pr_load ();
    FILE * input = stdin;

    screen = pr_open ("/dev/fb");
    clear_pixrect (screen);
    image = pr_load (input, NULL);
    pr_rop (screen, 100, 100, image -> pr_size.x, image -> pr_size.y,
            PIX_SRC, image, 0, 0);
    sleep (5);

    pr_close (screen);
}
clear_pixrect (pr)
struct pixrect *pr;
{
    pr_rop (pr, 0, 0, pr -> pr_size.x, pr -> pr_size.y, PIX_CLR,
            NULL, 0, 0);
}
```

Example 5.7 load_image.c - loading a pixrect image from a file

Having been compiled, the programs can be executed together by piping[4] the output of **save_image** to the input of **load_image** with

```
save_image | load_image
```

The simple effect of this is to display a black rectangle on the screen. This simple example demonstrates how an image can be built on a pixrect, stored in a file and then loaded again for further manipulation or display.

5.4.13. An explosion

The example presented in this final section will present a program which demonstrates all of the facilities discussed in this chapter. The source code of the program is shown in example 5.8, and the resultant output is shown in figure 5.4. The facilities demonstrated are:

* clearing a pixrect
* inverting a pixrect
* moving a pixrect
* using different rasterops
* writing of text on a pixrect
* drawing of lines on a pixrect

```
#include <stdio.h>
#include <pixrect/pixrect_hs.h>

#define MAXCIRCUITS        (4)
#define SCREENWIDTH        (screen->pr_size.x)
#define SCREENHEIGHT       (screen->pr_size.y)
#define BWIDTH             (100)
#define BHEIGHT            (100)
#define JUMP          (100)
#define RANDOM(maxval)     (random()%maxval)
#define DISPLAY_OP (PIX_SRC ^ PIX_DST)

struct pixrect *screen;
struct pixrect *bbox;

main ()
{
    int     circuit,
            x,
            y;
    int     startx,
            starty,
```

[4] See Chapter 2.

```
		endx,
		endy;


	screen = pr_open ("/dev/fb");
	clear_pixrect (screen);

/* Create the box on a memory pixrect */
	bbox = mem_create (BWIDTH, BHEIGHT, 1);
	clear_pixrect (bbox);
	kaleidoscope (bbox);
	label_box (bbox);

/* Let's go */
	for (circuit = 0; circuit < MAXCIRCUITS; circuit++)
	{
		startx = circuit * BWIDTH;
		starty = circuit * BHEIGHT;
		endx = SCREENWIDTH - BWIDTH - startx;
		endy = SCREENHEIGHT - BHEIGHT - starty;

	/*	Draw the top lane	*/
		y = starty;
		for (x = startx; x < endx; x += JUMP)
		{
			showbox (x, y);
		}
	/*	Draw the right hand lane */
		x = endx;
		for (y = starty + JUMP; y < endy; y += JUMP)
		{
			showbox (x, y);
		}
	/*	Draw the bottom lane	*/
		y = endy;
		for (x = endx; x > startx; x -= JUMP)
		{
			showbox (x, y);
		}
	/* Draw the left hand lane */
		x = startx;
		for (y = endy - JUMP; y > starty; y -= JUMP)
		{
			showbox (x, y);
		}
	}
	pr_close (screen);
}

showbox (x, y)
int	x;
int	y;
{
```

```
    invert_pixrect (bbox);
    pr_rop (screen, x, y, bbox -> pr_size.x, bbox -> pr_size.y, DISPLAY_OP,
            bbox, 0, 0);
}

clear_pixrect (pr)
struct pixrect *pr;
{
    pr_rop (pr, 0, 0, pr -> pr_size.x, pr -> pr_size.y, PIX_CLR,
            NULL, 0, 0);
}

invert_pixrect (pr)
struct pixrect *pr;
{
    pr_rop (pr, 0, 0, pr -> pr_size.x, pr -> pr_size.y, PIX_NOT (PIX_DST),
            NULL, 0, 0);
}

kaleidoscope ()
{
    int     loop,
            randx,
            randy;

    for (loop = 0; loop < 100; loop++)
    {
        randx = RANDOM (BWIDTH);
        randy = RANDOM (BHEIGHT - 20);
        pr_vector (bbox, BWIDTH / 2, (BHEIGHT - 20) / 2, randx, randy,
                PIX_SRC, 1);
    }
}

label_box (b)
struct pixrect *b;
{
    struct pr_prpos where;
    struct pixfont *font;

    where.pos.x = 5;
    where.pos.y = BHEIGHT - 5;
    where.pr = b;

    font = pf_open ("/usr/lib/fonts/fixedwidthfonts/screen.b.14");

    pf_text (where, PIX_SRC, font, "Explosion");
    pf_close (font);
}
```

Example 5.8 explosion.c - using all the pixrect facilities

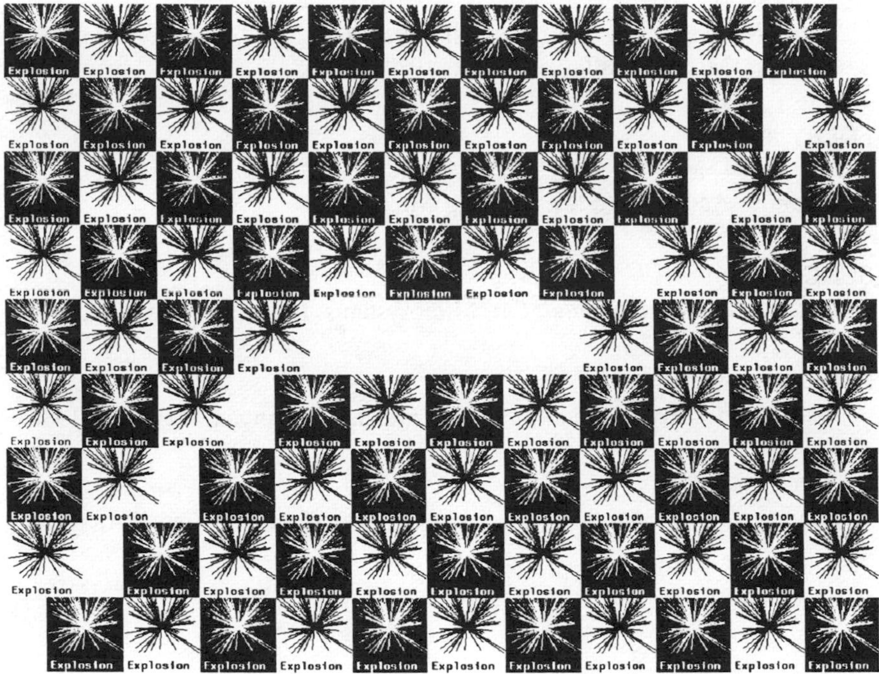

Figure 5.4 Computer art?

The effect of the program is to create a small pixrect containing a kaleidoscope image labelled with the word "Explosion". This is then moved around an imaginary rectangular circuit on the screen and displayed at various points. The **showbox()** routine first inverts the pixrect **bbox** and then displays it on the screen. Type the example in and run it to produce the effect shown in figure 5.4.

All sorts of different effects can be achieved by altering the following:

* the dimensions of the box being displayed (BWIDTH and BHEIGHT)
* the gap between each point where the box is displayed (JUMP)
* the raster operation used in displaying the box (DISPLAY_OP)
* slowing down the speed at which the box is displayed

Try altering these values and see what effects are produced. Also, the movement can be seen more closely if the speed of display is reduced. To do this insert a call to the system routine **sleep()** at the start of the **showbox()** routine - a value of 1 will allow the box to be seen more clearly.

References

[NEWMAN 79]
W.M. Newman and R.F. Sproull, *Principles of Interactive Computer Graphics*, McGraw-Hill, New York, 1979.

[FOLEY 82]
J.D. Foley and A. Van Dam, *Fundamentals of Interactive Computer Graphics*, Addison-Wesley, Reading MA, 1982.

[SUNCORE 86]
SunCore Reference Manual, Sun Microsystems, Mountain View CA, 1986.

[SUNCGI 86]
SunCGI Reference Manual, Sun Microsystems, Mountain View CA, 1986.

[PIXRECT 86]
Pixrect Reference Manual, Sun Microsystems, Mountain View CA, 1986.

6 Introduction to SunCore

6.1. Introduction

One of the fastest growing areas of computer use is in the generation of images. As the power of the computer has increased, so the complexity and range of images available has followed. This chapter deals with the *SunCore* package, which allows a user to create and manage a general graphics environment. Like many other similar packages SunCore is based around a particular set of definitions, namely the ACM Core. For those who are familiar with ACM core, dynamic output is supported to level 3C, including two and three dimensional translation, scaling and rotation. Input is supported to level 2, synchronous input.

The main purpose of this chapter is to describe how SunCore allows a graphical environment to be initialised and used. This includes looking at how SunCore is initialised to suit the requirements of the user, that is, drawing surfaces, input devices and type of operations available and the commands for drawing. Some knowledge of graphical terms is assumed, as well as that of the C programming language. Though C is used for the examples given here, SunCore can also be used with Pascal and FORTRAN. Further details can be found in the references given at the end of this chapter.

6.2. Overview

The main aim of SunCore is to allow the creation of and interaction with images on some output device, usually the workstation. The fact that this output device may not be the screen, but say a plotter, raises the need for some global representation of data which is then transformed into data relevant to the particular device. SunCore achieves this by having two different views of the data

(1) An internal representation of the world which is device-independent.

(2) An external representation of the world dependent on the output device.

In turn there are two interdependent sets of coordinate systems

(1) *World Coordinates* which the programmer uses to construct all graphical objects.

(2) *Normalised Device Coordinates* (NDC) which is a fixed coordinate system independent of physical devices. World coordinates are transformed to NDC and then to the physical device coordinates by a *device driver.*

The user defines an object, which is to be drawn, in 2 or 3 dimensional coordinates. This data is then transformed into NDC, and finally the NDC data is transformed into physical device coordinates and drawn on each *view surface*, a view surface is a physical device on which the final data is presented.

Further, the NDC space can be limited by defining a *viewport.* A viewport is a region of NDC space which the programmer selects and inside which the output will appear.

A *window* is a region defined in world coordinates, which limits the objects visible on the view surface. An *image* is a collection of output primitives: lines, polygons, text etc. These primitives are collected together into *segments*, and finally drawn on the view surface.

There are two distinct types of segment, namely *temporary* and *retained.* Temporary segments allow primitives to be drawn without the capability of applying any transformations once the segment has been closed. Primitives drawn in a temporary segment are not remembered; once a view surface is cleared or other primitives are drawn on top; the original primitives are lost. These are examined in more detail in section 6.6 Getting down to Drawing.

Steps required in Drawing a Picture

The following sequence of programming steps is usually found in a SunCore program and is explained further in the rest of the chapter.

1. Initialise SunCore
2. Initialise a View Surface
3. Select a view surface
4. Specify the viewing operation parameters
5. Set image transformation type
6. Create a segment
7. Draw objects by using output primitives
8. Close the segment
9. Repeat 4->8 for each image that makes up picture
10. Apply image transformations to relevant segments
11. Deselect the view surface
12. Terminate SunCore.

6.3. Initialisation and termination

SunCore, when initialised, is informed of the input and output levels and the number of dimensions (2 or 3) required. These values, once set, are valid until SunCore is terminated and cannot be changed. The form of the procedure call is as follows

initialize_core(OUTPUT_LEVEL, INPUT_LEVEL, DIMENSIONS);

The OUTPUT_LEVEL parameter may have one of the following constant values. These constants are defined in *<usercore.h>* which should be included in all SunCore source files.

BASIC - Only temporary segments maybe created.

BUFFERED - Retained and Temporary segments, with no image transformations allowed.

DYNAMICA, DYNAMICB, DYNAMICC - These have the same effect - Retained and Temporary segments with full segment attributes.

For the INPUT_LEVEL parameter there are two valid values

NOINPUT - No input required in environment

SYNCHRONOUS - Support of ACM Core up to input level 2

There is a third level in ACM Core not supported by SunCore.

The DIMENSIONS parameter is either TWOD or THREED. THREED encompasses TWOD setting, allowing three and two dimensional objects to be drawn.

Termination of SunCore, which should be performed when the user has finished with the SunCore package, is accomplished with the function call

terminate_core();

6.4. View surfaces

View surfaces, in SunCore, are the means with which the user communicates graphically with the outside world. Anything drawn must appear on a view surface, which in the simplest case could be the workstation screen but could also be a plotter or printer. Whatever the final physical device, the steps required in relating it to a view surface, and therefore SunCore, are the same. The steps are firstly to initialise the device as a view surface, and then to select it for output. Thus multiple view surfaces can be used for output at the same time. The initialisation is accomplished by

initialize_view_surface(surface_name, type);

The **surface_name** argument specifies a physical view surface and is a structure of type **vwsurf.** All of the field values in the structure are assigned when **initialize_view_surface** is called except one - the device driver routine.

type is a flag which should be set **TRUE** if hidden surface removal is required on the view surface, and **FALSE** otherwise.

There are two methods of assigning a relevant value to the **surface_name** device driver argument. First we can assign an explicit value to the **dd** field of the **vwsurf** structure, shown below

```
struct vwsurf {
        char screenname[DEVNAMESIZE];
        char windowname[DEVNAMESIZE];
        int windowfd;
        int (*dd)();          /* Device driver routine pointer */
        int instance;
        int cmapsize;
        char cmapname[DEVNAMESIZE];
        int flags;
        char **ptr;
            };
```

The **dd** field should point to a function which is a driver routine for a view surface. Valid function names are

bw1dd - Sun 1 monochrome bitmap display

bw2dd - Sun 2 or Sun 3 monochrome bitmap display

cg1dd - Sun 1 colour display

cg2dd - Sun 2 or 3 colour displays

pixwindd - Monochrome window used with suntools

cgpixwindd - Colour window used with suntools

gp1dd - Sun 2/160 or Sun 3/160 with a Graphics Processor

gp1pixwindd - Colour window in suntools running on a Sun 2/160 or Sun 3/160 with a Graphics Processor

In *<usercore.h>* a macro is defined, namely **DEFAULT_VWSURF**, which accomplishes the assignment

struct vwsurf mysurf = DEFAULT_VWSURF(pixwindd);

Here **mysurf** is initialised, with the device driver set to *pixwindd*, to use a SunView pixwin (Pixwins are explained in Chapter 4.)

The method of assigning to an explicit device driver is fine when only one surface is required and the environment in which the SunCore application is running is constant. If more than one view surface is required, or the application is to be run both outside and inside suntools, then the second method of assigning should be used.

This method involves the use of the **get_view_surface** function, which is in the SunCore library. The function call looks as follows

```
if (get_view_surface(&mysurf, argv))
      exit(1);
```

The function returns zero if it succeeds and non-zero otherwise. The **argv** argument is scanned for the **-d** option which can be followed by the name of a physical device, e.g. */dev/fb*. The advantages of using this function are two-fold. It automatically assigns the correct device driver when the application is run from inside and outside suntools, and when more than one surface is required, creates new windows. For example, if three surfaces are required you could have the following

```
struct vwsurf surf1, surf2, surf3;

if (get_view_surface(&surf1, argv))
      exit(1);
if (get_view_surface(&surf2, argv))
      exit(1);
if (get_view_surface(&surf3, argv))
      exit(1);
```

Run within suntools this would create two new windows, to connect with **surf2** and **surf3**, with **surf1** taking over the window from which the application was launched (as a *blanket window*). This blanket window is usually not wanted, as any standard input and output with the terminal is lost. The easiest way to overcome this is by the use of a false view surface variable, e.g.

```
struct vwsurf false;

if (get_view_surface(&false, argv))
      exit(1);

.
. /* other 'get_view_surface' and 'initialize_view_surface'
.     calls */
.
initialize_view_surface(&false, FALSE);
terminate_view_surface(&false);
```

It is also possible to set the position and size of windows. This is done by making use of the char **ptr** field in struct vwsurf. This is a pointer to a string of chars, which define the size and position of the window and icon used by the view surface

```
char *windowdata[] = { "100,100,250,250,800,100,50,50,0",
                       NULL };

struct vwsurf *surf;

if (get_view_surface(surf, argv)) exit(1);

surf->ptr = windowdata;

initialize_view_surface(surf, FALSE);
```

The first two numbers define the top left corner position of the window, with the second pair defining the size, 250 * 250 pixels. The third pair define the location of the top left corner of the icon for the window, with the fourth pair being the size, 50 * 50 pixels. The final zero (0) in the first string signifies that the window, when initialised, will be in the open state. If this value was set to one (1) then the window would be initialised in the closed, iconic, state. The last parameter, *NULL*, is a delimiter.

Once the relevant fields of the view surface structure have been assigned values, and **initialize_view_surface** has been called, all that remains before the surface can be used for drawing is to select it

```
struct vwsurf surf;
...
...
/* Assignment and Initialisation of surf */
...
...
select_view_surface(&surf);
...
...
/* Drawing stage */
...
...
deselect_view_surface(&surf);
```

After the user is finished with output to a particular view surface, for a time, then the **deselect_view_surface** routine is used. The view surface is still valid, but disabled from output and can be re-enabled by a further **select_view_surface** call. In order to terminate a view surface the **terminate_view_surface** routine is used

```
terminate_view_surface(&surf);
```

6.5. Viewing operations and coordinate transforms

Once a user has initialised the required number of view surfaces, the next step before drawing can take place is the specification of the range and type of view required. This can be compared to using a camera. Several variables can be set; where to place the camera; which direction to point it; what size of lens to use. SunCore allows each of these to be defined for one or more view surfaces. These can be thought of as viewing operations, and are listed below with their corresponding camera representation

set_view_reference_point
The location of the camera in World coordinates.

set_view_plane_normal
The direction in which the camera is pointing.

set_view_plane_distance
The angle of view.

set_view_depth
The depth of field, i.e. the distance of the front and back *clipping planes* from the view reference point.

set_view_up_2 and set_view_up_3
The 'up' direction in two & three dimensions.

set_window
Sets the area of interest by a window boundary

These routines all relate to a set of values which, when SunCore is initialised, have default values

View reference point = { 0, 0, 0 }

View plane normal = { 0, 0, -1 }

View Distance = 0

Front Distance = 0

Back Distance = 1

Window = (0, 1, 0, 0.75)

View Up Vector = (0, 1, 0)

The effect of changing these values, on the final view, is dealt with in detail in the references at the end of this chapter. For a pictorial view of the viewing system see figure 3.1 in Chapter 3 of the SunCore manual.

6.6. Getting down to drawing

We are now at the stage were SunCore has been informed of the number and viewing operations for each view surface, and are ready to start creating images. An image on a view surface is made up of a collection of *output primitives*. An output primitive can be thought of as an indivisible unit of an image - a line, a polygon, a piece of text. These primitives, in turn, are grouped together into *segments*. An application program describes an object by creating a segment, calling output primitive functions, and then closing the segment.

There are two types of segment, namely: *temporary* segments and *retained* segments. Retained segments have an *image transformation type* which specifies how they can be transformed. Retained segments can be made visible or invisible, detectible (via the pick input function) or undetectible, highlighted, and may be transformed.

Retained segments have names (actually numeric identifiers) so that by placing output primitives in such segments, the application programmer can selectively modify parts of the picture by deleting and recreating segments (which effectively replaces them) so that their images change. Retained segments are stored in the display list for later dynamic modification.

Temporary segments are not saved in the display list, are only drawn once, and may not be modified dynamically. A frame action (such as moving or resizing the window) deletes all portions of any temporary segments which have been drawn.

Retained segments have five attributes connected to them, one static and four dynamic. The static attribute is called the image transformation type, and can have one of the following values

NONE
: No transformations may be applied

XLATE2
: The segment may be translated in two dimensions

XFORM2
: The segment may be fully translated, scaled, and rotated, in 2D

XLATE3

The segment may be translated in 2 or 3D

XFORM3

The segment may be fully translated, scaled, and rotated, in 2 or 3D

These have been defined in *<usercore.h>* to have the relevant values. The transformation type is set, before the retained segment is created, by

```
set_image_transformation_type(type);
int type; /* NONE, XLATE2, XFORM2, XLATE3, XFORM3 */
```

Once the correct image transformation type has been set (the static attribute), the retained segment may be created:

```
create_retained_segment(seg_name)
int seg_name; /* Segment Identifier: 1-> 2,147,483,647 */
```

The identifier must be unique, and the segment will remain in the display list until it is deleted. The output primitive functions are now called to define the required image, with a final call to close the retained segment

```
close_retained_segment();
```

The four dynamic attributes can be set after the segment has been created. They are listed below:

Visibility

This is either TRUE or FALSE and defines whether the image is visible or not. It is set with a call to the following:

```
set_segment_visibility(seg_name, visibility)
int seg_name;
int visibility; /* TRUE or FALSE */
```

Highlighting

This can be either TRUE or FALSE and defines whether the segment is highlighted or not. When set to TRUE the segment defined is blinked once

```
set_segment_highlighting(seg_name, highlighting)
int seg_name;
int highlighting; /* TRUE or FALSE */
```

Detectability

This specifies the detectability of the named segment. A value is defined, in the range 0 to 2 to the 31st power, which is then used in conjunction with **await_pick** input function. A value of zero means that the segment cannot be detected. The higher the detectability the higher the priority a segment has when a user tries to select it via the input primitives explained in section 6.8.

```
set_segment_detectability(seg_name, detectability)
int seg_name;
int detectability; /* 0 -> 2^31 */
```

Image Transformation

These are a collection of routines which, depending on how the static attribute has been set, allow the segment to be transformed:

```
set_segment_image_translate_2(seg_name, tx, ty)
int seg_name;
float tx;     /* x Translation Value in NDC */
float ty;     /* y Translation Value in NDC */

set_segment_image_transformation_2(seg_name, sx, sy, a , tx, ty)
int seg_name;
float sx, sy;  /* x & y Scale factors */
float a;        /* Rotation value in radians clockwise about the z
              axis */
float tx, ty;  /* x & y Translation Values in NDC */

set_segment_image_translate_3(seg_name, tx, ty, tz)
int seg_name;
float tx, ty, tz; /* x, y & z Translation Values in NDC */

set_segment_image_transformation_3(seg_name, sx, sy, sz, ax,
ay, az, tx, ty, tz)
int seg_name;
float sx, sy, sz; /* x, y, z Scale Factors */
float ax;         /* Rotation Value in radians clockwise about the
                     x axis */
float ay;     /* Rotation Value in radians clockwise about the
                y axis */
float az; /* Rotation Value in radians clockwise about the
             z axis */
float tx, ty, tz; /* x, y, z Translation Values in NDC */
```

Temporary segments are created when the application programmer requires a transient image. These segments cannot be modified, and remain visible until a **new_frame()** action

```
create_temporary_segment()
...
...
/* Output Primitives */
...
...
close_temporary_segment()
```

The **new_frame()** action, aside from clearing any temporary segments, will redraw any visible retained segments.

6.6.1. Output primitives

Output Primitives are the means of creating an object, defined in world coordinates. SunCore supports eight different primitives, namely

Move
: alters the current position.

Line
: draws lines in world coordinates.

Polyline
: draws sequences of connected lines.

Polygon
: draws a closed polygon which is filled with a predefined colour.

Text
: draws character strings.

Marker
: draws markers whose symbols are displayed independently of any transformations.

Polymarker
: draws a sequence of markers .

Rasters
: draws an array of, one-bit or eight-bit deep, pixels.

All primitives use world coordinates to supply positional data, with some affecting the value known as the *current position*. This is the current drawing position in world coordinates and is initialised to the origin of the world coordinate system. Most output primitives have separate functions for drawing in absolute or relative mode, and 2 or 3D mode.

For each type of output primitive there is a set of routines, as follows:

Move

```
move_abs_2(x, y)
float x, y; /* x and y coordinates to move to */

move_abs_3(x, y, z)
float x, y, z; /* x, y and z coordinates to move to */

move_rel_2(dx, dy)
float dx, dy; /* x and y coordinate deltas */

move_rel_3(dx, dy, dz)
float dx, dy, dz; /* x, y and z coordinate deltas */
```

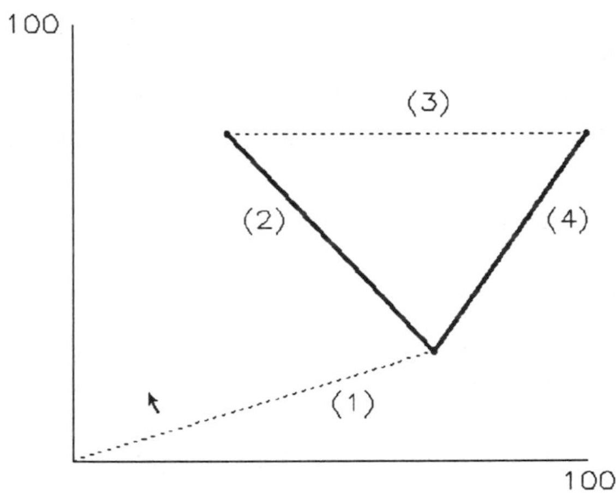

Figure 6.1

Imagine the dotted lines indicate move operations, then the 'V' shape in figure 6.1 is created by the sequence of calls

(1) move_abs_2(70.0, 25.0)

(2) line_rel_2(-40.0, 50.0)

(3) move_rel_2(70.0, 0.0)

(4) line_abs_2(70.0, 25.0)

in a window of size 100 x 100.

Line

```
line_abs_2(x, y)
float x, y; /* end coordinate of line - starting from current pos. */
```

```
line_abs_3(x, y, z)
float x, y, z; /* end coordinate of line - starting from current
pos. */

line_rel_2(dx, dy)
float dx, dy; /* relative end coordinate of line - from current
pos. */

line_rel_3(dx, dy, dz)
float dx, dy, dz; /* relative end coordinate of line - from current
pos. */
```

Polyline

```
polyline_abs_2(x_array, y_array, n)
float x_array[], y_array[]; /* x and y coordinates */
int n; /* number of array elements */

polyline_abs_3(x_array, y_array, z_array, n)
float x_array[], y_array[], z_array[]; /* x, y and z coordinates */
int n; /* number of array elements */
```

In both the above the current position is updated to the last point in the array.

```
polyline_rel_2(dx_array, dy_array, n)
float dx_array[], dy_array[]; /* x and y delta arrays */
int n; /* number of array elements */

polyline_rel_3(dx_array, dy_array, dz_array, n)
float dx_array[], dy_array[], dz_array[];
/* x, y and z delta arrays */
int n; /* number of array elements */
```

For these relative routines the current position is used as the starting point, with each element of the arrays being added to the corresponding value. The current position is updated to the end of the last line drawn.

Text

```
text(string)
char *string; /* The string is output from the current position */
```

Marker

```
marker_abs_2(x, y)
float x, y; /* Absolute x and y coords */

marker_abs_3(x, y, z)
```

```
float x, y, z; /* Absolute x, y and z coords */

marker_rel_2(dx, dy)
float dx, dy; /* x and y coordinate deltas */

marker_rel_3(dx, dy, dz)
float dx, dy, dz; /* x, y and z coordinate deltas */
```

The marker symbol is set by **set_marker_symbol(marker)** where the **marker** parameter is an integer in the range 32 to 127. This integer represents the ASCII value of a character symbol.

Polymarker

```
polymarker_abs_2(x_array, y_array, n)
float x_array[], y_array[]; /* Absolute x and y arrays */
int n; /* Number of Coordinates */

polymarker_abs_3(x_array, y_array, z_array, n)
float x_array[], y_array[], z_array[];
/* Absolute x, y and z arrays */
int n; /* Number of Coordinates */

polymarker_rel_2(dx_array, dy_array, n)
float dx_array[], dy_array[]; /* x and y deltas */
int n; /* Number of Coordinates */

polymarker_rel_3(dx_array, dy_array, dz_array, n)
float dx_array[], dy_array[], dz_array[];
/* x, y and z deltas */
int n; /* Number of Coordinates */
```

Polygon

```
polygon_abs_2(x_array, y_array, n)
float x_array[], y_array[]; /* x and y coordinates */
int n; /* Number of array elements */

polygon_abs_3(x_array, y_array, z_array, n)
float x_array[], y_array[], z_array[];
/* x, y and z coordinates */
int n; /* Number of array elements */

polygon_rel_2(dx_array, dy_array, n)
float dx_array[], dy_array[]; /* x and y deltas */
int n; /* Number of array elements */
```

```
polygon_rel_3(dx_array, dy_array, dz_array, n)
float dx_array[], dy_array[], dz_array[]; /* x, y and z deltas */
int n; /* Number of array elements */
```

For the polygon routines, the current position is set to the first point in the arrays, after execution.

Rasters

A raster is a rectangle of bits which represent an image. The raster output primitives may only be used in non-transformable segments as they cannot be scaled or rotated. They may, however, be picked or dragged in translatable segments.

The raster routines make use of the **suncore_raster** structure to define the area of view surface which is of interest:

```
struct suncore_raster {
        int width;
        int height;
        int depth;
        short *bits;
        };
```

In taking a raster image from a view surface, the following steps are required:

(1) A call to **size_raster()** to set the *width, height* and fldepth *fields of the* **suncore_raster** *structure.*

(2) A call to **allocate_raster()** to allocate space in memory for the raster and set the *bits* field.

(3) A call to **get_raster()** to copy the bits from the screen into the store allocated in (2).

Looking at these routines in more detail we find:

```
size_raster(surf_name, xmin, xmax, ymin, ymax, raster)
struct vwsurf *surf_name;
/* View surface containing area of interest */
float xmin, xmax, ymin, ymax;
/* Region of NDC space of interest */
struct suncore_raster *raster; /* Raster to be sized */

allocate_raster(raster)
struct suncore_raster *raster;
/* This allocates space for the raster structure */
```

```
get_raster(surf_name, xmin, xmax, ymin, ymax, x, y, raster)
struct vwsurf *surf_name;
float xmin, xmax, ymin, ymax; /* Region of NDC space */
int x, y; /* starting point of raster, relative top left */
struct suncore_raster *raster; /* Returned raster */
```

To write a raster to a view surface the following is used:

```
put_raster(raster)
struct suncore_raster *raster;
```

The raster image is entered into the current segment, on those view surfaces selected from the current position, which represents the lower left hand corner of the raster.

SunCore also supplies two routines for saving and retrieving rasters to disk, namely **raster_to_file** and **file_to_raster**. The file format is defined in *<rasterfile.h>*. Rasters can be interchanged with the Pixrect level by using the **pr_dump** and **pr_load** functions described in Chapter 5.

6.6.2. Attributes

Like Retained segments, output primitives have attributes connected with them. They define the style in which each primitive is output. The following list describes the attributes connected with each output primitive type

Line and Polyline

line index - this is an index to the colour lookup table to define the colour in which the lines will be drawn.

line style - this controls the appearance of lines drawn. It can have one of the values: SOLID, DOTTED, DASHED, or DOTDASHED. These constants are defined in *<usercore.h>*.

line width - this controls the width of the lines drawn.

Polygon

fill index - this is an index to the colour lookup table which defines the colour used in filling the polygons.

interior style - this controls the style of filling. It can have one of two values, PLAIN or SHADED.

Text

text index - this is an index to the colour lookup table which defines the colour used in drawing text.

font - defines which font to use in text output. The following are valid values; ROMAN, GREEK, SCRIPT, OLDENGLISH, STICK or SYMBOLS.

charsize - a pair of values which sets the size of characters in world coordinates.

charup - represents the direction of 'up' for characters in the form of a vector.

charpath - represents the direction in which text will extend, in the form of a vector.

charspace - specifies the space, in world coordinates, between individual characters.

charprecision - controls the quality of text output. Valid values are STRING or CHARACTER.

Marker

marker symbol - defines which character to use as a marker.

Raster

rasterop - specifies the boolean operation used when writing rasters.

Each of these primitives is changed by an appropriate **set_** function, e.g.

```
set_charsize(5.0,5.0);
set_linestyle(DOTTED);
set_fill_index(1);
set_marker_symbol((int)'|');
```

6.7. Example One

This example shows how to make use of several view surfaces, as well as the range of 2D output primitives. To compile it, and example two, use the following command line

```
cc exam1.c -o exam1 -lcore -lsuntool -lsunwindow -lpixrect -lm
```

The program should be run from a **gfxtool** window, inside **suntools**.

```
/* SunCore Example Program One */

#include <usercore.h>

/* View surface variables */
struct vwsurf *surf1, *surf2, *surf3;

/* View surface window sizes */
```

```
char *pos[]={"200,200,400,400,900,100,50,50,0",
              NULL},
     *pos2[]={"700,100,300,300,800,100,50,50,0",
              NULL};

/* Data arrays for drawing */
static float x[]={ 0.0, 25.0, 50.0, 75.0, 100.0 },
             y[]={ 0.0, 73.0, 54.0, 35.0, 44.0 },
             starx[]={ 10.0, 15.0, 20.0, 5.0, 25.0, 10.0},
             stary[]={ 10.0, 35.0, 10.0, 25.0, 25.0, 10.0},
             boxx[]={25.0, 0.0, -25.0, -0.0},
             boxy[]={0.0, 25.0, 0.0, -25.0},
             shapx[]={20.0, 27.0, 30.0, 40.0, 35.0, 30.0},
             shapy[]={80.0, 70.0, 90.0, 30.0, 40.0, 20.0};

main( argc, argv)
int argc;
char **argv;
{
int i;
/* Allocate space for view surface structures */
surf1 = (struct vwsurf*)(calloc(1,sizeof(struct vwsurf)));
surf2 = (struct vwsurf*)(calloc(1,sizeof(struct vwsurf)));
surf3 = (struct vwsurf*)(calloc(1,sizeof(struct vwsurf)));

get_view_surface(surf1, argv);
get_view_surface(surf2, argv);
get_view_surface(surf3, argv);

initialize_core(BASIC, NOINPUT, THREED);
surf2->ptr = pos;
surf3->ptr = pos2;

if (initialize_view_surface(surf1, FALSE)||
        initialize_view_surface(surf2, FALSE)||
        initialize_view_surface(surf3, FALSE)) {
            printf("This example must be run from inside suntools0);
            terminate_core();
            exit(1);
}

set_window(-10.0, 110.0, -10.0, 110.0);

/* Demo showing 'polyline' and 'polygon' */

select_view_surface(surf1);
create_temporary_segment();
set_linestyle(SOLID);

move_abs_2(10.0, 10.0);
polyline_abs_2(starx, stary, 6);
set_linestyle(DOTTED);
for(i=0;i!=100;i+=10) {
```

```
        move_abs_2(50.0+i, 50.0+i);
        polyline_rel_2(boxx, boxy, 4);
}
set_fill_index(1);
polygon_abs_2(shapx, shapy, 6);

close_temporary_segment();
deselect_view_surface(surf1);

/* Demo showing 'text' facilities */

select_view_surface(surf3);
create_temporary_segment();
set_charprecision(CHARACTER);

move_abs_2(20.0, 80.0);
set_charpath_2(1.0, -1.0);
set_charsize(5.0, 5.0);
text("Test string");
move_abs_2(10.0, 10.0);
set_charpath_2(1.0, 1.0);
set_charsize(3.0, 3.0);
text("and another!");
move_abs_2(80.0, 50.0);
set_charpath_2(-1.0, -1.0);
set_charsize(10.0, 10.0);
text("Hello!!");

close_temporary_segment();
deselect_view_surface(surf3);

/* Demo showing 'line' and 'polymarker' */

select_view_surface(surf2);
set_charpath_2(1.0, 0.0);
set_charsize(3.0, 3.0);
create_temporary_segment();

move_abs_2(0.0, 0.0);
set_linewidth(2.0);
set_linestyle(DOTTED);
line_abs_2(100.0, 0.0);
move_abs_2(0.0,0.0);
line_abs_2(0.0, 100.0);
move_abs_2(8.0, 100.0);
text("y");
move_abs_2(100.0,10.0);
text("x");
set_linewidth(1.0);
set_linestyle(DOTTED);
move_abs_2(0.0, 0.0);
polyline_abs_2(x, y, 5);
move_abs_2(0.0, 0.0);
```

```
set_marker_symbol((int)'*');
polymarker_abs_2(x, y, 5);

close_temporary_segment();
deselect_view_surface(surf2);

sleep(10);
terminate_core();
}
```

Example 6.1

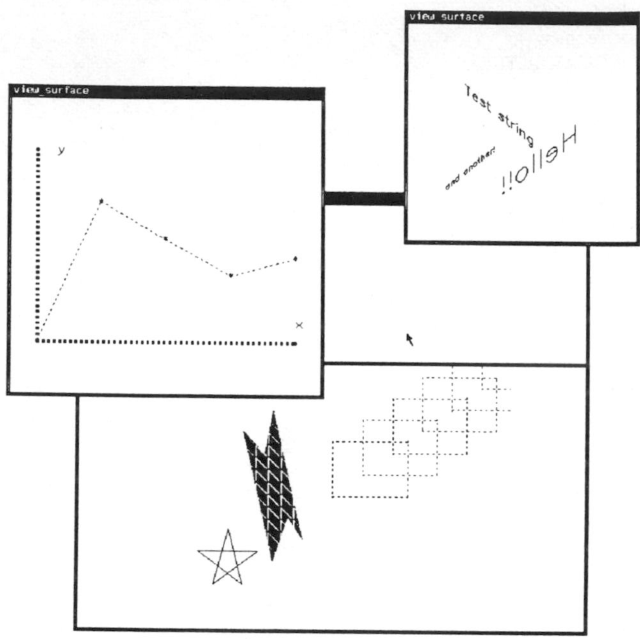

Figure 6.2 Output from Example One

6.8. Input primitives

SunCore supports 6 logical input devices to supply an interactive environment. They make use of the two physical devices, namely the mouse and keyboard, connected to the work station. The following is a list of the different types

Pick - used for identifying a segment or primitive within a segment using the mouse.

Keyboard - provides an alphanumeric form of input.

Button - a means of choosing among several alternatives, using the three mouse buttons

Stroke - supplies a sequence of positions in NDC space, using the mouse.

Locator - provides a position in NDC using the mouse.

Valuator - provides a scalar value using the mouse.

To make use of an input device the application programmer firstly has to initialise the device, by

```
initialize_device(device_class, device_number)
int device_class; /* PICK, KEYBOARD, STROKE, LOCATOR,
 VALUATOR, BUTTON */
int device_number; /* There are: */
/* 1 PICK device */
/* 1 KEYBOARD device */
/* 1 STROKE device */
/* 3 BUTTON devices */
/* 1 LOCATOR device */
/* 1 VALUATOR DEVICE */
```

Once a device has been initialised, the next step is for the form of output, the echo type, to be set. The different types of visual feedback available can be seen by running example 2. Each type of device has a choice of echo types connected with it, giving in the case of the **LOCATOR** type a choice of 7. They are listed in detail in the SunCore reference manual.

The device must then be connected to a view surface to allow input to commence. This is accomplished by

```
set_echo_surface(device_class, device_number, surf_name)
int device_class; /* PICK, KEYBOARD, STROKE, LOCATOR,
VALUATOR, KEYBOARD */
int device_number;
struct vwsurf *surf_name; /* view surface to connect with */
```

Example Two

This example shows the use of a variety of input primitives and should be compiled with the following command line

cc exam2.c -o exam2 -lcore -lsuntool -lsunwindow -lpixrect -lm

The runnable file, *exam2*, should then be run from a **gfxtool** window.

```
/* SunCore Example Program Two */
#include <usercore.h>
#define LEFTB 1
#define MIDDLEB 2
#define RIGHTB 3
```

```
struct vwsurf *surf1;

main( argc, argv)
int argc;
char **argv;
{
int button, length;
float val, x, y;
char string[80];

surf1 = (struct vwsurf*)(calloc(1,sizeof(struct vwsurf)));
get_view_surface(surf1, argv);

initialize_core(BASIC, SYNCHRONOUS, THREED);
initialize_view_surface(surf1, FALSE);

initialize_device(BUTTON, 1);
initialize_device(BUTTON, 2);
initialize_device(BUTTON, 3);
initialize_device(LOCATOR, 1);
initialize_device(STROKE, 1);
initialize_device(VALUATOR, 1);
initialize_device(KEYBOARD, 1);

set_echo(VALUATOR, 1, 1);
set_echo(STROKE, 1, 1);
set_echo(KEYBOARD, 1, 1);


set_valuator(1, 50.0, 0.0, 100.0);
set_echo_surface(VALUATOR, 1, surf1);
set_echo_surface(LOCATOR, 1, surf1);
set_echo_surface(KEYBOARD, 1, surf1);
set_echo_surface(STROKE, 1, surf1);

printf("Valuator - Hit Right mouse button to continue0);
while (button!=RIGHTB) {
        await_any_button_get_valuator( 10, 1, &button, &val);
        if (val!=50.0) printf("Value is = %f0, val);
}

set_echo(LOCATOR, 1, 2);
set_echo_position( LOCATOR, 1, 0.5, 0.5);
printf("Locator - Hit Left mouse button to continue0);
while (button!= LEFTB) {
        await_any_button_get_locator_2(10, 1, &button,
                &x, &y);
}

set_echo(LOCATOR, 1, 3);
printf("Locator - Hit Middle mouse button to continue0);
set_echo_position( LOCATOR, 1, 0.5, 0.5);
while (button!= MIDDLEB) {
```

```
        await_any_button_get_locator_2(10, 1, &button,
                        &x, &y);
}

set_echo(LOCATOR, 1, 4);
printf("Locator - Hit Right mouse button to continue0);
set_echo_position( LOCATOR, 1, 0.5, 0.5);
while (button!= RIGHTB) {
        await_any_button_get_locator_2(10, 1, &button,
                        &x, &y);
}

set_echo(LOCATOR, 1, 5);
printf("Locator - Hit Left mouse button to continue0);
set_echo_position( LOCATOR, 1, 0.5, 0.5);
while (button!= LEFTB) {
        await_any_button_get_locator_2(10, 1, &button,
                        &x, &y);
}

set_echo(LOCATOR, 1, 6);
printf("Locator - Hit Middle mouse button to continue0);
while (button!= MIDDLEB) {
        await_any_button_get_locator_2(10, 1, &button,
                        &x, &y);
}

set_echo_position( KEYBOARD, 1, 0.5, 0.5);
printf("Keyboard - enter a 'q' to end0);
while (string[0]!='q') {
        await_keyboard(100000000, 1, string, &length);
}

terminate_core();
}
```

Example 6.2 Input primitives

Further Reading

W.M. Newman, R.F. Sproull,
Principles of Interactive Computer Graphics, McGraw-Hill, New York, 1979.

J.D. Foley, A. Van Dam,
Fundamentals of Interactive Computer Graphics, Addison-Wesley, Reading MA, 1982.

SunCore Reference Manual, Sun Microsystems, Mountain View CA, 1986.

7 Administration of Workstations

7.1. Introduction

Administration of a Sun Workstation includes such diverse tasks as installing new versions of the operating system, reconfiguring the kernel, installing new application software, creating new user accounts, closing down and restarting the system.

Not all of these tasks are described in detail. In particular, the installation procedure and the method of reconfiguring the kernel are only described in outline.

7.2. Background

This section provides an overview of disks and network services from the point of view of the system administrator.

7.2.1. Disks and file systems

A large physical disk is normally divided into several *hard partitions*. Each hard partition can be thought of as a logical disk drive in its own right. Disks can have a maximum of eight hard partitions, named 'a' through 'h', and corresponding to each there is a unique entry in */dev*.

Disks are attached to disk controllers; the first disk on a SCSI (Small Computers Standard Interface) is referred to as */dev/sd0*. The 'a' partition of this disk is thus /dev/sd0a. The 'b' partition of the second disk on the same controller is */dev/sd0b*, for example.

Each hard partition has an offset and a size. Hard partition offsets must be in cylinders but the size can be specified in cylinders or sectors. Disks need not use all of the available hard partitions. The exact configuration of the hard partitions is encoded at the start of the disk in an area called the disk label.

The label is written on the disk by the **diag(8)**[1] program and can be

[1] This notation means the **diag** entry in Section 8 the Sun UNIX manual.

changed by the **setup(8)** program. On a running system, the program **dkinfo(8)** can be used to print out the contents of the disk label:

```
# dkinfo xy0
xy0: Xylogics 450 controller at addr ee40, unit # 0
821 cylinders 10 heads 32 sectors/track
a: 15884 sectors (49 1 , 6 tracks, 12 sectors)
   starting cylinder 0
b: 33440 sectors (104  l, 5 tracks)
   starting cylinder 50
c: 262720 sectors (821 cyls)
   starting cylinder 0
d: No such device or address
e: No such device or address
f: No such device or address
g: 213120 sectors (666 cyls)
   starting cylinder 155
h: No such device or address
```

Conventionally, certain hard partitions are assigned to specific functions. For example, on a standalone system 'a' is the *root* partition, 'b' is the *swap* partition and 'g', which occupies the rest of the disk, is the */usr* partition. 'c' is usually used to reference the whole disk.

The bottom layer of the Sun UNIX operating system is the *kernel.* One of the major functions of the kernel is to implement the *file system.* The file system is a higher level structure imposed on the hard disk partitions. It is a tree-structured hierarchy of directories and files.

The kernel itself occupies a file called *vmunix* which is found at the root of the file system. Normally, vmunix and several important directories */etc, /bin, /dev, /lib, /stand, /lost+found, /mnt, /private, /pub,* and */usr* are all found on the same partition. This partition is known as the *root* partition.

The files forming the sub-tree under */usr* occupy too much space to fit on the root partition. They are kept together on a separate partition (often 'g'), which is then referred to as the */usr* partition. The **mount(8)** command is used to attach the file system in the */usr* partition to its appropriate point in the file system hierarchy. This is known as *mounting* the file system. It is normally carried out at system startup time by entries in */etc/rc(8).*

Thus the **mount** command is used to tell the kernel that a file system is to be attached to the tree-structure at a given directory, or *mount point.* **umount(8)** is used to un-mount or remove a file system from the hierarchy. The file */etc/mount(5)* is maintained by **mount** and **umount**; it contains a list of currently mounted file systems. **mount** with no arguments lists the currently mounted file systems:

```
# mount
/dev/xy0a on / type 4.2 (rw)
/dev/xy0g on /usr type 4.2 (rw)
```

A very important command for the system administrator is **fsck(8)**. This is the file system check program. It is used to check the consistency of a file system and, if any inconsistencies are found, it can be used to repair them. A file system can become corrupted in several ways. The most common are the system being incorrectly shutdown, crashes and hardware faults. **fsck** must always be executed on unmounted file systems (but the root file system is always "mounted") and it should always be run at system startup time from the */etc/rc* file.

fsck must only be run on the root file system when in single user mode. If **fsck** reports and corrects any inconsistencies, then the system should be rebooted, immediately, without issuing a **sync(8)**.

Some other commands which operate on file systems include **newfs(8)**, which is really a front-end for **mkfs**(8), which is used to initialise a file system on a hard partition, **dumpfs**(8) which can print out file system information, and **tunefs(8)**, which can be used to change certain file system parameters.

7.2.2. Sun network services

Network services are dealt with in more detail in the next chapter.

Network services are based on servers, which provide resources, and clients, which consume them. Thus a *server* is a machine or process which provides any of the network services. A *client* is a machine or process that accesses a network service.

There are three network services of interest:

1. Network Disk (ND).
2. Network File System (NFS).
3. Yellow Pages (YP).

Network disk is a method of providing diskless nodes with a virtual disk. Typically a public partition (*/pub*) is shared between a server and all of its clients. Each client will have its own root and swap partitions on the server's disks.

Hard partitions are defined by the label written on the beginning of a disk. The **nd**(8) command is able to subdivide a hard partition into *soft partitions*; the soft partitions are defined by the file */etc/nd.local*. These soft partitions provide the shared public partition and the root and swap partitions of the diskless clients. Amongst other things, *nd.local* defines which hard partitions are divided into soft partitions, the size of these soft partitions, and which clients may access the soft partitions as root and swap partitions. On a server, part of the *nd.local* file might look like:

```
user 0 1 /dev/xy0f 0 10120 -1
user moser 0 /dev/xy0g 0 16560 0
user moser 1 /dev/xy0g 16560 34040 -1
user hinault 0 /dev/xy0g 50600 16560 1
user hinault 1 /dev/xy0g 67160 50600 -1
```

Thus on this server, the public partition is situated on the hard partition */dev/xy0f* and the root and swap partitions for machines *moser* and *hinault* on */dev/xy0g*.

On a server, the clients' root partitions are referenced through */dev/ndl**, where the * corresponds to 0 for *moser* and 1 for *hinault*. It is defined by the last entry in the *user* lines in *nd.local*.

On a client, the public partition is referenced through */dev/ndp0*, the root partition through */dev/nd0*, and the swap partition through */dev/nd1*.

The **nd** command is executed on */etc/nd.local* when a server is started up, by an entry in */etc/rc.local*. The *nd.local* file is created on a server when the system is installed.

The **network file system** allows clients to remote mount a file system from a server machine. All of the clients may then share the same file system.

The server controls which clients may access the file system via the */etc/exports* file. (See **exports(5)**.) Typical entries in the */etc/exports* file might be

```
/usr/man
/usr/dcl-ism1        dcl-ism2 dcl-ism3
```

These mean that */usr/man* is exported to all machines, but */usr/dcl-ism1* is only exported to machines *dcl-ism2* and *dcl-ism3*.

To mount a remote file system on a client the **mount** command is used.

Example

To mount the manual pages from the server machine *dcl-ism1* on a client issue

```
mount dcl-ism1:/usr/man /usr/man
```

on the client.

Usually a client will mount the file systems it needs (both local and remote) at startup time by entries in */etc/fstab* (see **fstab(5)**). Typical entries might be

/dev/sd0a / 4.2 rw 1 1
/dev/sd0g /usr 4.2 rw 1 2
dcl-ucrel:/usr/man /usr/man nfs ro,hard 0 0

which mounts the partitions 'a' and 'g' on the local SCSI disk on root and */usr*, respectively, and mounts the remote file system */usr/man* from machine dcl-ucrel on the directory */usr/man*.

The third network service, **yellow pages**, is a lookup database, from which a server process provides information to client machines. This can be used to assist the task of system administration in a local network.

Yellow pages is a distributed system, that is, the database is replicated at several machines known as *slave servers*. One server is designated a *master server*. The yellow pages serve information stored in maps which are a set of keys and associated values. Most maps are derived from the ASCII files found in */etc* (*passwd*, *group*, etc; these are described later). Programs that wish to access the information from a server, must know the name of the map or *mapname* and must provide a key. A server process will then respond with the associated value. This could be any server.

For more information on the yellow pages, see Chapter 8.

7.3. Installing Sun UNIX

7.3.1. The setup program

Usually when a Sun workstation is installed, a Sun engineer will complete the hardware installation and then install the system software. This will consist of initially copying a primitive UNIX system from cartridge tape onto disk, booting this UNIX system and then using the **setup** program to install the complete system. Since a system administrator will need to provide some of the information needed by the **setup** program, a brief description of this utility is given. For a full description see the document "Installing UNIX on the Sun Workstation".

When run on a Sun workstation with a bit–mapped display, **setup** presents a series of five electronic "forms", which can be completed in any order, using input from the keyboard and mouse. The five forms are the Workstation Form, the Defaults Form, the Optional Software Form, the Clients Form, and the Disk Form.

The **Workstation Form** provides information about the workstation, such as whether the workstation is a standalone system or a file server, whether the workstation is tapeless and which ethernet interfaces are present. An example Workstation Form follows in figure 7.1.

The **Defaults Form** is used to change some of the default values assumed by variables of the **setup** program.

The **Clients Form** provides details of the diskless clients of a server.

The **Optional Software Form** specifies which optional software packages are to be installed.

The **Disks Form** allows us to change the hard partition information for all the disks on the system being configured. Example Disks Forms are given in figures 7.2 and 7.3.

Not all of the forms need be completed in every installation. For the case of a standalone system only the Workstation, Defaults and Optional Software Forms are used. Since there are no clients, the Clients Form is not needed and the default disk partitions are likely to be adequate, so the Disks Form is not needed. For the case of a server and clients, all of the forms are likely to be completed. The software for a server and each client are installed together. If all forms are to be completed, Sun advise that they are completed in the order

Workstation Form,
Defaults Form,
Optional Software Form, and then
Disk Form.

Before proceeding with **setup**, the system administrator will need to decide the name of each machine, the internet address of each machine, and the ethernet address of each diskless client.

Each machine on a local network has a unique hostname or machine name. This may be up to 32 alphanumeric characters but alphabetic characters must be lower case. The hostname is specified in the Workstation Form.

An internet address consists of two parts. A network number followed by a host number. The host number, which must be in the range 1-254, uniquely identifies a machine on a local network. The network number is used to identify the network. This number will either be the number assigned by ARPA, or the Sun default of 192.9.200. (Internet Addresses are discussed more fully in Chapter 8.) The network number is specified on the Defaults Form, and with Automatic Host Numbering turned off on that form, the host number is the number specified on the Workstation Form.

A machine's hardware ethernet address is displayed in the monitor power-up banner as a six-byte hexadecimal address. Each client machine should be powered-up and this address noted. For each client of a server, the client's ethernet address is specified on the Clients Form.

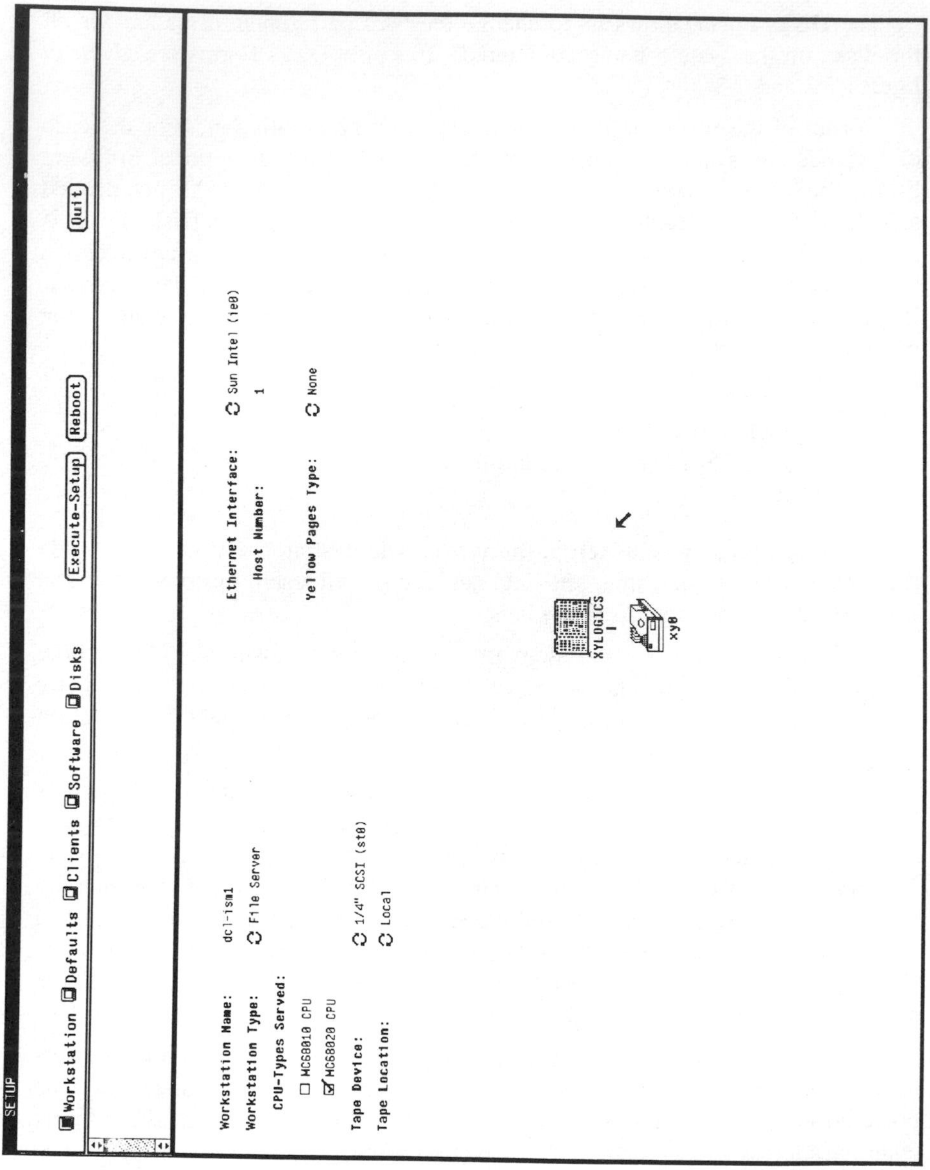

Figure 7.1 A workstation form

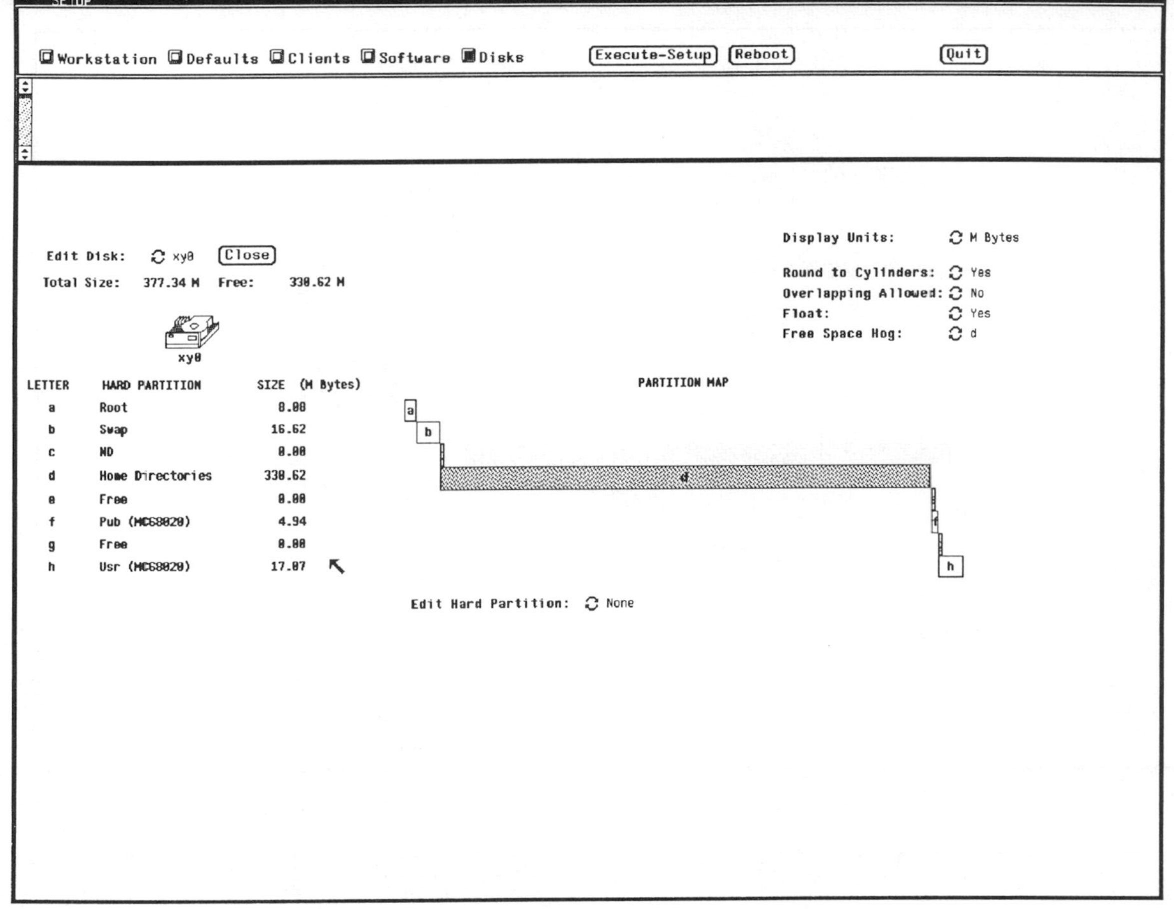

Figure 7.2 A disks form

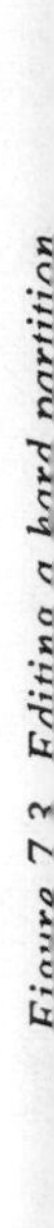

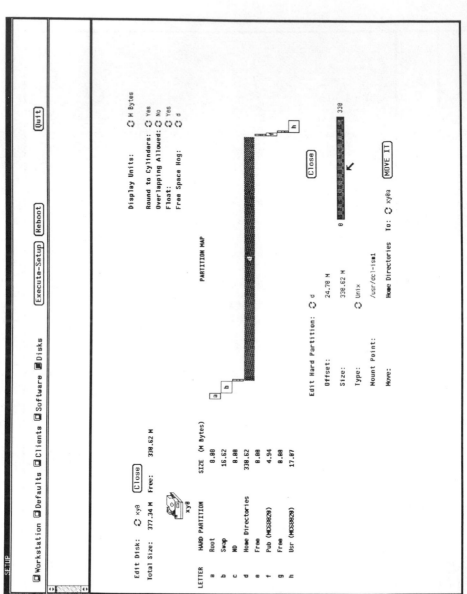

Figure 7.3 Editing a hard partition

After completing all the necessary forms **setup** may now be executed by moving the arrow over the ''execute setup'' field and pressing the leftmost mouse button. After confirmation, setup will proceed with software installation, provided that setup finds no errors in the choices specified. From time to time, the operator will be asked to change tapes. **Setup** will eventually finish with the message ''Installation complete'', and the new system may be booted.

7.3.2. Configuring UNIX

After installing the UNIX system, and booting the machine, the system administrator must logon to the machine and set the root password. The system kernel should then be remade.

As installed the system runs a *generic* kernel. This kernel is capable of driving every kind of device that Sun supports. This kernel thus takes up more main memory than is necessary. The kernel must be reconfigured to contain only those device drivers that the system needs. The kernel should also be configured to set the correct time zone, to set the maximum number of simultaneous users of the system, and various options such as system accounting, and the quota system, for example.

The details of rebuilding the kernel are beyond the scope of the book. Refer to Chapter 8, ''Configuring the System Kernel'', of the Sun Document ''Installing UNIX on the Sun Workstation''.

7.4. Adding user accounts

Creating a login name for a new user of the system is a simple process. It can be automated easily. Firstly, an entry in the password file (*/etc/passwd*) is created for the user. Then the user's login or home directory must be created. Next, the user's environment on login may be defined by creating several *setup* files in the user's home directory (such as *.login*, *.cshrc* etc). Finally, **chown(8)** is used to set the ownership to the user of the home directory and any setup files, and **chgrp(1)** is used to set the group ownership of these to the user's default group.

7.4.1. The password file

The password file is described in **passwd(5)**. It is an ASCII file consisting of a series of lines, one line per user. Each line is further divided into seven fields which are separated by colons. At the start of the password file are some system entries, for root, daemon, etc. Then follow the entries for the users. A typical entry might look like:

kirti:5LsTxkbzMsuCY:169:10:& Walpole:/usr/users/kirti:/bin/csh

The fields in a password file entry are:

1. The login or user name. This must be unique within the password file. Uniqueness can be checked by using a command of the form

```
grep "^name:" /etc/passwd
```

2. The encrypted password. When creating the entry for a new user this is often left blank. This corresponds to no password required. However, this can pose a security problem and it might be better to set an initial password for the user, not based on the user's name etc.

3. The user identifier UID.

The user identifier must be unique in the password file and on a local network a login name must have the same user identifier on all machines. It is easier to ensure that the user identifier is unique if the password file is kept sorted on user identifier.

4. The group identifier GID. Group identifiers are used to class together users who are related in some way; for example, those working on the same project may have the same group identifier.

The user identifier and the group identifier are numeric values used by UNIX to identify the ownership of files and processes, and to protect them.

5. The "comment field". This often contains information about the user such as the user's full name, telephone number, and room number etc. An ampersand may be used used here as a shorthand for the user's login name.

6. The location of the user's login directory.

7. The initial shell on login. If this field is left blank then (by default) the Bourne Shell */bin/sh* is obtained. A popular choice is */bin/csh* which gives the C–shell.

The password file can be edited only by the superuser. It should be edited using **vipw(8)** which locks the password file to prevent several processes from gaining simultaneous access to the file. If the file is already being edited, a second attempt will result in a warning to try again later.

Each user can set up or change their password by using the **passwd(1)** program. The **chsh(1)** program allows a user to change the login shell field in the password file. If no shell is specified, the shell reverts to the default Bourne shell (*/bin/sh*). Only superuser can specify a shell other than */bin/csh* or */bin/sh*.

The file **/etc/group(5)** is a database consisting of groups and their respective members. It is an ASCII file consisting of a sequence of lines, one line per group, with the lines divided into fields which are separated by colons. Typical entries are:

```
uucp:*:9:peter,stephen,kirti
cosdist:*:11:jon,john,gordon
```

The fields in the group file are:

1. Group Name.
2. Encrypted Password. This is usually an asterisk.
3. Numerical Group Identifier.
4. A comma separated list of all users allowed in this group.

Users need not be added to their default group as defined by their password file entry.

The */etc/group* file can be used to control access to files. For example, all people working on project called ipse can be included in a group named ipse. All files related to project ipse can then have read/write owner and group permission set to allow access but preventing access via the 'other' permission bits.

7.4.2. Creating the home directory and environment

Users home directories are often kept in a directory called *users*, which is a subdirectory of the */usr* directory. Home directory names correspond to the users login name and so for the user with login name kirti, the home directory would be

```
/usr/users/kirti
```

This arrangement is not compulsory. One alternative is to subdivide further the users directory into subdirectories, each subdirectory corresponding to a group of users. For example, in an academic institution one might identify groups of users such as staff, postgraduates, and undergraduates. The users directory would then contain subdirectories

```
staff
pgrad
ugrad
```

corresponding to the groups. An individual's home directory would be a subdirectory, of staff, pgrad or ugrad, depending on status.

The users directory need not be a subdirectory of */usr*, but could be mounted on the root directory as */users*.

Assuming that all home directories are subdirectories of the directory */usr/users*, the following command sequence can be used to create a home directory for user kirti:

```
cd /usr/users
mkdir kirti
chown kirti kirti
chgrp staff kirti
```

This sequence first changes to the parent directory, creates the home directory, changes the ownership to the user's login name (kirti) and changes the group to the users' group (staff).

The command interpreters or shells (Bourne Shell and C shell) and many interactive programs such as **mail** and the **vi** editor are described as having an *environment*.

The environment is, roughly, those options that modify how the program responds to the user. The shells and interactive commands allow users to tailor the environment to their own needs. It is possible to change terminal settings, to change prompts, to change command names, and to change search paths. This is achieved through the use of various *setup* files, for example, *.profile* for the Bourne shell, *.cshrc*, *.login* and *.logout* for the C shell, *.exrc* for **vi** (and the editor **ex**), and *.mailrc* for **mail**.

A system administrator often creates default setup files for a new user in the user's home directory, which reflect local standards. They should have ownership set to the user's login name, and group set to that of the user. In Release 3 of Sun UNIX, examples of the startup files may be found in the directory */usr/lib* in the files

Cshrc
Exrc
Login
Logout
Mailrc

7.4.3. Removing user accounts

Removing a user account is straightforward but has some implications. If the system administrator believes that some of the user's files may be useful at a later date then they should be saved. For example, they could be moved to a secure area and have their ownership changed, or else, they could be dumped to tape using **tar** and the tape stored in a secure place.

All files on the system owned by the user can be deleted using the **find(1)** command. For example, with

find / -user <login-name> -exec rm -f {} \;

where <login-name> represents the user's login name. However, this will not delete any file that has a link made to it. Perhaps, the other users should be warned so that they can adopt the ownership of these files.

The users's entry in the password file should be deleted, and any reference to the user in the file */etc/group* should be deleted. Any **mail** aliases set up in */usr/lib/aliases* should be removed.

7.5. Dumping and restoring

A very important task for any system administrator is that of performing regular backups of all the UNIX file systems on a workstation. Taking a backup means making a copy of the file system onto some other exchangeable medium, such as magnetic tape.

There are two reasons for taking backups. Firstly, something unusual may occur (such as a disk crash) damaging all or part of a file system. Secondly, a user may inadvertently delete one or more files, realising later that they are still needed. This might be due to error, a program with a bug, or a program used incorrectly. In the first case it is likely that the whole file system would have to be restored, but in the second case just the files lost. In either case, the system administrator can restore versions only as recent as those on the last backup copy.

The media containing the backup copies, usually cartridge or reel magnetic tape, must be stored in a secure place. A record of dumps should be kept and the media clearly labelled. The dump tapes should be stored in a secure place, certainly not in the same room as the workstation.

7.5.1. The dump command

The command **dump(8)** copies a file system to some suitable backup medium, such as magnetic tape. Further, it allows a whole file system to be dumped, called a *total* or *full* dump, or else part of a file system to be dumped, called a *partial* or *incremental* dump. This is done by specifying a *dump level* as an argument to **dump**. Legal dump level arguments are 0-9.

Dump level 0 causes the whole file system to be dumped. A dump at level n will cause only those files, modified since the last dump at a level lower than n, to be copied to the dump tape.

The file */etc/dumpdates* is used by **dump** to record the level and date of a dump. It is used by **dump** to calculate whether a file should be included in an incremental dump. The argument 'u' to **dump** causes this file to be updated. If it is missing, there will be no record of the dump. It is therefore important that this argument be used each time a dump is taken.

A complete level 0 dump of every file system, on even a medium sized workstation, will take several tapes (reel or cartridge) and will take a long time to complete. In an installation with many workstations, and possibly a large number of file systems, it would be impractical to **dump** at level 0 every dump. So, in practice, a level 0 dump is taken and this is followed by some sequence of incremental dumps. The strategy chosen for doing full or incremental dump combinations has some implications for the way in which restores are performed. This will be illustrated in the methods described below.

Care must be taken to avoid two extremes: the dumps are taken so infrequently that the files on a dump tape are hopelessly out of date, or the dumps are taken so often that all of the systems time is spent in dumping.

It is possible that a different strategy is adopted for different file systems. For example, a disk partition might be devoted to the user's home directories. The files in this file system will be constantly changing and so the file system might be dumped daily. Another disk partition might contain the */usr* file system. The information contained in this file system will not be changing so critically and so it is possible that this file system might be dumped weekly. In fact, the way in which a large disk is partitioned and file systems assigned to these partitions should take into account the intended dumping strategy. It might be appropriate to chose partition sizes in order that a completely full file system will fit on a single dump tape, for example.

Some commonly proposed strategies include:

1. Take a full dump once per week. On subsequent days, dump only those files that have been modified since the previous day's dump. This can be achieved by taking a level 0 dump on the first day and dumps at levels 1,2,3,4 on the following days.

This method has some implications for the way in which files are restored. To completely restore the file system involves restoring the level 0 dump and then each incremental dump in turn, a time-consuming process. For a single file (or a few files) it is not easy to judge on which dump tape the most recent version of that file exists.

2. Take a full dump once per week; on each subsequent day, take an incremental dump at the same level (probably level 9). Thus, on each day the complete set of files changed since the last total dump will be dumped. The dumps will be progressively bigger and take longer to complete. However, to restore the complete file system requires only the last total dump and the last incremental dump tape.

3. Depending on the size of the file system, method 2 can be modified to take advantage of the other incremental levels available. A full level 0 dump is taken. Each subsequent day a level 9 dump is taken, and these are kept for a week. Once a week a level 5 dump is taken. These tapes are kept for a month. Once a month a level 3 dump is taken and these tapes are kept for a year. Once a year a full level 0 dump is taken.

In the first two methods, there would be two sets of incremental tapes which are alternated weekly. The level 0 tapes might be kept indefinitely. In fact, the system administrator will have to decide how long these tapes are kept. If the information on the tapes is valuable, and not easily reproduced, then the longer the tapes should be kept. For some file systems it is possible to re-use the tapes, keeping a cycle of say three sets of tapes. A reasonable compromise method is:

4. A level 0 dump is taken. On subsequent days, level 9 dumps are taken. Three level 9 tapes are used which are cycled. Whenever a level 9 dump would occupy more than one tape a level 0 dump is taken. The sequence of level 9 dumps then continues on the following days. Three complete sets of level 0 dump tapes are retained and re-used cyclically. This method has the advantage of being conservative in its use of tapes and restores are straightforward. However, it is unlikely to back up *transient* files, that is files that existed for a short time in January would not be available in June. Nor does it keep many backup *versions* of files.

It can be seen that ensuring a system is securely backed up needs a large commitment in time (machine and human) and resources (machine and tapes). It is important that the system administrator decide on a strategy and then ensure the dump tapes are made. Also, the strategy should be amended in the light of experience.

7.5.2. Using dump

A workstation might have :

1. A cartridge tape unit with one of two types of controller.

    a. A sun archive controller (/dev/st0).
    b. A SCSI controller (/dev/st0).

2. A 1/2" tape unit, which would have a controller capable of writing at 1600 bpi (/dev/mt0) or a controller capable of writing at the higher density of 6250 bpi (/dev/mt0).

3. None of these.

However, if it is assumed that the workstation is on a local network where at least one of the workstations has a local tape, unit then the **dump** command can be used to dump file systems to magnetic tape.

Examples

Examples 1,2 and 3 illustrate the use of the **dump** command.

1. To take a level 0 dump of the root file system of a SCSI disk to a local SCSI tape.

The root partition is normally located in partition /dev/sd0a. The **dump** command is

```
dump 0ucbf 126 /dev/rst0 /dev/rsd0a
```

This illustrates several important features of the **dump** command. The flags must be grouped together: 0ucbfd.

If a flag is further qualified (by a file name, say) then this argument follows the group of flags directly. If there is more than one such argument, they must appear in the order implied by the order of the flags. The raw devices are used (note the 'r' in */dev/rst0* and */dev/rsd0g*) to make the dump go faster.

The flags have the following meaning:

'0' - It is a level 0 dump.

'u' - Update the file */etc/dumpdates*, to ensure a record of the dump is made.

'c' - This indicates that the dump is to cartridge tape, and it must be present.

'b' - Sets the blocking value to 126. This is more efficient for SCSI cartridge tape.

'f' - Dump to the dump device specified, not the default (/dev/rmt8).

2. To take a level 9 dump the 'g' partition of a SCSI disk (/dev/sd0g) to a remote 1/2" reel tape located on another machine.

Suppose the partition to be dumped is on the machine with host name *millar*, and the remote tape unit is on the machine with host name *kelly*.

/etc/hosts on machine *millar* must have an entry for machine *kelly*, and */etc/hosts* on machine *kelly* must have an entry for machine *millar*. On the machine *kelly*, the file */.rhosts* must have an entry for machine *millar*.

For a 1600 bpi tape drive the **dump** command is:

```
dump 9uf kelly:/dev/rmt8 /dev/rsd0g
```

For a 6250 bpi drive the **dump** command is:

```
dump 9uf kelly:/dev/rmt0 /dev/rsd0g
```

There is no need for the 'c' flag and the default blocking factor is adequate.

3. To dump a diskless client's root partition to the server's local SCSI tape.

Suppose machine *yates* is a file server with 1 SMD disk drive and a local SCSI tape unit. Machine *moser* is a diskless client of *yates*. The 'g' partition of *yates* (/dev/xy0g) will be used to provide the soft *public* partition (/pub) for *yates* and its clients. Further, the network disk provides soft partitions to support the client's root and swap partitions. The file */etc/nd.local* defines these partitions:

```
...
user moser 0 /dev/xy0g 0 16560 0
user moser 1 /dev/xy0g 16560 34040 -1
user hinault 0 /dev/xy0g 50600 16560 1
user hinault 1 /dev/xy0g 67160 50600 -1
...
```

The first entry for *moser* defines the root partition and indicates that it can be referred to from *yates* as */etc/ndl0*, for the block device, and */dev/rndl0* for the character (or raw) device.

Dumping the /pub partition with

```
dump 9ucbf 126 /dev/rst0 /dev/rxy0g
```

will dump only */pub*; it will not dump the other soft partitions in */dev/xy0g*. (It still must be done.) Therefore, it would not dump *moser's* root partition. This can be achieved with:

```
dump 9ucbf 126 /dev/rst0 /dev/rndl0
```

The following points should be kept in mind:

Dump is one of those few programs that ignore the hierarchical structure of file systems but instead directly accesses i-nodes, and uses the information stored there. (The date of the last modification of a file is stored in its i-node, for example.) Because **dump** deals directly with i-nodes it needs access to the device on which the file system resides. For security reasons, these devices are only readable by root, and thus only root can successfully execute **dump**.

Commands to dump the various file systems on a workstation could be gathered together into a shell script. The file script should have ownership *root* and have the *setuid* bit set. A simple C program could then be written which checked that a user was entitled to run the shell script and if so *exec'd* the file script. This would enable *trusted* users to perform dumps, without their knowing the root password. Alternatively, a new group *operator*, say, could be created and the group ownership of the shell script set to operator. This would enable anyone in the group operator to execute the dump.

Because root alone can execute **dump**, in the case of a remote dump the */.rhosts* is necessary on the remote machine, since this file allows root on the local machine to execute commands on the remote machine.

Whenever a file system is being dumped it should have as little activity on it as possible. Preferably, it should be unmounted. For network disk partitions the corresponding client should be powered down. Also the file system should be consistent. The **fsck(8)** program should be executed on that file system correcting any inconsistencies before the file system is dumped. (It is necessary to unmount the file system before running **fsck** on it.)

If a system has several disks, it might be possible to designate some of the partitions as *backup partitions* for other partitions of a similar size. A **cron(8)** entry could be created to copy (using **dd(1)**, say) a partition to its backup at night when the system is quiet. The system administrator can then take tape backups, during the next working day, from the dump partitions. The backup partitions could be mounted read only (except when being copied to) and users would be able to find *yesterday's* copies of files there, if needed.

7.5.3. Using restore

restore(8) is the utility program provided by the Sun UNIX system for copying to disk files on a dump tape created by **dump**. **restore** can be used to restore an individual file, or group of files; it can be used to restore a subtree of a file system from a given point and hence can restore a complete file system. **restore** can be used in batch mode or interactively, where it provides a shell-like interface, and can be used to restore files across the ethernet.

Care should be taken to restore files from the correct dump tape. For this reason, it is important to make sure that proper records of all dumps are kept. When restoring files which may be on one or more incremental tapes, the tapes should be used in order of increasing dump level.

Example

Consider a workstation with two SCSI disk drives and suppose it has the following partitions in use:

```
/dev/sd0a mounted as root
/dev/sd0g mounted as /usr
/dev/sd1g mounted as /usr/users
```

(in fact, */dev/sd1g* corresponds to the whole of the second disk drive and contains all the users home directories). Suppose that a very recent backup of the home directories has been taken at level 0 to a local SCSI tape, with the command

```
dump 0ucbf 126 /dev/rst0 /dev/rsd1g
```

This can be used to illustrate some features of restore.

For user kirti, files within her directory with names a, b, c, say, that is with absolute names

```
/usr/users/kirti/a
/usr/users/kirti/b
/usr/users/kirti/c
```

appear on the dump as

```
/kirti/a
/kirti/b
/kirti/c
```

It is these names that must be used when restoring files by name, as in

```
restore bxf 126 /dev/rst0 /kirti/b
```

say.

A second point is that files are extracted relative to the current working directory. Thus, to restore the file into kirti's directory, first

```
cd /usr/users
```

then

```
restore bxf 126 /dev/rst0 /kirti/b
```

There is no need for the c option but the blocking factor (126) must be specified with the b flag.
The flag x means extract the named files. The list of file names to be extracted appears last on the command line.

If the tape unit is situated on the remote machine *kelly* (as in the dump examples) then the command form is:

```
restore bxf 126 kelly:/dev/rst0 /kirti/b
```

Since this command is executed by root the name of the local machine *millar* must appear in the */.rhosts* file on the remote machine *kelly*.

Sometimes it is a bad idea to restore a file to its original place. It is possible to take advantage of the fact that restore works relative to the current working directory by restoring files to */tmp* or */usr/tmp* say, then, after checking that they are the correct versions, copying them to the correct location.

For a few files, it is convenient to restore them using **restore**'s *interactive* mode of operation. This mode can be used on a local or remote tape. For example restoring the file *Makefile* into user ron's compiler directory. This directory is a subdirectory of *~ron/SySL*.

```
% restore -if dcl-csvax:/dev/rmt8
restore > cd users/ron/SySL/compiler
restore > add Makefile
Warning: ./users: File exists
Warning: ./users/ron: File exists
Warning: ./users/ron/SySL: File exists
Warning: ./users/ron/SySL/compiler: File exists
restore > extract
You have not read any tapes yet.
Unless you know which volume your file(s) are on you should start
with the last volume and work towards the first.
Specify next volume #: 1
set owner/mode for '.'? [yn] y
restore > quit
```

7.5.4. Restoring an entire file system

This would have to be done after a serious disk crash. It is possible to move a file system from one disk partition to another by first dumping the file system and restoring it in the second file system, to a larger partition, perhaps.

Assume that the partition to which the file system is to be restored is a hard partition, and not the root partition, for example, */dev/xy0e* on an SMD disk.

First, an empty file system is created on the partition:

```
newfs /dev/rxy0e
```

The empty file system is mounted on a suitable directory, /mnt for example:

```
mount /dev/xy0e /mnt
```

From within the mounted directory, the file system is restored from the last level 0 dump:

```
cd /mnt
restore rvbf 126 /dev/rst0
```

(assuming a SCSI tape unit.) Any incremental dumps are then restored.
The r flag indicates that the complete tape is to be read into the current directory.
After a complete restore, **restore** leaves a file *restoresymtable* in the current working directory. This can be removed

```
rm restoresymtable
```

The restored file system should be checked:

```
cd
umount /dev/rxy0e
fsck /dev/rxy0e
```

A full dump of the file system should be taken, which can then be mounted on its proper mount point.

As will be seen, restoring a root file system presents some difficulties. The utilities needed for the restore are located on the file system itself. (**mount, dump, restore, fsck,** and **umount** are usually kept in */etc*.) In this case, as done during the initial system setup, a mini UNIX system is loaded from the boot tape into the swap partition (partition 'b' on the first disk). When this system is then booted, it contains enough utilities to restore root.

It is also difficult to restore a file system to the */pub* partition or to a soft client partition. For details, see the document "System Administration for the Sun Workstation".

7.5.5. The tar command

At some sites it may be impossible to take dumps of all the file systems on a daily basis. Users who are worried about the security of their own file store allocation can be encouraged to take their own copies of their file store, to tape, using the **tar(1)** command.

Example

For user kirti to create a tar image of all her files to a local SCSI tape:

```
cd ~kirti
tar cvfb /dev/rst0 126 .
```

The flags are:

'c' create a new tar image.

'v' set verbose mode, this causes **tar** to display which files are being copied, as they are being copied.

'b' set the blocking factor, (126 for cartridge tape).

The **cd** ensures that the user is in the home directory. The '**.**' indicates the current working directory. If the list of file names includes the name of a directory, then the sub-tree from that directory is copied.

To extract an individual file, type

```
tar fx /dev/rst0 <filename>
```

As with **restore**, <filename> must exactly match the name of the intended file on the tape.

To extract the whole contents of the tape, type

tar fx /dev/rst0

7.6. Managing disk space

The system administrator will need to monitor regularly disk space usage. Even the largest workstation will occasionally run out of file space. In the worst case, the message *filesystem full* will be printed on the system console. This will prevent any useful work from being done until some disk space is freed. Clearly, it is better to monitor usage and not be caught in this situation. If a disk becomes too full (>90%) system performance may deteriorate drastically. (See the document ''UNIX File System'', a tutorial in ''System Administration for the Sun Workstation''.)

7.6.1. Checking disk usage

There are several commands available for summarising disk usage.

df(1) returns information about the disk partitions given in the argument list, or if none is specified, the file mounted file systems (gleaned from */etc/mtab*). The information given includes, the file space occupied by the file system, the space used and the space available, how much of the file system's total capacity has been used, and the mount point of the file system.

Example output from **df** (with no arguments).

Filesystem	kbytes	used	avail	capacity	Mounted on
/dev/xy0a	7735	5889	1072	85%	/
/dev/xy0f	4771	3786	507	88%	/pub.MC68020
/dev/xy0h	104923	60811	33619	64%	/usr.MC68020
/dev/xy0e	181051	1956	100989	38%	/usr.MC68020/yates

The file capacity is based on an optimum total file capacity which is 90% of the total physical capacity available. The amount of reserved free space may be changed from 10% (the default) with the **tunefs(8)** command. Therefore, the amount of reserved free space can be reduced. This would be at the cost of system degradation, but it might be feasible on a file system with very little traffic.

For a hard partition divided into soft partitions, **df** returns values only for the first soft partition.

After checking the amount of free space on the file systems with **df**, if any system is over-full, the system administrator can use the following commands to check for any excessive usage.

du(1) summarises the disk usage in kilobytes below the current working or the named directories (if given as arguments). Totals are displayed for each sub-directory. If the -s flag is given only the grand total is printed.

Thus, if the users home directories are all contained in the same place, the following command can be used to summarise the disk usage for each user:

```
du -s *
```

quot(8) must be executed by root. It summarises the number of blocks owned by each user in the named file systems. Execution of **quot** can be slow, and on large disks it is best run at a low priority.

ls(1) ls -s gives the size in kilobytes of the files in the current directory.

If **quot** gives an unexpectedly high result for a particular user, kirti say, then **ls** can be used in conjunction with **find(1)** to gather more information about a users files:

```
find / -user kirti -exec ls -lisad {} \;
```

Another way to control disk usage by users is by the quota system. This is the subject of the next section.

7.6.2. Disk quotas

The disk quota system provides a means to regulate the disk space usage by users. Quotas may be set for individual users on any file system. Usually, quotas are enforced on a file system containing the user's home directories. It is inadvisable to enforce quotas on */tmp*.

The quota system introduces a little system overhead in cpu time consumed in writing a new block to disk.

The quota system imposes two limits on a user. There is a limit on the amount of disk space (in units of 1K blocks) that the user can own and there is a limit to the number of files the that user can create.

There are two types of limit, a soft limit and a hard limit. Different values may be set for limits for different users. Whenever a user exceeds the soft limit, that user is warned, and if the user does not reduce usage to below the soft limit within a specified time, then the user is considered to have exceeded the hard limit. Whenever a hard limit is exceeded by a user, then no more resources are available to that user. The user's usage must be decreased or the system administrator must increase the user's quota. The soft and hard limits, and the time-limit by which a user may exceed a soft quota are decided and set by the system administrator on a file-system basis using **edquota(8)**. Individual users may check their usage using the **quota(1)** command.

It is straightforward to set up the disk quota system. The UNIX kernel must be configured to include the disk-quota sub-system, that is, the system configuration file must contain the line

```
options QUOTA
```

If necessary, the system must be rebuilt after adding this line.

On the root directory of each file system on which quotas are to be enforced, create an empty file called *quotas*. This can be done with the **touch(1)** command:

```
touch quotas
```

The command **edquota** is used to specify initial limits for the users. The command **edquota -t** is used to set the over quota time limit for the specified file systems.

Then the file */etc/fstab* is edited to mark each read-write file system that is to have quotas as being read-write with quotas (rw,quota). For example, change

```
/dev/xy0e /usr.MC68020/yates 4.2 rw 1 2
```

to

/dev/xy0e /usr.MC68020/yates 4.2 rw,**quota** 1 2

(See **fstab(5)** for further details of the file */etc/fstab*.)

Then add the lines

```
/usr/etc/quotacheck -a   >/dev/console
/usr/etc/quotaon -a
```

to the file */etc/rc.local*. (In fact these lines are in rc.local, but commented out.)

The **quotacheck(8)** command is run on all file systems that are defined in */etc/fstab* as having quotas. It checks that a file systems quota file (*quotas*) is consistent with the actual numbers of blocks and files allocated to a user. The **quotaon** command turns on the quota system for each file system in */etc/fstab* that is defined as having quotas.

Whenever the system administrator creates a new user account on a system with quotas, then a quota should be created for the user. When a user is removed from a system with quotas enforced, then the user's quota limits should be set to zero.

The system administrator can use **quota** to examine the usage and quotas for any user and

```
repquota -a
```

to obtain a summary of the usages and limits for all users on all file systems, on which quotas are enforced.

7.6.3. Freeing space from a file system

In the event that a file system becomes full or nearly full, the system administrator must free space by deleting files or moving files to another file system.

Should the space in the root file partition become exhausted, it will probably be due to obsolete files accumulating in the */tmp* directory. These files can be deleted. If the problem persists, then the */tmp* directory can be moved to another disk partition (with more free space) and a symbolic link created to it from the root directory.

If the */usr* file system runs out of space then there are several options. The directory */usr/adm* contains accounting information. The files in this directory can become very large. They can be truncated with

```
cp /dev/null acct
cp /dev/null messages
cp /dev/null wtmp
cp /dev/null lastlog
```

(This can be done automatically using the **cron** command.)

The directories */usr/tmp* and */usr/spool* and its subdirectories can be checked for obsolete files. (On a server or client */usr/adm*, */usr/spool* and */usr/tmp* are symbolic links to */private/usr/adm*, */private/usr/spool/* and */private/usr/tmp* respectively.)

The manual files in */usr/man* or some sub-sections of the manual files could be deleted. (See the next section.)

The directory *sys* (which is in fact symbolic link to */usr/sys*) can be moved to another file system and a symbolic link created to it. If the system is stable, that is, the system administrator does not envisage changing the system kernel, then this directory can be archived to tape and then deleted.

7.6.4. Optimising disk space with NFS

Much disk space can be wasted in a *heterogenous* environment, that is, a local network that has standalone workstations as well as file servers and diskless clients. This is due to duplication of information. If there are several standalone machines, then the information in */usr* will be duplicated in each of the machines, for example. Also, a common problem is that if a user has a login name on several machines then that user is likely to keep duplicate copies of files on several machines. The NFS network service can be used to minimise this duplication.

To minimise the disk space duplication by users, the directory containing the home directories on each machine is cross mounted onto all the other machines. Each user has a home directory on one machine only and the */etc/passwd* file is maintained to reflect this.

Example

Suppose that we have two machines with host names *ipse1* and *ipse2* respectively. The home directories on *ipse1* are under */usr/ipse1* and the home directories on *ipse2* are under */usr/ipse2*.

To cross mount the directories, first create the directory */usr/ipse2* on machine *ipse1* and the directory */usr/ipse1* on the machine *ipse2*. Next, edit the file */etc/exports* on *ipse1* to add the entry */usr/ipse1* and edit the file */etc/exports* on *ipse2* to add the entry */usr/ipse2*. Edit the */etc/passwd* file on *ipse1* and on *ipse2* so that each user appears on both systems but with a home directory in one of */usr/ipse1* or */usr/ipse2*. Thus, if user kirti's home directory is to be on *ipse1* and user cathy's home directory is to be on *ipse2*, then the */etc/passwd* files on both machines should have the entries:

```
cathy:fWpbaJSf1Ebn6:135:10:& Taylor:/usr/ipse2/cathy:/bin/csh
kirti:5LsTxkbzMsuCY:169:10:& Walpole:/usr/ipse1/kirti:/bin/csh
```

(It might be safest to use the YP network service to maintain the password files.)

On *ipse1* execute the following command:

```
mount -o soft -t nfs ipse2:/usr/ipse2 /usr/ipse2
```

On *ipse2* execute the following command:

```
mount -o soft -t nfs ipse1:/usr/ipse1 /usr/ipse1
```

Thus the users kirti and cathy will be able to logon to either machine but they will have only one home directory each.

The file */etc/fstab* on both *ipse1* and *ipse2* must be edited to add the lines

```
ipse2:/usr/ipse2 /usr/ipse2 nfs rw,soft 0 0
```

and

```
ipse1:/usr/ipse1 /usr/ipse1 nfs rw,soft 0 0
```

respectively. This will ensure that if either machine is rebooted, then the remote file systems will be automatically mounted.

Clearly, this method can be extended to more than two machines.

NFS can also be used effectively to reduce the disk space usage on a standalone machine by mounting the */usr* directory, or just some of its subdirectories, from a *server* machine after first archiving and then deleting the contents of the local directories. The server need not be a file server as such, it could be another standalone system. However, Sun advise that, for the best performance, the following rules are followed:

1. Both machines run the same version of UNIX.

2. The server is a Sun-3, or a Sun-2 with all Sun-2 clients. That is, a Sun-2 cannot act as a server to a Sun-3.

3. The server has a SMD disk controller.

4. The server should not be a time sharing system.

Example

Consider cross-mounting the */usr/man* directory from the machine with machine name *itm1*, say, to the machines with machine names *itm2* and *itm3*.

On the machine *itm1* edit the file */etc/exports* to add the line

```
/usr/man itm2 itm3
```

On machines *itm2* and *itm3*, issue the command

```
mv /usr/man /usr/man.orig
```

and then issue the command

```
mkdir /usr/man
```

This creates an empty directory, where the remote file system will be mounted.

On *itm2* and *itm3*, edit the file */usr/fstab* to add the line

```
itm1:/usr/man /usr/man nfs ro,hard 0 0
```

Now reboot the machines *itm2* and *itm3* (using **/etc/shutdown**), or issue the command

```
mount -o hard,ro -t nfs itm1:/usr/man /usr/man
```

on both *itm2* and *itm3*.

If everything appears to be working properly, then delete the directory */usr/man.orig* on both *itm2* and *itm3*.

This method can be extended to more directories, and more client machines. Most space would be gained by mounting the whole of */usr*. However, just mounting */usr/man*, */usr/lib*, */usr/ucb*, */usr/etc*, and */usr/bin* is a good compromise. For more details, refer to Appendix H in ''Installing UNIX on the Sun Workstation''.

8 Networking

8.1. Introduction

The advent of workstations, such as the Sun, has led to computer systems consisting of not one single machine with terminals attached, but rather a multitude of interconnected autonomous machines. The interconnection is brought about by one of the several local area network (LAN) enabling technologies that exist: with the Sun this is typically an Ethernet LAN. The resulting networked system opens up opportunities for the development of distributed applications, along with the provision of facilities to allow file transfers, remote logins, electronic mail, etc, while retaining the user's access to a powerful local processing capability.

Sun UNIX allows the attachment of the workstation to an Ethernet, and provides various programming tools that allow the user to exploit the possibilities that a networked machine offers.

This chapter describes those facilities in a top-down fashion. The structure of the chapter is as follows. A brief overview of Ethernet is given followed by a discussion of Sun's networking tools: these include NFS (Network File System), Yellow Pages, RPC (Remote Procedure Call) and XDR (External Data Representation). Some new tools provided with Sun V3.0 are also touched upon. Next, we describe the interprocess communication primitives that provide the basis for the above facilities; these were first provided with Berkeley 4.2 BSD UNIX and have been carried over to Sun UNIX.

Before we start, note that networking itself is such a vast subject that volumes can (and have!) been written about it. The networking facilities on the Sun are also pretty extensive and again much can be written describing them. We therefore have much to pack into a single chapter. The level of discussion will be "mid-way": it will neither be kept solely at a beginner's level nor will it become too advanced in nature. The discussion will be kept as useful as possible, and we believe the pattern that the chapter follows is as logical as it can be.

8.2. Ethernet

The Ethernet local area network was originally developed at Xerox PARC. This first Ethernet specification, called the experimental Ethernet, was later superseded by a joint specification from Digital, Intel and Xerox, called the DIX Ethernet. More recently, the IEEE have produced the 802 standard which closely resembles the DIX Ethernet specification. It is this specification that is most widely accepted today.

Ethernet is based on a coaxial cable bus and uses the CSMA/CD protocol (CSMA/CD stands for Carrier Sense Multiple Access with Collision Detection). Using this protocol, machines on the Ethernet listen to the communication medium to determine whether any transmission is currently in progress. If there is any transmission in progress, then the machine waits for silence; otherwise it starts transmitting. Since multiple machines have access to the Ethernet, it is possible for more than one of them to detect silence and begin transmitting simultaneously. When this happens the transmitted data becomes corrupted. This event is called a collision. To detect collisions, transmitting machines also listen to the communications medium. After a certain time period (the time it takes for the message to reach the far extremities of the Ethernet), the machine is said to have acquired the communications medium. When a collision is detected, the machines involved back off for a period before attempting to retransmit.

One of the main reasons for the wide acceptance of Ethernet is that it supports broadcasting and multicasting of messages very efficiently. This is a useful feature for developing higher level distributed systems on top of Ethernet.

In the following sections we move on to look at Sun's own networking tools.

8.3. Sun's networking tools

In this section we look at the facilities that are provided by Sun to enable workstations to operate in the network environment. The main philosophy behind these facilities is to maintain the autonomy of individual workstations whilst, at the same time, allowing them to take advantage of the resources that are available over the network as a whole. Central to this philosophy is the *Client Server* model of distributed computing. Servers provide resources to the rest of the network and clients consume them. Sun's networking facilities allow workstations to act as clients and servers. This principle is exhibited most clearly by the use of the network disk (ND) protocol. ND allows diskless workstations to be supported on the network. For each diskless workstation client there is an associated server which provides it with disk space. Other networking facilities allow clients and servers to be represented by processes rather than machines. In this way, an individual workstation may be a client, a server or may run both client and server processes, depending on the context.

Sun's networking facilities consist of the Network File System (NFS), the Yellow Pages (YP), the Remote Procedure Call (RPC) protocol, and the External Data Representation (XDR) package. These facilities are discussed in the following sections.

8.3.1. Network File System (NFS)

The Network File System (NFS) is provided to ease the problems of sharing data between a network of machines. Rather than forcing users to copy files between machines or do remote logins to access remote data, NFS provides a distributed file system. NFS is not Sun specific and it is possible to use it in a heterogeneous network of machines and operating systems. Under NFS, remote files can be accessed in place with no more difficulty than local file access. This is achieved by allowing machines to mount remote file systems. Subsequent interaction then takes place over the network connection using the Remote Procedure Call (RPC) protocol (see section 8.3.3.).

As with other Sun networking facilities NFS is designed to operate in an environment of client and server workstations. NFS servers present parts of the file system to the clients on the network. Access to the file system is usually presented in the form of a UNIX file system. However, clients may set up their own file system interface according to their requirements.

A server presents part of its file system to a client by adding a line to the file */etc/exports*. Each line in */etc/exports* contains the part of the file system to be exported and the name of the client to which it is made available. If no client name is specified, then any client can remote mount the file system. In this way a server can restrict access to its exported file systems. The **showmount** command is provided to allow system administrators to see which file systems have been remote mounted.

The NFS architecture contains three different interfaces. At the highest level there is the operating system interface. This is typically presented in the form of a UNIX file system. Below this is the virtual file system (VFS) interface. The VFS interface provides the mapping from network wide unique file identifiers, *vnodes,* to the local operating system representation. For UNIX file systems this interface maps *vnodes* onto UNIX *inodes.* For each file in a UNIX file system there is a corresponding *inode* which contains administrative information about the file. *Inodes* are assigned identification numbers that are unique within a single machine. However, these may not be unique over the network as a whole. *Vnodes* are used above the VFS interface to ensure that files are uniquely identified throughout the network.

The VFS interface may be either local or remote. The local VFS interface connects to the file system on the local machine. The remote VFS interface defines the NFS interface. This uses the RPC protocol and the XDR package which are discussed in sections 8.3.3 and 8.3.4.

Figure 8.1 shows the flow of a **read** request from a client to a remote server and illustrates the positions of the three interfaces mentioned above.

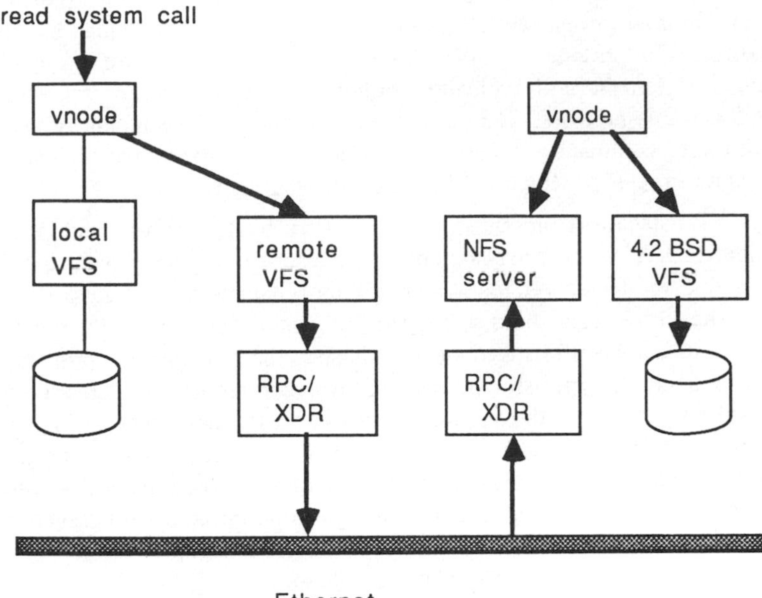

Figure 8.1 Read request from a client (top left) to a remote file system.

The NFS interface is defined so that a server can be stateless. The main advantage of a stateless server is that it enables the system to be robust in the face of client, server, or network failure. Because of this, NFS servers do not support the UNIX **open** operation since this would require the server to maintain state information about an open file. The **open** operation is still provided in the UNIX operating system interface, but the open file information is maintained locally by the client. Sun are considering implementing file locking, replicated data and other features implying state, but these will not be part of the basic NFS definition.

8.3.2. Yellow Pages (YP)

The Yellow Pages (YP) is an optional facility which is designed to ease the problems of administrating a network of machines. YP allows administration information such as passwords and host names to be stored in a single global database. This simplifies the tasks of adding new users and machines to the network and makes large networks more manageable. The YP database is replicated over several machines. The information stored by YP was formerly stored in ASCII files in the */etc* directory. These include the *passwd, group, hosts, network* and *protocol* files. Each of these files is represented in YP by a *map*. Maps contain a set of keys and associated values and are stored in files in */etc/yp* in *dbm* format. *Dbm* files are produced from ASCII files by running **makedbm.** To provide a higher level of naming, maps are grouped into *domains*. A domain will typically contain the maps that are relevant to a single local area network. The current domain can be determined by using the **domainname** command. Domains are represented by subdirectories with the same name in */etc/yp,* which hold the appropriate maps.

The YP database is presented to the network by YP servers, and is used by YP clients. A YP server may be either a master or a slave. For each YP map there is one master server, on which all the changes to that map should be made. The slaves each hold a copy of the map that is held by the master. Once a map has been changed on the master, the changes are propagated to the slaves using the **yppush** command. Slaves can request the latest copy of a map explicitly by using the **yppull** command. Each new map is timestamped when it is created, but no provision is made for regaining consistency if changes are made to a copy of the map on a slave. Hence all updates must be made on the master. It is possible for servers to be masters with respect to one map, but slaves with respect to another, but it is simpler if one server is designated as the master for the whole database.

YP clients do not contain any information themselves. When they require information from YP they communicate with a YP server using RPC. When a client machine boots up, the **ypbind** command is executed to bind the client to a nearby server. The current server can be determined by using the **ypwhich** command.

Several commands are provided to manipulate information that is stored, by default, in YP maps. An example is the **yppasswd** command for changing user passwords.

8.3.3. Remote Procedure Call (RPC)

RPC is an integral part of NFS but it can also be used on its own. RPC is also built on the client server model of distributed computing. With RPC, clients and servers are processes. Servers register the procedures that they want to make available to other processes on the network. Clients then execute these procedures by making remote procedure calls. A client procedure call results in a message being sent to the server. On receipt of the message, the server performs some processing and returns the results to the client; the procedure call then returns to the client (see figure 8.2).

The RPC interface is divided into three layers. The highest layer hides the use of RPC from the programmer, who simply uses a library of available procedures. The middle layer uses a small number of RPC routines, and the lowest layer involves the use of UNIX sockets (see section 8.4).

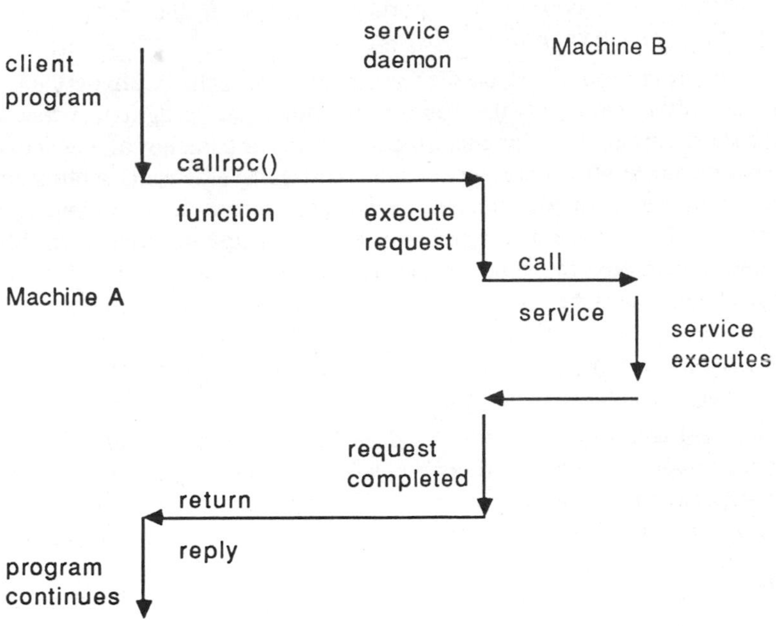

Figure 8.2 The RPC paradigm for communication.

Highest layer

The highest layer of RPC is provided so that the programmer can make use of remote programs without even knowing about RPC. This is accomplished by providing a set of RPC routines that can be called from within a C program. The standard routines are included in the C library *libc.a*. Some examples of standard RPC routines are: **rstat()** which gathers remote performance statistics, **ypmatch()** which gleans information from the yellow pages, and **rnusers()** which returns the number of users logged on to a remote machine.

Middle layer

The middle layer of RPC provides an interface that explicitly makes RPC calls. Each RPC procedure is defined by a *program* number, a *version* number and a *procedure* number. The program number is used to define a group of related procedures, each of which has a different procedure number. The version number refers to the program, so that a minor change to a remote service (i.e. adding a procedure) does not result in the need for a new program number.

To access a remote service, the user looks up the appropriate program, version and procedure numbers in a manual and then uses the routines in the

RPC library. The two most important routines in the RPC library are **callrpc()** and **registerrpc()**.

The **callrpc()** routine is used to make an RPC call. **Callrpc()** has eight parameters: the name of the remote machine, the program, version and procedure numbers, two parameters defining the arguments of the RPC call, and two parameters for the return value of the call. **Callrpc()** returns zero on success and nonzero on failure. Two parameters are required for the argument of RPC, since data types may be represented differently on different machines; therefore, the type of the argument as well as a pointer to the argument itself must be provided. Two parameters are required for the result, for the same reason. **Callrpc()** uses the Internet User Datagram Protocol (UDP) as its transport protocol and returns an error code if no answer is received after a number of retries.

The **registerrpc()** routine is used to register a particular RPC routine within a server. A server registers the RPC calls that it plans to handle using *registerrpc()* and then goes into an infinite loop waiting for requests using the **svcrun()** call. **Registerrpc()** has six parameters: the program, version and procedure numbers of the procedure to be registered, the name of the C procedure implementing the procedure, and the types of the input to and the output from the procedure.

RPC handles arbitrary data types by always converting them to the XDR standard before sending them over the network.

A programming example is presented in section 8.3.3.1 to demonstrate the use of **callrpc()**, **registerrpc()** and **svcrun()**.

Lowest layer

The use of the lowest layer of RPC allows the defaults of the higher layers to be changed. One of the defaults of **registerrpc()** and **callrpc()** at the higher layers is that the UDP protocol is used. This can be changed in the low level server by calling the **svctcp_create()** routine instead of the **svcudp_create()** routine that is called by **registerrpc()**. In the low level client the **clnt_call()** routine is used instead of **callrpc()**. The arguments to **clnt_call()** are a CLIENT pointer, the procedure number, the XDR routine for serialising the argument, a pointer to the argument, the XDR routine for deserialising the return value, a pointer to where the return value will be placed and the time in seconds to wait for a reply. To get a CLIENT pointer the **clnttcp_create()** routine can be used instead of the **clntudp_create()** routine that is used by **callrpc()**.

The **svctcp_create()**, **svcudp_create()**, **clnttcp_create()** and **clntudp_create()** routines require the use of UNIX sockets (see section 8.4). If unbound sockets are used, then a port mapper is used on the server machine to allocate port numbers.

Before returning results to a client the server routine must convert them to the XDR standard. This is done by using the **svc_sendreply()** routine which takes as its arguments, a transport service handle, the appropriate XDR routine for the data type, and a pointer to the data to be returned.

RPC supports broadcast RPCs as well as the standard RPC. The main differences between broadcast RPC and standard RPC are:

More than one answer is expected with broadcast RPC.

Broadcast RPC can only be used with connectionless protocols (ie UDP/IP).

All unsuccessful responses are filtered out as garbage with broadcast RPC.

All broadcast messages are sent to the portmap port. Therefore, all services that want to be accessible via broadcast RPC must be registered with their local port mapper.

The **clnt_broadcast()** routine is used to make a broadcast RPC with the following arguments: the program, version and procedure numbers, the XDR routine for the arguments, a pointer to the arguments, the XDR routine for the results, a pointer to the results and a routine that is called for each valid result obtained (the **eachresult()** routine). The **eachresult()** routine returns a boolean that indicates whether or not the client wants more responses.

Programming example

A simple programming example is presented at this point to illustrate the use of the middle layer of RPC. The example is in two parts: a client program, and a server program. The server provides a procedure that takes a number as its input and produces the square of the number as output. Note that this example also makes use of the XDR package which is described in the next section. The client program takes the name of the server machine and the number to be squared as arguments.

Client

```
/* File: square.h */
/* This header file is included in both client and server */

#define    PROG    20000000
#define    VERS    1
#define    SQUARE  1


/* File: client.c */
/* This program calculates the square of a number via a */
```

```
/* rpc to a server routine on a specified host machine */

#include <stdio.h>
#include <rpc/rpc.h>
#include "square.h"


main (argc,argv)
    int argc;
    char **argv;

{
        char *servername;
        int n;
        unsigned int n_sqrd;

        servername = argv[1];          /* the server machine name and the  */
        n = atoi(argv[2]);                  /* number to be squared are obtained */
                                            /* from the argument list             */

        if (callrpc(servername,PROG,VERS,SQUARE,xdr_int, &n,
                    xdr_u_int, &n_sqrd) !- 0) {

                perror("callrpc");          /* print error code on failure */
                exit(1);
        }
        printf("The square of  %d  is  %d\n", n, n_sqrd);
        exit(0);
}
```

Server

```
/* File: server.c */

/* The following procedure calculates the square of a number */

#include <rpc/rpc.h>
#include "square.h"


char *
squareit(indata)

int *indata;
{
        int f = *indata;
        static int sq;

        sq = f*f;
        return((char *)&sq);
}
```

```
main()
{

        registerrpc(PROG, VERS, SQUARE, squareit, xdr_int, xdr_u_int);

        svc_run();                      /* never returns */
        exit(1);
}
```

8.3.4. External Data Representation (XDR)

XDR is a facility that allows data to be transmitted across a network in a machine-independent fashion. The need for a facility such as XDR has arisen as a result of the interconnection of multiple machines with different architectures. In such an environment, programs that pass data between machines can experience problems due to the fact that data is sometimes represented in different ways by different machines. An example of this is the representation of long integers on VAX and Sun machines. On both machines a long integer is represented by 4 bytes; however, the order of the bytes differs. Further problems occur with pointers, strings and structures.

The XDR facility has three main components, a set of library routines for handling standard C data types, a set of *streams* which are used to transmit data on various different interfaces (e.g. standard I/O, UNIX files, memory locations and TCP/IP connections), and a definition of the XDR standard.

XDR library routines

To use the XDR routines within a C program the file *<rpc/rpc.h>* must be included. In the XDR library, primitive filter routines are provided for converting the following C types into the XDR standard: int, unsigned, long, u_long, short, u_short, float, double. In addition to these, primitive filter routines for converting strings, arrays, unions and pointers to structures are also provided. These primitive filter routines can be used to encode user defined data structures before transmission between machines. The process of converting a data structure from the machine specific representation into the standard XDR representation is called *serialisation*. The reverse process is called *deserialisation*.

XDR streams

All of the primitive filter routines mentioned above take a parameter that represents an XDR stream. This specifies the operations that are to be performed on the data item in question. XDR streams are created by calling one of the standard creation routines that are held in *<rpc/rpc.h>*. The following creation routines currently exist:

xdrstdio_create(): for passing data from/to standard input/output.

xdrmem_create(): for passing data from/to locations in local memory.

xdrrec_create(): for passing data from/to a UNIX file or a TCP/IP connection.

To pass data using UDP/IP the **xdrmem_create()** primitive is used to store encoded/decoded messages in memory before sending/receiving.

Three operations are defined on an XDR stream:

XDR_ENCODE: for serialising data.

XDR_DECODE: for decoding data.

XDR_FREE: for freeing memory that has been allocated by one of the XDR primitive filter routines.

These operations specify the direction of the data flow on an XDR stream. The same XDR primitive filter routines are used for both serialising and deserialising data. Serialisation involves conversion of a machine representation of a data structure into the XDR standard representation. The XDR standard is based on the assumption that bytes are represented in the same way on all machines, and that the meaning of a byte is preserved across hardware boundaries. Data items are then represented in multiples of 4 bytes. For example, integers, shorts and longs are all represented by 4 bytes. Byte strings are appended with up to 3 bytes to make up a multiple of 4 bytes.

The following section introduces some additional networking tools provided by Sun.

8.3.5. Other tools

In addition to NFS, RPC and so on, there are a number of user commands that are useful in a networked environment. These include:

traffic(1)
perfmeter(1)
perfmon(1)
etherfind(8C)
netstat(8C).

traffic provides the user with a graphical display of Ethernet traffic. It is, in effect, a window-based Ethernet monitor that provides basic information on the network state. Parameters such as packet size, packet source, packet destination and protocol in use may be selected for display. **etherd(8C)** is the related daemon process that gathers the statistics from which the traffic command filters and displays the information.

perfmeter is an iconic meter that allows various system statistics to be observed, including the number of Ethernet packets per second, the number of collisions detected on the Ethernet and the number of received packets in error. **perfmon** is a similar idea, but in a graphical window-based format rather than iconically.

etherfind is a more advanced form of network monitor, the output being displayed textually. The user can detail those packets to be traced with a finer granularity than with the traffic command. Packets can be selected on source, destination, source port, destination port, less than or greater than a certain packet size and protocol type. Other parameters, such as recognition of a broadcast packet are possible.

netstat prints, in a simple table format, the network status. The contents of various network-related data structures can be viewed, but the command is possibly most useful for checking the state of all operational sockets (see the following sections for a discussion on sockets).

NIT(4P) is worth mentioning. NIT is a Network Interface Tap Protocol introduced with Sun release 3.0. It allows the programmer to delve to an even lower level than the socket interface. Based on the raw socket code the programmer can set up the interface to perform packet filtering and data selection on incoming packets. Example code roughly follows the pattern of normal socket usage (again see later), with packets being sent and received via the **send** and **recv** system calls.

8.4. Interprocess communication

The previous sections in this chapter have dealt with proprietary facilities provided by Sun UNIX. All the facilities discussed have been at a relatively high level, so far as the user or system administrator is concerned, and all are based on interprocess communication primitives that reside at a lower level in the operating system. Efficient interprocess communication facilities are essential in the construction of distributed computing applications. With Sun UNIX, the interprocess communication primitives are accessible by the programmer. Tools such as RPC are intended to allow programmers to remain at a higher level and indeed even dissuade them from using the lower level primitives. However, there are many instances where it is preferable to descend to the lower level. Even if this can be avoided, it is better to have some idea of what is actually going on at a lower level in the system.

The abstraction for the low level primitives is based on *sockets* and the following sections give the reader a feel for their use, culminating in a simple programming example.

8.4.1. The Internet protocol family

Sockets are an abstraction that supply an interface to an implementation of the TCP/IP communication protocol suite, originally developed for the U.S. Department of Defense Arpanet wide area network. Although other protocol suites are available, TCP/IP provides the *de-facto* standard for communication between Sun (and BSD) UNIX systems. A little background on how the protocol operates is useful.

The Internet protocol implements two basic functions: *addressing* and *fragmentation*. The model of operation is that each host possesses an internet module with common rules for interpreting address fields and for fragmenting/reassembling internet datagrams. Internet uses the concept of encapsulation to move packets across each constituent network of a multinetwork system, permitting the constituent network to function independently of the details of the Internet protocol. Figure 8.3 shows how the Internet Protocol ties in with Sun UNIX.

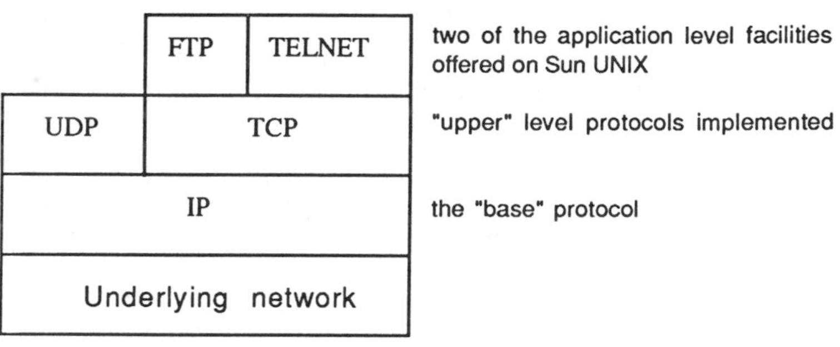

Figure 8.3. The Internet Protocol family and Sun UNIX

Addressing

There is a distinction between names, addresses and routes: a name is what is sought, an address shows where it is, and a route how to get there. The Internet protocol deals primarily with addresses, leaving higher level protocols to map from names to addresses. The Internet module maps internet addresses to local network addresses. Lower level procedures map from local network addresses to routes. Addresses are a fixed length of four bytes (32 bits): the first byte is the network number, followed by a three-byte local address. For human consumption this is often written in an "a.b.c.d" style.

Fragmentation

Fragmentation is the division of a large datagram, that originated in a network allowing a large packet size, into smaller datagrams on reaching networks where this exceeds the maximum packet size. This is done by splitting the packet into the minimum number of packets and duplicating the original header field in each one - the difference being the addition of a sort of "sequence number" field to allow packets to be reassembled correctly at the other end. Packets may be marked "don't fragment", but if fragmentation is found to be necessary they are just discarded.

Internet is a simple datagram protocol. All packets carry full source and destination address information. The user interface to the datagram service is via the *User Datagram Protocol* (UDP). A virtual circuit service (a method of packet transmission whereby a route is established and all packets follow the same path thereafter - there are distinct "call set up" and "call close down" phases, analogous to a telephone call) also exists that sits on top of the Internet protocol known as the *Transmission Control Protocol* (TCP).

8.4.2. Sockets

Before the Berkeley 4.2 BSD release, UNIX was weak in the area of interprocess communication facilities; the only standard mechanisms were *pipes* and *signals*. Pipes are restrictive in that the two communicating processes must reside on the same machine and be related through a common ancestor. They are also uni-directional in nature. With Sun UNIX and sockets, processes may rendezvous in several ways - either through a UNIX file system-like name space (where names are pathnames) or through a network name space. The latter is of most interest here, as it allows communication between processes across both local and wide area networks.

Many existing Sun UNIX commands make use of socket facilities in their operation. Examples include: **rwho** - which shows all the users on the network and **ruptime** - which shows the status of machines on the network. RPC, NFS etc, are all ultimately based on sockets.

A socket is defined as a bidirectional endpoint of communication. Names may be *bound* to sockets and each socket in use has a particular *type*, and one or more associated processes. Sockets themselves exist within *communication domains* and Sun UNIX supports two separate communication domains: the *UNIX domain*, and the *Internet domain*. Communicating processes residing on the same machine may use the UNIX domain and processes across networks the Internet domain. The Internet domain uses the DARPA standard protocols outlined earlier.

Sockets are typed according to the communication properties visible to the user, and processes are presumed to communicate only between sockets of the same type. Five types of socket have, so far, been identified, of which three are implemented in Sun UNIX:

* A *stream* socket provides for bidirectional, reliable, sequenced, and unduplicated flow of data, without record boundaries (c.f. virtual circuits).
* A *datagram* socket supports bidirectional flow of data, but this is not guaranteed to be sequenced, reliable, or unduplicated. A process receiving messages on a datagram socket may find messages duplicated and possibly in an order different from which they were sent. An important characteristic of a datagram socket is that record boundaries in data are preserved. However, an equally important characteristic is that datagram sockets closely model the facilities found in many contemporary packet switched networks, such as Ethernet. As such, and considering the low error rates in local area networks, they are often an adequate means of interprocess communication in such environments.
* A *raw* socket provides access to the underlying communication protocols which support socket abstractions. These are normally datagram oriented and are not intended for the general user. Rather, they are for those interested in developing new protocols or for gaining low level access to an existing one.

The other two socket types highlighted are the *sequenced packet* socket and the *reliably delivered message* socket. A sequenced packet socket is identical to a stream socket except that record boundaries are preserved. This interface is similar to that provided by the Xerox Network Systems (XNS) Sequenced Packet protocol. The reliably delivered message socket is similar to the datagram socket, but with reliable delivery.

8.4.3. System calls and library routines

There are a number of system calls, and library routines, that provide the programming interface to the interprocess communication primitives. This section gives a flavour of their use.

System calls

As interprocess communication is based on the socket abstraction, the most important system call is **socket.** To create a socket:

```
socket_id = socket (domain, type, protocol);
```

The call creates a socket in the specified domain, of the requested type, and adhering to the specified protocol. It returns a small integer number, a descriptor, for future reference to the socket. Two domains are implemented in Sun UNIX: AF_UNIX (Address Format, the UNIX domain) and AF_INET (the Internet domain). Example calls are:

```
socket_id = socket (AF_INET, SOCK_DGRAM, 0);
```

meaning use datagrams (User Datagram Protocol (UDP)) within the Internet domain. The third parameter to the call, a "0", means that the system will select the protocol most appropriate to the user's chosen domain.

```
socket_id = socket (AF_INET, SOCK_STREAM, pp->p_proto);
```

meaning use stream sockets within the Internet domain. The "pp->p_proto" refers to a field of a structure that contains the protocol type. The structure may be filled in, before the socket call, using the **getprotobyname** library routine

```
struct protoent *pp; 1
pp = getprotobyname ("tcp");
```

Using this routine makes programs a little more readable - rather than just using the numeric identifier for a protocol.

Having created a socket, a name has to be affixed to it, and until this is done processes cannot make reference to a socket. We **bind** a name as follows:

```
bind (socket_id, name, namelen);
```

Example calls:

```
bind (socket_id, "/dev/foo", sizeof("/dev/foo") - 1);
```

demonstrates a UNIX domain call and

```
bind (socket_id, &server, sizeof(server));
```

demonstrates an Internet domain call. The UNIX domain name is a UNIX pathname, whereas "server" is a structure of type *sockaddr_in* - one of the commonly used socket related structures - the contents of which must be

[1] Note: We do not, of course, usually put declarations immediately before system calls or library routines. This is done purely to emphasise the structure type being dealt with.

completed within the user program. Figure 8.4 shows the component fields of the structure.

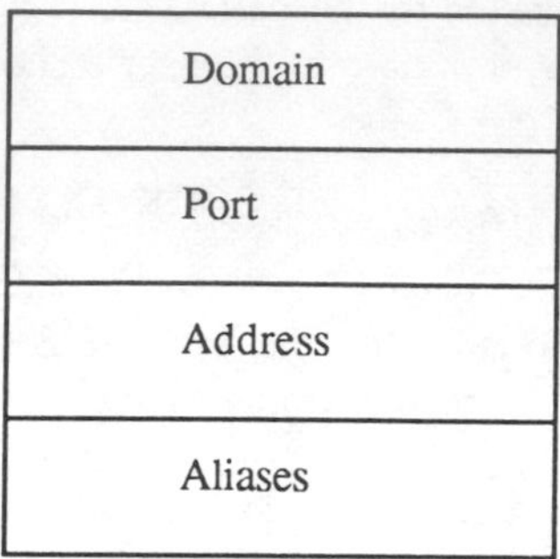

Figure 8.4. The "sockaddr_in" structure

The bind call can fail if the port number is wrongly chosen. Port numbers should be greater than 1023, as numbers less than this are reserved for privileged processes. The programming example shows how the programmer may select a correct port number.

There are two models of communication: *connection oriented* (TCP virtual circuit type) and *connectionless* (UDP datagram). The typical method by which two processes use the interprocess communication facilities is by a *client-server* relationship. One process, the client, requires a service provided by the other, the server. The client calls the server, the server executes the requested task and returns the result to the client.

Following the socket and bind calls the next step depends on whether we aim for a connection oriented or connectionless environment. Note that there is no reason for a server not to offer both virtual circuit and datagram interfaces to the service that it provides (this would require differing port numbers for each). The connection oriented, virtual circuit, method is considered first.

Connection Oriented Environment

A client process requests services from the server by initiating a connection to the server's socket. The server process must listen, for incoming requests, on its socket when it is ready to provide its services.

The first thing that the server does is to execute a **listen** call:

```
listen (server_socket_id, 5);
```

meaning listen on the socket identified by "server_socket_id" and allow 5 connections to be queued for processing (any connection requests after 5 are in the queue are simply ignored). Following the listen, the server waits in an **accept** call for an incoming connection:

```
struct sockaddr_in from;
fromlen = sizeof (from);
newsd = accept (server_socket_id, &from, &fromlen);
```

The "from" structure is filled in with the client's details on an incoming call. The accept call returns a new socket descriptor so that the client and server are "spliced" together, leaving the original socket descriptor free to look for other clients. (In many applications the use of accept is followed by a **fork** - the child process carrying on with the new descriptor.)

A client attempts a connection, in the Internet domain, by:

```
struct sockaddr_in server;
connect (client_socket_id, &server, sizeof(server));
```

The servers details are completed, by a mixture of library routines and assignations, before the **connect** call.

With the client and server connected, data transfer can take place. The standard **read** and **write** calls may be used here, but the new calls **send** and **recv** should be used in preference - if only to highlight that sockets are being used:

```
send (socket_id, buf, sizeof(buf), flags);
recv (socket_id, buf, sizeof(buf), flags);
```

"buf" is a character array containing the data to be sent. "flags" allows several options: for sending, it allows out of band data - a concept that we will not discuss here; for receiving, the ability to look at data before actually reading it is available.

Once a socket is finished with, it should be discarded by the **close** call:

```
close (socket_id);
```

Pending data will still be attempted to be received, even after a close. If the user has no use for such data, the socket may be forcibly closed by **shutdown** (this is not the same as the system maintenance command shutdown - the clash of names is a little unfortunate).

The same server processes on each machine have the same port numbers - only the machine address is different. A client on one machine who wants to make use of a service provided on another machine can find out the necessary port/protocol information by examination of the "/etc/services" file on his machine by using various library routines.

To summarise thc connection oriented method, an illustration of the calls that the client and server execute, with respect to time, is given in figure 8.5.

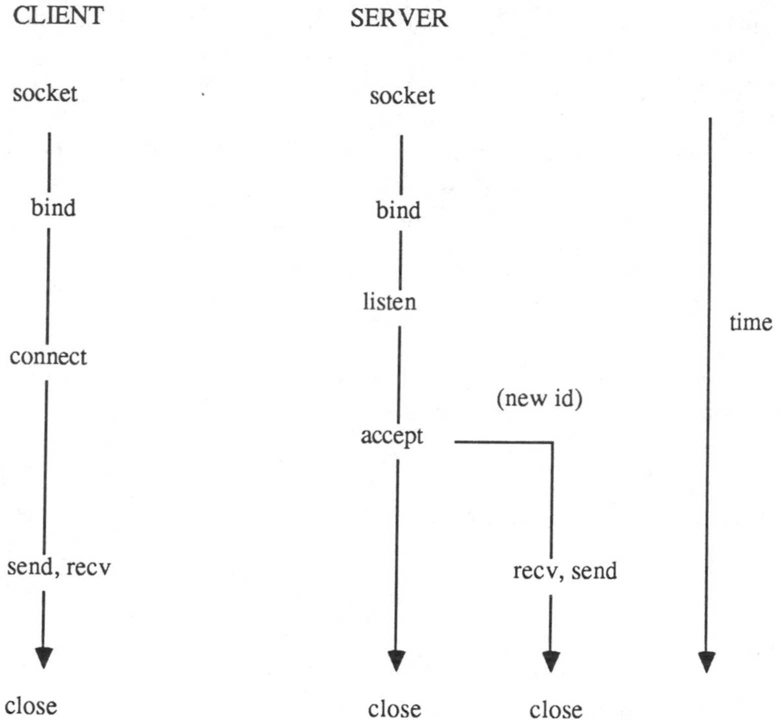

Figure 8.5. Time diagram of connection based communication

Connectionless Sockets

These have no call set up and close down phases. Instead, all packets include the destination address. The sockets are created and bound as before. (Connect, listen and accept are not used here.) To transfer data the **sendto** and **recvfrom** calls are used.

sendto (socket_id, buf, buflen, flags, &to, tolen);

sends the data in "buf" to the socket whose details are contained in the sockaddr_in structure "to".

recvfrom (socket_id, buf, buflen, flags, &from, &fromlen);

puts the received data in "buf" and fills in where it came from into "from". (recvfrom blocks on calling).

In developing socket based applications, it often becomes necessary to have a process that is listening on a socket *and* looking for input from the users terminal, or another file descriptor, at the same time. This may be achieved by the **select** system call. Details of these calls may be found in section 2 of the UNIX programmer's manual.

Library routines

Complementing the system calls are a series of network library routines that exist primarily to allow the manipulation of network addresses. Locating a service on a remote host requires several levels of mapping before the client and server may communicate. The service name and remote host must be translated into a network address. The address must then be used in locating a physical location and route to the service (this is not really applicable in the local area network environment).

Routines are provided for the following:

* mapping host names to network numbers
* network names to network numbers
* protocol names to protocol numbers
* service names to port numbers
* selecting the protocol to use in communication

In Sun UNIX a file, "/etc/hosts", contains Internet addresses in the "a.b.c.d" format alongside the corresponding host names, and any aliases.

The routines **gethostbyname, gethostbyaddr** and **gethostent** return a *hostent* structure - an intermediate data structure that may be used for filling in the sockaddr_in structures. Similarly, routines exist for mapping network names to numbers, and vice versa: these routines return a *netent* structure. They are **getnetbyname, getnetbynumber** and **getnetent.** For protocols a *protoent* structure is completed by **getprotobyname, getprotobynumber** and **getprotoent** routines.

Service names are a little more complicated. Services must exist on well known ports. In other words, a service must have the *same* port number on each machine. A file, akin to "/etc/hosts", exists called "/etc/services", where the service to port number relationships are retained. *Servent* structures are returned by the routines **getservbyname, getservbyport,** and **getservent.**

The component fields of the "hostent", "netent", "protoent" and "servent" are shown later, in figure 8.6.

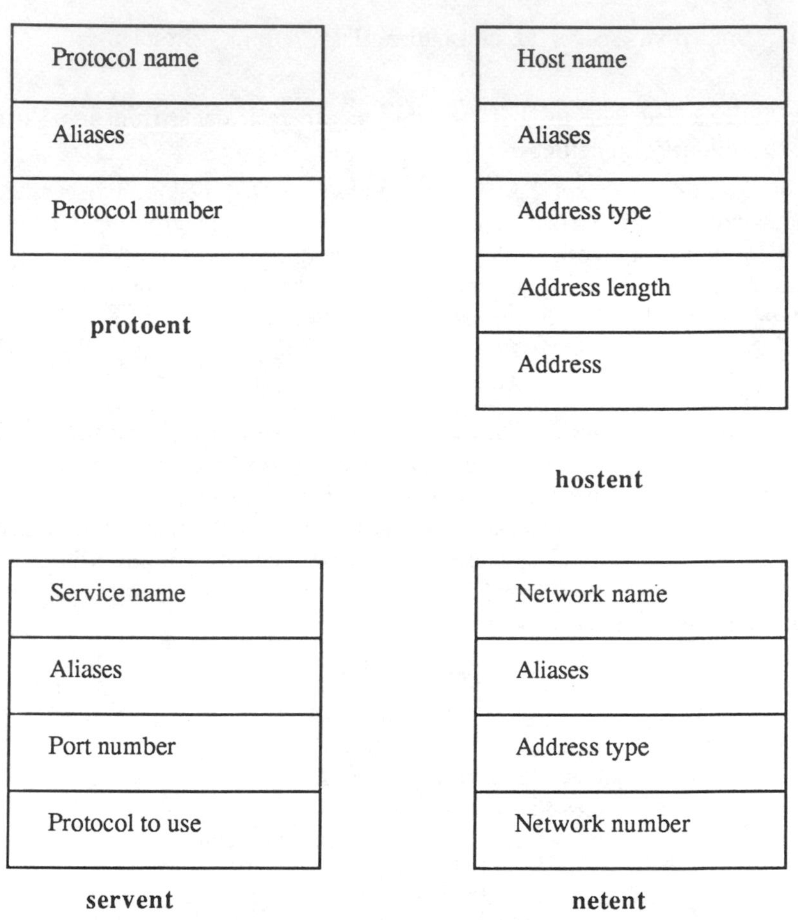

Figure 8.6. The fields of the other common socket structures

Details of these library routines may be found in section 3N of the UNIX programmer's manual.

8.4.4. Broadcasting

With TCP/IP sockets the programmer may enable his application to *broadcast* to the network. Using a datagram socket, this is achieved by using a special address in the destination field of the packet to be sent. *All* nodes on the network will receive packets containing this special address. Consequently, programmers should be cautious in their use of broadcast sockets, or the traffic load on the network will increase significantly.

8.4.5. Miscellaneous

By using the routines mentioned in the previous section, application programs should rarely have to deal directly with addresses as such, decreasing the network dependency a little. However, there are other routines provided to tackle some other problems such as byte swapping. The routines in the previous section return addresses in what is known as network byte order. On a VAX this is reversed and programs are required to byte swap quantities. This is especially true if the programmer wants to print out an address, perhaps in the debugging of his program. These routines are **htonl, htons, ntohl** and **ntohs** (host to network/network to host long/short). (These routines may be found under byteorder(3N).)

8.4.6. Programming example

At this point the socket discussion will be rounded off by presenting a brief programming example, simple enough to illustrate the mechanisms involved. There are two parts: a sender and a receiver. The sender will merely send a message to the receiver and the receiver will reply to the sender. The example will present the connectionless socket paradigm and in both parts the code only will be shown. The previous discussion and the commentary within the code should be sufficient to give an idea of what is going on.

Sender

```
/* This is the sender part of the example.
 * All it does is create a socket on the machine it is run on;
 * it sends a message to the specified host and gets a reply from that host.
 * To run it the user would type:
 *
 *          sender hostname message.
 */

#include <stdio.h>
#include <strings.h>
#include <sys/errno.h>
#include <sys/types.h>
#include <sys/socket.h>
#include <netinet/in.h>
#include <arpa/inet.h>
#include <netdb.h>

#define     RECIPIENT_PORT     2001 /* hardwired port for example only */

extern int  errno;
```

```
struct protoent *getprotobyname ();
struct hostent *gethostent (), *gethostbyname ();

int     sender_id, sender_port;

struct protoent *pp;
struct servent *ss;
struct hostent *sender, *recipient;
struct sockaddr_in  sender_sock, recipient_sock;
struct in_addr  sender_addr, recipient_addr;



main (argc, argv)
int     argc;
char    *argv[];
{
    char    myhost[40], recipient_host[40], message[BUFSIZ];
    int     length;

    if (argc < 3)
    {
        fprintf (stderr, "usage: sender host message\n");
        exit (1);
    }

    /* look up the hosts name... */
    if (gethostname (myhost, 40) != 0)
    {
        perror ("gethostname");
        exit (1);
    }

    /* and use it to find out the address details */
    if ((sender = gethostbyname (myhost)) == 0)
    {
        perror ("gethostbyname");
        exit (1);
    }
    bcopy (sender -> h_addr, (char *) & sender_addr, sender -> h_length);
    /* bcopy preserves the address - gethost* routines return information
     * to the same memory area each time, hence the need to save the address
     */

    if ((pp = getprotobyname ("udp")) == 0) /* get the udp id */
    {
        perror ("getprotobyname");
        exit (1);
    }

    /* now create the socket the sender will use */

    if ((sender_id = socket (AF_INET, SOCK_DGRAM, pp -> p_proto)) == -1)
```

```
{
    perror ("socket");
    exit (1);
}

/* fill in a few details... */
sender_sock.sin_family = AF_INET;
sender_sock.sin_addr = sender_addr;

/* find a suitable port to use, and bind the socket */
for (sender_port = IPPORT_RESERVED; sender_port <= 32767; ++sender_port)
{
    sender_sock.sin_port = htons ((u_short) sender_port);
    if (bind (sender_id, &sender_sock, sizeof (sender_sock)) >= 0)
        break;
    if (errno == EADDRINUSE || errno == EADDRNOTAVAIL)
        continue;
    perror ("bind");
    close (sender_id);
    exit (1);
}

strcpy (recipient_host, argv[1]);
strcpy (message, argv[2]);

/* now look up details of the destination of the message... */
if ((recipient = gethostbyname (recipient_host)) == 0)
{
    perror ("gethostbyname");
    exit (1);
}
bcopy (recipient -> h_addr, (char *) & recipient_addr, recipient -> h_length);

recipient_sock.sin_family = AF_INET;
recipient_sock.sin_addr = recipient_addr;
recipient_sock.sin_port = htons ((u_short) RECIPIENT_PORT);

fprintf (stderr, "sending to (address, port): %s, %d\n",
        inet_ntoa (recipient_sock.sin_addr),
        htons (recipient_sock.sin_port));

/* ... and send it */
if (sendto (sender_id, message, sizeof (message), 0, &recipient_sock,
            sizeof (recipient_sock)) < 0)
{
    perror ("sendto");
    exit (1);
}

length = sizeof (recipient_sock);
/* should get a response */
if (recvfrom (sender_id, message, sizeof (message), 0, &recipient_sock,
            &length) < 0)
```

```
    {
        perror ("recvfrom");
        exit (1);
    }

    /* print it and exit */
    fprintf (stdout, "Recipient replies %s\n", message);
    close (sender_id);
}
```

Receiver

```
/* This is the recipient side of the example.
 * It creates a socket and listens for an incoming packet.
 * On receipt of a message it prompts the user for a suitable
 * reply and sends it back to the source.
 */

#include <stdio.h>
#include <strings.h>
#include <sys/errno.h>
#include <sys/types.h>
#include <sys/socket.h>
#include <netinet/in.h>
#include <arpa/inet.h>
#include <netdb.h>

#define     RECIPIENT_PORT     2001 /* hardwired port for example only */

struct protoent *getprotobyname ();
struct hostent *gethostent (), *gethostbyname ();

int     recipient_id;

struct protoent *pp;
struct servent *ss;
struct hostent *recipient;
struct sockaddr_in  recipient_sock, sender_sock;
struct in_addr  recipient_addr;


main ()
{
    char    myhost[40], message[BUFSIZ];
    int     length;


    if (gethostname (myhost, 40) != 0)/* look up own hosts name */
    {
        perror ("gethostname");
        exit (1);
    }

    /* and use it to find out the address details */
```

```
if ((recipient = gethostbyname (myhost)) == 0)
{
   perror ("gethostbyname");
   exit (1);
}
/* preserve the address */
bcopy (recipient -> h_addr, (char *) & recipient_addr, recipient -> h_length);

if ((pp = getprotobyname ("udp")) == 0)  /* get the udp id */
{
   perror ("getprotobyname");
   exit (1);
}

/* now create the socket the recipient will use */

if ((recipient_id = socket (AF_INET, SOCK_DGRAM, pp -> p_proto)) == -1)
{
   perror ("socket");
   exit (1);
}

/* fill in a few details... */
recipient_sock.sin_family = AF_INET;
recipient_sock.sin_addr = recipient_addr;
recipient_sock.sin_port = htons ((u_short) RECIPIENT_PORT);

/* now bind the socket */
if (bind (recipient_id, &recipient_sock, sizeof (recipient_sock)) == -1)
{
   perror ("bind");
   exit (1);
}

fprintf (stderr, "listening on (address, port): %s, %d\n",
      inet_ntoa (recipient_sock.sin_addr),
      htons (recipient_sock.sin_port));

length = sizeof (sender_sock);
if (recvfrom (recipient_id, message, sizeof (message), 0, &sender_sock,
         &length) < 0)
{
   perror ("recvfrom");
   exit (1);
}

fprintf (stdout, "message from %s\n", inet_ntoa (sender_sock.sin_addr));
fprintf (stdout, "your reply? ");
gets (message);

if (sendto (recipient_id, message, sizeof (message), 0, &sender_sock,
         sizeof (sender_sock)) < 0)
{
```

```
        perror ("sendto");
        exit (1);
    }

    close (recipient_id);
}
```

8.4.7. Some comments

The socket abstraction is provided only with Sun (and 4.2 BSD) flavours of UNIX, and upward. Consequently, communication between machines running earlier versions of UNIX, or another common operating system, such as Digital Equipment Corporation's VMS, is difficult, though not impossible. Proprietary packages that implement the appropriate protocols and emulate the system calls are available. However, these can be somewhat expensive.

Most problems encountered in the programming of socket-based applications involve socket addresses - either wrong choice of address/port, accidental re-use of an address/port, or address/port pair. Byte swapping is also a nuisance. Care should be exercised in these areas and should an application fail to work these are the first suspects in the debugging process.

As a final point, if the Yellow Pages system is running the local "/etc/hosts" file is mapped out. Rather, the information is returned via an RPC call to a YP server. The application programmer should note that this happens. Any C programs that use any of the *get** routines will need to be relinked, if YP is running.

8.5. Concluding comments

As stated at the outset of this chapter, a networked Sun workstation opens up a whole new range of possibilities to the user and programmer. Careful use of NFS and ND allow users to save on disk space throughout their networked system. YP assists in the administration of the network. RPC allows programmers to develop their own distributed applications. Likewise, sockets do so, but at a lower level.

In short, all the ingredients are available on which to build a powerful networked system and Sun workstations really should be networked in order to gain the most from them.

Further reading

This chapter has merely provided a summary of the networking capability of the Sun workstation. For further details the obvious place to look is in the Sun manual pages themselves and, for background to the wider subject of networking, the following books are highly recommended:

R Cole, *Computer Communications* (2nd Edition), Macmillan, London, 1986, ISBN 0-333-39501-8.

F Halsall, *Introduction to Data Communications and Computer Networks* Addison-Wesley, Reading MA, 1985, ISBN 0-201-14540-5.

A S Tanenbaum, *Computer Networks* Prentice-Hall, Eaglewood Cliffs, New Jersey, 1981, ISBN 0-13-165183-8.

9 Software Development on the Sun

9.1. Introduction

There are several approaches to software development and the one chosen for a particular project will depend on several factors; the size and number of people involved; whether the project is experimental or highly structured; the existing methods adopted by a particular organisation. In general, though, most software development goes through the following cycle:

(1) Analyse the requirements of the project,

(2) Design the software,

(3) Implement the system,

(4) Test the system.

In a highly structured project, such as an air traffic control system, each phase would be fully documented before proceeding to the next and if, for example, changes in the design were found to be necessary after testing, then a formal review procedure would have to be followed before the changes were incorporated. At the other extreme, a highly experimental project involving one person may be only loosely defined and the act of implementing the system would reveal new requirements. This highly *iterative* process would continue until the experiment was complete.

UNIX systems offer support mainly in the area of implementation. There are writing tools (like those used to write this book) that help us to document the phases of development, but none supplied with the standard system that support, requirements analysis, design or system testing. Tools like SCCS (*source code control system*), **make** and **dbxtool**, which we shall discuss here, are aimed at software management and production.

SCCS and **make** are BSD UNIX tools; **Dbxtool**, however, is Sun specific. It is a SunView version of **dbx**, a *source level* debugging tool from BSD UNIX, used to find and correct errors (or *bugs*) in programs. **dbxtool** extends the facilities of **dbx** and, in conjunction with SCCS and **make**, it can be used as an interactive program development tool. The examples given below use the C language, but they should work in Pascal or FORTRAN, except where indicated.

9.2. From design to source files

Most of the example programs in this book have been fairly short. However, many more realistic programs are several thousands of lines long, and as with the directory browser in Chapter 3, consist of many separate functions. This size and complexity is usually handled at the design stage, and one approach to design is to first describe the system in a *Program Design Language* (or PDL). A PDL consists of English statements mixed with programming language constructs. This allows the system to be dealt with at a higher level, ignoring some of the implementation details found in programming languages. So, for example, the main *module* of the directory browser could be described as;

```
main()
{
frame = init_tool_frame(FRAME);

top_panel = init_top_panel(frame,PANEL);

list = build_directory_list();

bottom_panel = init_bottom_panel(frame, PANEL, list);

window_main_loop(frame);
}
```

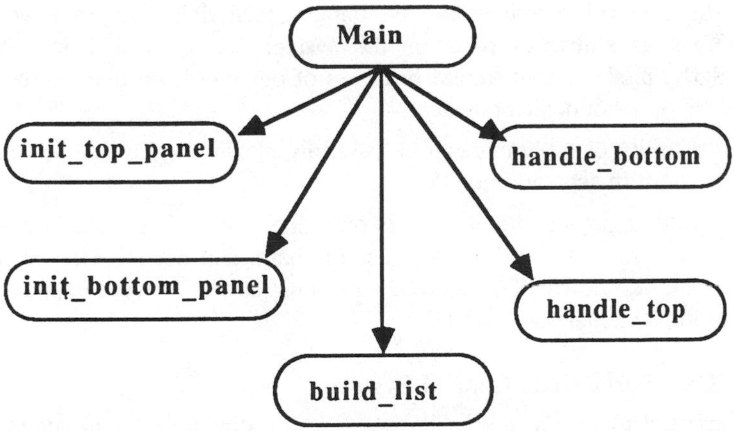

Figure 9.1

We could break down *main* into further modules, each describing the next level of detail required as shown in figure 9.1. The process of *top-down* design description would continue until we are ready to fill in the details at the programming language level. The modules, shown in figure 9.1, would then be mapped to source files in our working directory, e.g.

```
% ls
main.c
init_tool_frame.c
init_top_panel.c
build_directory_list.c
init_bottom_panel.c
%
```

If the program was very large, then the modules above would be broken down further, so those modules shown above would be mapped to directories, each containing more source file modules.

The modular approach has several advantages over the single source file approach:

(1) Different modules can be given to different programmers for concurrent implementation.

(2) Smaller modules are more manageable in software development (and subsequent maintenance).

(3) It is easier to isolate errors within a module.

(4) Higher level functions can be implemented first, leaving lower level functions as stubs, so parts of the system can be tested in isolation. Similarly, modules in different branches of our top-down tree can be tested in isolation from other branches.

(5) Portability of programs can be eased by placing highly specific parts of the program in separate modules.

The design approach shown here is only one, fairly simple method. Others include data flow charts, program structure charts and object oriented design. However, the top-down PDL approach demonstrates how we can move from design to implementation in UNIX.

9.3. SCCS: Source Code Control System

Having created the initial entries in our working directory (or directories) we need a method of controlling changes during subsequent development. The standard tool available on Sun workstations is *SCCS, the source code control system.* It provides facilities for keeping records of changes made to any file registered with SCCS. The record keeping mechanism also ensures that only one person can update a file at a time and allows the different versions of a file to be kept and restored.

To use SCCS we first create a *SCCS* directory within our working directory (or directories), i.e.

```
% mkdir SCCS
```

SID keywords

Each file to be registered with SCCS should contain an identity keyword (or SID) which SCCS uses to put version control information in released files. So, a file with the initial keywords %W% and %G% would have these replaced by the file name, SID and SCCS symbol, and the date of the last changes respectively. For example, in the C file, *main.c*, the declaration

```
static char sccsid[] = "%W% %G%";
```

would be replaced by SCCS with

```
static char sccsid[] = "@(#) main.c 1.1  05/28/87"
```

The variable name *sccsid* can be changed to something more suitable to your project, and one practice is to have a unique name for every source file, e.g. *sccsid01*, *sccsid02*, *sccsid03*, and so on.

SCCS entries can then be created, and any temporary files removed by:

```
% ls
SCCS append.c list.c main.c
% sccs create *.[ch]
   output from SCCS
% ls
,append.c ,list.c ,main.c SCCS append.c list.c main.c
% rm -i ,*
```

We would then be left with read-only copies of our sources files in the working directory, and entries termed *s-files*, which keep track of changes, in the *SCCS* directory. Note that all SCCS commands have the form sccs <sccs-command> <arguments>

Files can have changes made to them with the **edit** command, e.g.

```
% sccs edit main.c
New delta 1.2
% ls -l main.c
-rw-r--r-- 1 de    256 May 31 16:58  main.c
```

where SCCS informs us that we are creating a new version (or *delta*) of *main.c*. *New delta 1.2* means that this is release 1, version 2 of this file. When we have finished editing the file, and have no more changes to add to delta 1.2, the changes can be recorded by the **delta** command, e.g.

```
% sccs delta main.c
1.2
25 inserted
0 deleted
75 unchanged
% ls -l main.c
main.c not found
```

which tells us that between deltas 1.1 and 1.2, 25 lines have been added, none have been deleted and 75 were not changed. Each time a delta is saved the version number is incremented by one, i.e. 1.1, 1.2, 1.3 ... 1.12 and so on. To retrieve the latest delta, for compilation or printing, say, we use the **get** command, e.g.

```
% sccs get main.c
1.2
100 lines
% ls -l
-r--r--r-- 1 de    256 Jun  1 17:08  main.c
```

where we are told that delta 1.2 was retrieved with 100 lines.

There are further SCCS commands that help us manage changes, like the *info* command to tell us who is editing a file, and various other commands that allow us to retrieve old deltas or forget old changes. However, SCCS does not control the nature of changes made to files or say anything about how those changes may effect other files. Some team projects appoint one member as a project librarian to monitor these effects.

9.4. Make

Whereas SCCS controls the changes to the source files of a system, **make** describes how the system is constructed from the source files. The construction sequence is described in *makefiles* which contain *dependency* rules and construction rules. The left-hand side of a dependency rule gives the name of the *target* (or *targets*) to be built, while the right-hand side gives the names of the files on which the target depends. If the target is out of date with respect to its constituent parts the construction rules following the dependency rules are executed.

9.4.1. Compilation

Before we explain the details of makefiles we will look at the compilation process. **Make** can be used to build any objects which depend on other UNIX files (e.g. building a book from its chapters with **nroff**); however, it is mainly used to build software systems.

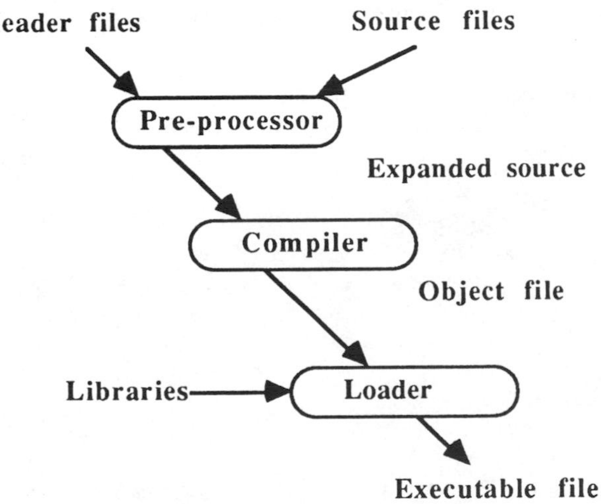

Figure 9.2 The compilation process

In figure 9.2 a source file is taken and initially passed through the *pre-processor*. Here any # symbols are interpreted. For *#include*, the following filename is included into the source text, and for *#define* the symbol definition is replaced in the text. The expanded source file is then passed to the compiler to produce an object file. Object files in the directory have the *.o* suffix. Finally the linker, **ld**, takes one or more object files, together with any required library files, and produces the desired executable file. If we type, for example

```
% cc main.c list.c append.c -o listprog
main.c:
list.c:
append.c:
% ls
append.c append.o list.c list.o listprog main.c main.o
```

the compiler has taken each *.c* file in turn to produce its respective object file, and the linker has taken the three object files to produce the executable file, *listprog*.

9.4.2. Example makefile

In the above compilation example *listprog* depended on three object files, *main.o*, *append.o* and *list.o*. The object files in turn depended on their respective C source files. We could create a text file called *makefile* (or *Makefile*) to describe the construction of *listprog* as follows;

```
listprog: main.o list.o append.o
	cc -g main.o list.o append.o -o $@

.o:
	cc -c -g $<
```

Typing

```
% make
```

would cause **make**, by default, to use the file *makefile* (or *Makefile*) in the current directory, and build the system described in that file.

The first line has the target to be built, *listprog*, on the left-hand side of the first dependency rule, followed by a colon and a space. The right-hand side gives the names of the files on which *listprog* depends. The next line, which must be indented by a *tab* character, gives the rule to construct *listprog* from the object files.

The next dependency rule tells **make** how to construct the object files required for the first dependency rule. Only the *.o* suffix is required to instruct **make** how to build object files, though it would be possible to have a rule for each object file if we wish to treat each of them differently (e.g. by using different compiler options in the construction rules).

The two symbols with the *$* prefix are built-in *macros* which are a useful shorthand notation. *$@* is expanded to the name of the target for that dependency rule, i.e. *listprog*, while *$<* is expanded to the name of the files from which we expect to build the target. In this case *$<* is expanded to the name of the C file required to build its respective object file.

9.4.3. User-defined macros

The above example is fairly small and simple. During the development of the program we may wish to add new source files or change compilation options. To make these changes throughout the makefile would become tedious; **make**, therefore, provides a *macro* facility to allow the users to define their own symbols. For example, the previous *makefile* could be amended as follows:

```
OBJS=main.o list.o append.o
CFLAGS= -g
HDRS= defs.h struct.h
LIBS=-lsuntool -lsunwindow -lpixrect

listprog: ${OBJS}
	cc ${CFLAGS} ${OBJS} ${LIBS} -o $@

.o: ${HDRS}
	cc -c ${CFLAGS} $<
```

Here four macros have been defined, *OBJS*, *CFLAGS*, *HDRS* and *LIBS*. When **make** is executed the macros are expanded to their respective values.

When **make** is typed with no arguments the first target in *makefile* is built by default. In the above example this is *listprog*. Other targets can be added and we can specify which target to build on the command line. Two commonly used targets are *install* and *clean*, where, *install* would put *listprog*, and any other runtime files associated with *listprog* in their correct locations, and *clean* would remove any temporary files. For example, adding these two entries to our previous *makefile*:

```
DESTINATION = /usr/local
DEST_LIB = /usr/local/lib
install:
        cp listprog ${DESTINATION}/listprog
        cp .listrc ${DEST_LIB}/.listrc

clean:
        rm *.o listprog
```

9.4.4. Using SCCS with make

It is possible to use SCCS to retrieve source files for **make** by specifying a dependency rule to construct the source files, e.g.

```
SRCS = main.c list.c append.c
sources: ${SRCS}
${SRC}:
        sccs get $@
```

Our final *makefile* would be as follows, with comment lines prefixed by the # symbol:

```
# makefile for the listprog system by J. Smith
# Next line is for SCCS control
# %W% %G%

OBJS = main.o list.o append.o
SRCS = main.c list.c append.c
# -g for use with dbx, -s -O for final version
CFLAGS = -g
HDRS = defs.h struct.h
LIBS = -lsuntool -lsunwindow -lpixrect
# Change the next two entries to appropriate directories
DESTINATION = /usr/local
DEST_LIB = /usr/local/lib

listprog: ${OBJS}
        cc ${CFLAGS} ${OBJS} ${LIBS} -o $@

.o: ${HDRS}
        cc -c ${CFLAGS} $<
```

```
sources: ${SRCS}
${SRC}:
        sccs get $@

install:
        cp listprog ${DESTINATION}/listprog
        cp .listrc ${DEST_LIB}/.listrc

clean:
        rm *.o listprog
```

9.5. Development with dbxtool

A program may compile correctly and have no syntax errors. However, it is highly likely that it will contain logical errors (or bugs) which occur when the program is executed. One approach to finding and correcting bugs is to use a *source level* debugging tool, like **dbxtool. Dbxtool** allows the program source code to be traced and examined, either after the program has crashed or while it is running. Figure 9.3 shows the layout of **dbxtool.** It can be started from the root menu or from a **shelltool** by typing:

% dbxtool program_object_name

Where *all* the object modules of *program_object_name* have previously been compiled with the **-g** compiler option.

```
dbxtool
Awaiting Execution
File Displayed:   ./dir_main.c                                    Lines: 21-40

                                        FRAME_ARGS,       argc,argv,
                                        FRAME_LABEL,      "Directory Browser 3.2",
                                        FRAME_ICON, &icon,
                                        0);

        init_control_panel();

        init_confirm();

        if (argc > 1)
                sprintf(name,"%s",argv[1]);

        build_list(name);

        init_dir_panel();

        window_fit_height(dir_panel);

        window_fit_height(base_frame);

 print  print *  next  step  stop at  cont  stop in  clear  where
                       up    down     run

(dbxtool) trace draw_dir_panel
(1) trace draw_dir_panel
(dbxtool) run
Running: dir
calling draw_dir_panel() from function init_dir_panel
returning from draw_dir_panel

execution completed, exit code is 0
program exited with 0
(dbxtool)
(dbxtool)
(dbxtool)
```

Figure 9.3 Dbxtool

Dbxtool consists of a status window, a editing subwindow which shows the portion of source code currently being executed, a panel with some common dbxtool commands, and a command subwindow (similar to the **cmdtool**), where dbxtool commands are entered and dbxtool output can be edited[1].

If **dbxtool** has been started from the root menu the object program can be loaded by typing

(dbxtool) **debug program_object_name**

in the dbxtool command window.

[1] The use of textedit windows and scrollbars is explained in Chapter 1.

In the following examples two modes of failure are considered:

(1) A crash causing a *core dump*. Roughly a core dump gives the state of a program at the time it crashed. The program will fail giving a message such as:

> segmentation fault (core dumped) or
> bus error (core dumped).

(2) Incorrect program behaviour.

Debugging crashed programs

When a program crashes, a file called *core* is created. When a crashed program is debugged with **dbxtool**, the *core* file is also read. It is possible to get a trace of the function calls which led up to the crash via the **dbxtool** command **where** as shown below.

Table 9.1 where listing

```
(dbxtool) debug dir
Reading symbolic information...
Read 5010 symbols
(dbxtool) run
Running: dir
signal SEGV (segmentation violation) in pw_rop at 0x2c248
pw_rop+0x358:                movl   a0@,a0
(dbxtool) where
pw_rop(0x8adec, 0x204, 0x2e, 0x2c, 0x14, 0x0, 0x0, 0x0, 0x0) at 0x2c248
... listing of internal SunView function calls ....
window_main_loop(0x89588) at 0x15be3
main(argc = 1, argv = 0xefffe04, 0xefffe0c), line 42 in "dir_main.c"
(dbxtool)
```

Generally, the most significant line is the last function to be called. This is the function which caused the crash. From the **where** output it might be apparent what caused the crash. For example, a function may have been passed the wrong type of parameter, given an incorrect number of parameters or, in C, been passed a variable rather than a pointer to that variable. Errors such as this escape the C compiler, but would have been noticed by the Pascal compiler. The parameters to the function may be examined via the **print** command. The error can then be corrected and the program re-built for re-testing.

Debugging badly behaved programs

A program may not crash fatally, but may still be producing incorrect output. The object program is loaded into **dbxtool** as before, but this time the **run** command is used to execute the program from within **dbxtool. Run** can also be given the command line arguments that the object program usually takes as parameters.

Usually, before running the program in this way, some additional commands are used to show the behaviour of program as it runs. These include:

Trace

A variable, function name or source line will be traced as the program executes. For example,

(dbxtool) **trace i**

prints out the value of i as it changes and

(dbxtool) **trace function_x**

traces each call to the function **function_x.**

When using **trace**, it helps to have a rough idea of which variable or function to examine. In the extreme it is possible to type **trace** alone, in which case every source line is printed as it is executed.

Display

The values of variables are displayed in the lower text window as they change. For example,

(dbxtool) **display counter**

The panel subwindow contains buttons to allow us to execute some **dbxtool** commands with the mouse. Whereas the typed in commands are usually followed by some parameters, the button commands take the last *text selection* as an argument. The buttons act as follows:

print/print *

Prints out the value of the variable marked by the text selection in the editing subwindow. **print *** prefixes the variable with an asterisk to examine pointer variables.

next/step

Execute the next source statement after the program has stopped at a breakpoint. **step** will go into functions and procedures, whereas **next** will skip them.

stop at

Stops execution of the program at the line previous selected in the editing subwindow. **print** can then be used, for example, to examine the state of the program at this point.

stop in

Stops execution at the first line of the function named in the text selection.

cont

Continues execution after a breakpoint, like **stop at** or **stop in**, has been reached.

clear

Removes any breakpoints set.

where

Gives a *where* listing of the function call stack, as described in table 9.1.

up/down

Allows us to move up and down the function call stack so that we can examine local variables.

run

Executes the currently loaded executable file.

Using the above commands, it is possible to follow the path of function calls and the changes in variable values so that errors can be isolated and pinned down. Corrections can than be made and the program re-built. The new object program can then be examined by typing:

(dbxtool) **debug new_object_code**

so that the changes previously made can be checked.

There are other options to the commands shown here and other **dbxtool** commands. **Quit** quits **dbxtool** and **help** gives a brief summary of a command's action. The interested reader should follow the references at the end of this chapter, having mastered the basic commands shown here.

Using make and sccs with dbxtool

It is possible to work almost entirely from within **dbxtool**, editing text and re-compiling the source when changes are made. The initial object file would be loaded and run to discover bugs. Any changes could be made and saved using the editing subwindow. The object would then be re-made using the dbx **make** command, which would execute the *makefile* in the current directory.

If the source code was controlled by **sccs** any source files would first have to be put into sccs edit mode by issuing a shell command from within **dbxtool** or another window. The sequence of operations within **dbxtool** could then be as follows

(debug) **debug prog**
... insert trace and breakpoint statements
(debug) **run prog**
... locate source of error
(debug) **sh sccs edit <filename.c>**
... load, edit and save filename.c in the editing subwindow
(debug) **sh sccs delta <filename.c>**
(debug) **make prog**
... re-test the new version

The newly released writeable version of the file would have to be explicitly loaded into the editing subwindow in order that changes could be made, and then saved prior to re-making. If you attempt to quit Bdbxtool with the tool menu a message will appear if you have not saved any changes made in the editing window. However, if you quit bxtool with the **quit** command in the command subwindow, no prompt will be given and the changes will be lost.

9.6. Alternative debugging strategy

An alternative approach to using a source level tool like **dbxtool** is to insert statements at important points in the program to observe the program's behaviour. These debugging statements can be used to demonstrate that the program is running as expected, as well as indicating any errors in the program. It is more akin to testing than the **dbxtool** approach above. The statements would print out the values of important program variables and calls to functions. When a runtime error occurs, the value of the variables and the point of execution in the program can be traced. In C, debugging statements would be of the form

```
fprintf(debug_fp,"Value of counter %d0,loop_counter);
```

where **debug_fp** is a pointer to a file where the statements are written. The statements could also be written to a separate window. For example, if we wished to make use of the scrollbars in a **cmdtool** window which was started as a *console* window, **debug_fp** would be obtained from

```
debug_fp = fopen("/dev/console","w+");
```

which would be placed in the initialisation module of the program.

9.6.1. Conditional debugging

Rather than delete debugging statements from the final version of the program, it is possible to switch them off at compile time. This is achieved via the **-D** option on the compiler command line. When compiling a C program the user would type

```
% cc -DDEBUG source_file.c
```

and the debugging statements would be modified to

```
#ifdef DEBUG
fprintf(debug_fp,"Value of counter %d0,loop_counter);
#endif
```

The line **#ifdef DEBUG** means that if the symbol **DEBUG** is defined on the command line, then any lines up to the next **#endif** are included in the compiled program, otherwise they are ignored by the compiler.

Pascal and Fortran debugging statements are written in a different way as they do not use **#ifdef**. Instead, the symbol on the command line is given a value, e.g.

```
% pc -Ddebug=2 pascal_prog.p
% f77 -DDEBUG=2 fortran77_prog.F
```

and the value of **DEBUG** is tested by normal language **if** statements. For example,

In Pascal:

```
if ( debug = 2 ) then
    writeln('Counter value',counter);
```

In Fortran:

```
if ( DEBUG .eq. 2 ) then
    write (0,*)  "Value is " , counter
endif
```

The Fortran filename should end with a capital F if the file is to be processed by the C pre-processor to define the symbol on the command line.

9.6.2. Conditional compilation

The use of **#ifdef** is not confined to debugging statements. It can be used to control the compilation of any statements. It is useful, for example, when a program must run on two machines with slightly different versions of Berkeley UNIX 4.2.

The token defined on the command line can also be defined as a *macro* in a *makefile*, for example;

```
DEBUG=DEBUGGING
main: main.c
        cc -D${DEBUG} main.c -o main
```

Here the macro **DEBUG** is expanded to **DEBUGGING** when the C compiler is executed. Within *main.c*, **#ifdef** would be used to check if **DEBUGGING** was defined. At a later run of **make** the makefile could be edited to:

```
DEBUG=
main: main.c
        cc -D${DEBUG} main.c -o main
```

to switch off debugging statements.

Except in the case of locally, isolated errors, an error in a program may indicate a flaw in its design and it is advisable to re-think the implementation of that design in order to make the program more reliable.

Further Reading

Programming Utilities for the Sun Workstation, (sections on **make** and **sccs**), Sun Microsystems Inc., Mountain View CA, 1986.

Debugging Tools for the Sun Workstation, Sun Microsystems Inc., Mountain View CA, 1987.

FORTRAN Programmer's Guide, Sun Microsystems Inc., Mountain View CA, 1986.

Pascal Programmer's Guide, Sun Microsystems Inc., Mountain View CA, 1986.

B W Kernighan, D M Ritchie,
The C Programming Language, Prentice Hall, Englewood Cliff NJ, 1978.

I Sommerville
Software Engineering, 2nd edition, Addison-Wesley, Reading MA, 1985.

Index